Migration, Immigration and Social Policy

Migration, Immigration and Social Policy

Edited by

Catherine Jones Finer

Blackwell
Publishing

CONTENTS

Notes on Contributors   vi

1   Editorial Introduction   1
Catherine Jones Finer

2   From Border Control to Migration Management: The Case for
a Paradigm Change in the Western Response to Transborder
Population Movement   5
Savitri Taylor

3   European Union Policy on Asylum and Immigration. Addressing
the Root Causes of Forced Migration: A Justice and Home
Affairs Policy of Freedom, Security and Justice?   29
Channe Lindstrøm

4   A Sledgehammer to Crack a Nut: Deportation, Detention and
Dispersal in Europe   48
Liza Schuster

5   Governance, Forced Migration and Welfare   63
Peter Dwyer

6   The Experiences of Frontline Staff Working with Children
Seeking Asylum   81
D. Dunkerley, J. Scourfield, T. Maegusuku-Hewett and N. Smalley

7   When the Export of Social Problems Is No Longer Possible:
Immigration Policies and Unemployment in Switzerland   93
Alexandre Afonso

8   Why It Is Bad to Be Kind. Educating Refugees to Life in
the Welfare State: A Case Study from Norway   109
Anniken Hagelund

9   How Studies of the Educational Progression of Minority
Children Are Affecting Education Policy in Denmark   124
Bjørg Colding, Hans Hummelgaard and Leif Husted

10   New Destinations? Assessing the Post-migration Social Mobility
of Minority Ethnic Groups in England and Wales   137
Lucinda Platt

Index   161

NOTES ON CONTRIBUTORS

Alexandre Afonso is a PhD student at the Institute for Political and International Studies, University of Lausanne, Switzerland.

Bjørg Colding is Research Fellow at the Institute of Local Government Studies-Denmark, Copenhagen, Denmark.

David Dunkerley is Professor of Sociology at the University of Glamorgan.

Peter Dwyer is Senior Lecturer in Social Policy in the School of Sociology/Social Policy, University of Leeds.

Anniken Hagelund is Senior Researcher at the Institute for Social Research in Elisenberg, Oslo.

Hans Hummelgaard is Research Director at the Institute of Local Government Studies-Denmark, Copenhagen, Denmark.

Leif Husted is Senior Research Fellow at the Instutute of Local Government Studies-Denmark, Copenhagen, Denmark.

Channe Lindstrøm is currently seconded by the Danish Refugee Council Professional Emergency Roster as Reporting Officer to UNHCR Branch Office in Accra, Ghana.

Tracey Maegusuku-Hewett is a PhD student at the University of Glamorgan.

Lucinda Platt is Lecturer in the Department of Sociology, University of Essex.

Liza Schuster is Lecturer in the Department of Sociology, City University.

Jonathan Scourfield is Senior Lecturer in Cardiff School of Social Sciences.

Nina Smalley is a social researcher and occupational psychologist, who has recently worked at Cardiff School of Social Sciences and Cardiff Law School.

Savitri Taylor is Senior Lecturer in the Law School at La Trobe University, Australia.

1
Editorial Introduction

Catherine Jones Finer

Rarely can the title of this series—Broadening Perspectives on Social Policy—have seemed more apposite; and rarely can the wording of a title—Migration, Immigration and Social Policy—within this series have proved more telling. Migration, *per se*, is a neutral term, referring to the facts of the case: the movement of people (and peoples) around the world—to escape danger or in search of a better life—which commonly involves the crossing of borders between countries. *Im*migration, by contrast, refers to a part of this phenomenon, as seen from the various perspectives (welcoming? unwelcoming? ignorant/innocent? calculating? discriminating? ambivalent?) of a migrants-receiving society (likewise *e*migration in respect of a migrants-sending/losing society). As such, immigration poses issues of policy for the societies concerned—as well as for those other societies (and/or their supranational representatives) with or within which they maintain, or hope to maintain, good working relationships. Against this backcloth, social policy—at least in the sense of regulations and services capable of actual delivery on the ground—remains, so far, society-specific.

The tensions implicit between European welfare statism and notions of mass immigration have long been apparent, albeit too often unacknowledged hitherto, by *aficionados* of these self-same welfare states. Box 1 illustrates the range of contradictory aspirations and inspirations. Not that difficulties over "mass" immigration have been confined to the self-declared welfare states (and/or their latter-day reformulations). These can apply to *any* developed society, as the present collection of papers makes clear.

Over and above the nation state, the one supranational body so far possessed of any credibility—and pretension—regarding the (re)direction of at least regional trends in migration is the European Union (EU), itself still a fledgling entity in institutional terms, in danger of growing beyond its corporate strength while still searching for a popular, if not populist, base of support. As a would-be container and controller of migration—or rather of immigration into EU Europe—its efforts remain in danger of being dissipated and distorted by the very nationalistic pressures it is supposed to be rising above.

In the meantime, the movements of people continue, seemingly regardless of anything the governments of developed countries "on target" might be

---

Box 1

The multicultural welfare state problematic

- . . . in Titmuss' view social policies had two purposes, to provide the best possible social services according to need rather than economic means, and to serve as moral exemplars of the good society and the good life. They would advance the values of collective altruism and function as an institution of social integration, in contrast to the competitive egoism of the economic market and its divisive effect on society. (Pinker 1990: 35–6)
- [There is] an assumption that the establishment of social welfare necessarily and inevitably contributes to the spread of humanism and the resolution of social injustice. The reverse can be true . . . Welfare, as an institutional means, can serve different masters. A multitude of sins may be committed in its appealing name . . . Welfare may be used to narrow allegiances and not to diffuse them. (Titmuss 1987: 312)
- Welfare states are national states, and in every country welfare is a national concern, circumscribed by the nation's borders and reserved for its residents alone . . . Seen in this perspective, a welfare state is not only a national system, it is also anti-international: a socially secure society is also a closed shop. (De Swaan 1994: 102)
- How is democratic consensus to be achieved on issues of morality, custom and legislation when subsections of the population adhere to distinct systems of morality or faith? (Coleman 1997: 1460)
- Migration is an integral part of the European Union's formation and development. Consequently, migration has always been an issue on the agenda of the European institutions. (Niessen and Schibel 2003: 21)

Source: Adapted from Jones Finer (2004: 77–8).

---

attempting to do about them. Such, certainly, is the starting point of the first paper in this collection.

"Western countries need not, should not and [manifestly] cannot *control* transborder movement in the manner attempted up until now", observes Savitri Taylor. Written from an Australian perspective, which nonetheless encompasses Western concerns in general, this wide-ranging paper puts the case—ambitious yet ostensibly pragmatic—for the worldwide *management* of migration instead, in such a manner as to benefit all the stakeholders in the process. From a comparable and no less ambitious perspective in its way, Channe Lindstrøm's paper next puts the case for (at least) the EU's developing a common policy on (at least) asylum and immigration: one which goes beyond containment to tackle the root causes of migration flows into Europe. "The EU possesses the potential means and authority to produce a real and positive impact along the relief-development continuum", she affirms, if only "institutional competence is coordinated and funds are made available".

Meanwhile, EU member governments are continuing to respond, not so much to the realities of the immigration situation as to their voters' presumed perceptions of it. Liza Schuster exposes the *normalization* of deportation, detention and dispersal programmes by the governments (in particular) of France, Italy, Germany and the UK—at a time when "there is no asylum 'crisis' and it is contentious whether there is an undocumented migration crisis". This paper is an indictment of policies and practices whose harm "extends beyond the people targeted [and damages] the society that tolerates them". Peter Dwyer then follows through by demonstrating how the welfare rights of forced migrants are being hollowed out "upwards, sideways and downwards" in EU Europe—away from anything approaching what its *citizens* can expect. This he does with particular reference to Leeds—a major location for dispersed UK asylum-seekers—wherein the vagaries of their sociolegal status, coupled with the makeshift complexities of local, multi-agency "governance", can leave migrants with welfare rights virtually "hollowed out to extinction". David Dunkerley and colleagues complete this group of papers with their own telling account of how welfare professionals can feel about being employed to operate services in such a context.

There then follow three contributions exceptionally revealing in respect of what might be dubbed the opposite ends of developed Europe's continuum of outlook on the integration of immigrants. Alexandre Afonso offers a rare explanation, not merely of Switzerland's traditional resistance to the very idea of immigration (other than as a temporary, expedient, labour market device), but of the institutional barriers that have built up to inhibit the development of even modest moves in aid of "integration"—however much these might now be desired in some key quarters. In dramatic contrast, Anniken Hagelund then offers a no less forthright account of why, how and to what effect (so far), the Norwegian welfare state—for so long the arche-typal proponent of "kindism" towards migrants from poorer countries—is now embarked on a proactive integration programme designed to make functioning Norwegian citizens out of newly arrived refugees, in as short a time as possible. It is intriguing, after this, to take in Bjørg Colding and colleagues' account of how education authorities in Denmark (again "not a traditional country of immigration") are comprehensively being encouraged to tackle not merely the low educational staying-power characteristic of certain categories of ethnic minority youth (distinguished by age/"generation" of entry as well as by countries of origin), but the lack of practice of teachers at responding "multiculturally"—and the reluctance of many employers to offer apprenticeships to ethnic minority youth.

The collection concludes, fittingly, with a (retrospective) eye to the longer term. Drawing on material from the Office for National Statistics' (UK) Longitudinal Study, Lucinda Platt offers an analysis of post-migration social mobility in Britain from 1971 to 1991 and 2001. This permits the effects of migration origins and histories to be separated, for the first time, from the effects of within-Britain experiences (notably in respect of education and employment) on the respective fortunes, over two generations, of members of different ethnic minority groups. In a field so charged with competing loyalties, value judgements and presuppositions, it is satisfying to be able to finish on so dispassionate and constructive a note.

My thanks to all of the contributors, in all their generosity and resilience, for making this collection possible.

References

Coleman, D. A. (1997), Origins of multi-cultural societies and problems of their management under democracy. In *Proceedings of the 23rd International Population*, Liege: International Union for the Scientific Study of Population.

De Swaan, A. (1994), Perspectives for transnational social policy in Europe: social transfers from West to East. In A. De Swaan (ed.), *Social Policy beyond Borders: The Social Question in Transnational Perspective*, Amsterdam: Amsterdam University Press.

Jones Finer, C. (2004), The quest for an ideal multi-cultural welfare state? Dutch experience viewed from a British Perspective. In E. de Gier, A. de Swaan and M. Ooijens (eds), *Dutch Welfare Reform in an Expanding Europe: The Neighbours' View*, Amsterdam: Het Spinhuis, pp. 77–99.

Niessen, J. and Schibel, Y. (2003), *EU and US Approaches to the Management of Immigration: Comparative Perspectives*, Brussels: Migration Policy Group.

Pinker, R. (1990), *Social Work in an Enterprise Society*, London and New York: Routledge.

Titmuss, R. M. (1987), Social welfare and the art of giving. In R. H. Tawney (ed.), *The Concept of Equality* (1964). Quoted from P. Alcock, H. Glennerster, A. Oakley and A. Sinfield (eds), *Welfare and Wellbeing: Richard Titmuss's Contribution to Social Policy*, Bristol: Policy Press.

From Border Control to Migration Management: The Case for a Paradigm Change in the Western Response to Transborder Population Movement

Savitri Taylor

Introduction

During the 500-year period of European empires (Abernethy 2000), trans-continental movement was undertaken mostly by Europeans (Juss 2004: 304–5; Habermas 1998: 231), who by migrating to the colonies improved both their personal economic situation and the economic situation of the home country (Habermas 1998: 231). The 15 million Asians and Africans who moved continents between 1500 and 1900 accounted for only a small fraction of total movement (Juss 2004: 304), and in many instances were individuals transplanted from one colony to another by a colonizing power in order to meet labour needs (Gledhill 1994: 6).

The proposition (now undisputed) that, subject to very limited international legal obligations, it is the sovereign right of states to exclude non-citizens from their territory, is only of late nineteenth-century origin (Juss 2004: 298). Its most vigorous defenders are the Western nations which benefited so greatly from free movement in earlier times. The reason for this is not difficult to discern. Net international migration now occurs from the rest of the world to the West (UN Department of Economic and Social Affairs 2004: 32), prompted by various combinations of poverty, violence, injustice and persecution, and facilitated by global communication and transport systems.

State-endorsed opportunities for migration are at present far outstripped by the demand for such opportunities. Given the sorts of circumstances producing the demand, it is no wonder that some individuals decide or are forced to take matters into their own hands. Western countries are concerned by the fact that about one-third to one-half of all movement across their borders is irregular and that the trend is upward (International Organization for Migration 2003a: 58–60).

In responding to irregular movement, Western governments often try to draw a sharp distinction between those forcibly displaced and economic migrants. However, classifying individuals as belonging to one group *or* the other is very problematic (Special Rapporteur of the Commission on Human

Rights on the Human Rights of Migrants 2000: para. 30). Above the level of pure survival, the desire for economic betterment rarely constitutes sufficient motivation in itself for persons to incur the emotional and other costs associated with migration (authorized or otherwise). Massey *et al.* have pointed out (1998: 9):

> Migration typically has not ended with the equalization of wages, but with the attainment of bearable conditions of life in areas of origin, after which people find migration not worth the effort. Despite the absence of legal barriers to movement and the persistence of a significant wage differential, sustained net migration between Puerto Rico and the USA mainland effectively ended in the early 1970s, as did migration between Spain and Germany.

Moreover, the fact that a small number of countries, which are "neither the poorest nor the least developed", produce the "vast majority" of international migrants suggests that the explanation for most international migration is to be found in a combination of economic and non-economic factors rather than economic factors alone (1998: 10).

In the long run, the only policy responses to irregular migrant and asylum-seeker movement likely to be effective are those which address the root causes. In other words, it is necessary to take steps towards the elimination of poverty, armed conflict and human rights abuse in the countries producing the irregular movers, so that migration becomes truly "a choice and not the only option" (Sorensen *et al.* 2003: 19). Unfortunately, however, the trade, investment, aid and other initiatives which can effectively address root causes do not come cheap in economic or political terms—and can only yield results in the long term (see e.g. Martin 1997: 25; Puchala 1997: 342; Suhrke and Zolberg 1999: 170; Widgren and Martin 2002; Chimni 2002). In the short term, some of the necessary initiatives may even lead to increases in irregular asylum-seeker and migrant flows (see e.g. Widgren and Martin 2002; Martin 1997: 25). Since politicians in the West have to win elections in the short term, their self-interest is best served by talking of the need to deal with root causes, without actually making a sustained effort to do so (see e.g. Fagen 2003; Rotberg 2002; Crawford 2001; Lucas 1999: 142). Talk of addressing root causes is often used, in fact, as a "moral alibi" for restrictive immigration policies and tough border controls.

The main argument advanced in this article is that Western countries need not, should not and cannot *control* transborder movement in the manner attempted up till now. Rather they can and should cooperate with countries of origin, countries of transit and other receiving countries to *manage* migration in a manner which benefits all stakeholders, including would-be migrants. The cooperative regulation of migration is not being proposed here as a substitute for policies seeking to eliminate migration push factors, but rather as an addition to such policies: to provide solutions for the individuals affected by the push factors while they continue to operate (which may be for a very long time indeed).

Overview of Formal Migration Programmes

While most countries allow non-citizens to enter for temporary purposes such as tourism, study and business, most make little or no provision for such people to enter and remain within their territory on a non-time-limited basis. There are over 191 countries in the world, but only four of these (Australia, Canada, New Zealand and the United States) have formalized general programmes of permanent immigration (International Organization for Migration 2003a: 17). In absolute terms, the United States' immigration programme (with an intake of 1,063,732 persons in 2002) is almost three times the size of the other three countries' programmes put together. Looked at from a different perspective, however, Australia's annual immigration intake (105,429 persons in 2001/2) represents about 0.54 per cent of its existing population, Canada's intake (228,575 persons in 2002) about 0.71 per cent, New Zealand's intake (53,000 persons in 2001/2) about 1.3 per cent, and the United States' intake about 0.36 per cent of its existing population, making the United States the least rather than the most generous of the traditional immigration countries.

For the calendar year 2002 or financial year 2001/2, the family reunification category constituted 36 per cent of Australia's total migration programme, 29 per cent of Canada's, 27 per cent of New Zealand's and 63 per cent of the United States'. In the same period, the skilled migration category constituted 51 per cent of Australia's total migration programme, 60 per cent of Canada's, 68 per cent of New Zealand's and 16 per cent of the United States'. Finally, the humanitarian category constituted 12 per cent of Australia's programme, 11 per cent of Canada's, 5 per cent of New Zealand's and 12 per cent of the United States'.[1]

The United States, Canada, Australia and New Zealand make a proportion of their humanitarian category places available to refugees referred for resettlement by the Office of the United Nations High Commissioner for Refugees (UNHCR). Denmark, Finland, the Netherlands, Norway and Sweden are also traditional resettlement countries for UNHCR. The United States, Canada and Australia between them provide most of the resettlement places, collectively offering (though not necessarily filling)[2] about 81,700 places annually (UNHCR 2003a). By contrast the European countries named provide only about 4,000 places per year between them. In recent years, UNHCR and a number of the traditional resettlement countries have been taking active steps to encourage expansion of the base of resettlement countries (UNHCR 2002: para. 14; Troeller 2002: 85–6). Benin, Brazil, Burkina Faso, Chile, Iceland, Ireland and most recently the United Kingdom have started providing an annual quota of resettlement places for UNHCR (UNHCR 2003a).[3] In addition to the countries which make an annual commitment, countries such as Belgium, France, Germany, Italy, Luxembourg, Spain and Switzerland assist UNHCR with resettlement places on an *ad hoc* basis (UNHCR 2003a; Feller 2001). The bottom line, however, is that the need for resettlement places far exceeds the present supply (Van Selm *et al.* 2003: 17–18).

Rationales of Immigration Control

Preserving national culture

Until the late 1950s the four traditional immigration countries—Australia, Canada, New Zealand and the United States—restricted non-white immigration while encouraging white immigration through settlement schemes (UN Department of Economic and Social Affairs 2004: 71–2). However, over the course of the 1960s and 1970s all these countries were forced to dispense with their restrictions on non-white immigration partly because the supply of European immigrants was drying up and partly because racial discrimination was becoming less acceptable internationally (2004: 72).

The author's own country, Australia, phased out its notorious White Australia Policy over the period 1966 to 1973 (Garnaut *et al.* 2003: 11), according to the then prime minister Gough Whitlam, in order "to turn a decent face to the world" (Marr and Wilkinson 2003: 35). However, Australian authorities believed that public acceptance of the policy's removal depended on non-white immigrants being chosen with a great deal more care than was the case with white immigrants, and acted accordingly (*ibid.*). Even now many white Australians are strongly opposed to non-white immigration (Reynolds 1998: 147; Sheridan 1998: 170; Roberts 2005). Joseph Carens has put the best possible argument for their position rather well (though he is not convinced by it). This is that the fundamental issue is one of culture, not race. Cultural homogeneity increases the likelihood that members of the political community will "want the same things and thus be able to cooperate on common projects and to provide collective benefits" (Carens 1988: 46). Moreover, since Australia's settler society was founded by persons of British stock, the existing Australian population values the achievements of British civilization and wishes to "recreate Britain" in Australia. In order to achieve both of these quite reasonable objectives—so runs the argument—it is necessary to ensure that immigrants to Australia are "as much like the British as possible", in other words, come from white societies (1988: 47).

Carens is right not to be convinced by this argument. It is already too late for Australia to preserve British culture in all its purity. For good or ill, Australia is now a multicultural society; so preservation of cultural homogeneity can no longer serve as a reason for immigration control. The horse has already bolted. (An equivalent proposition holds true for European Union countries as well; Espiner 2004: 17.)

Defending liberal values and the rule of law

A slightly different rationalization of immigration control is based on the observation that "liberal institutions are not only scarce, but hard won and fragile" (Whelan 1988: 17). It follows that

> a liberal may properly compromise liberal principles in practice, in the non-ideal world, when this appears necessary *in order* to preserve or strengthen them where they have a foothold . . . In this spirit a liberal

might, as things stand in the world today, not only uphold the traditional (and admittedly nonliberal) sovereign power over borders and
admission to citizenship, but might also support restrictive policies on
these matters, insofar as there were good reasons to believe that uncontrolled cross-border movement of people—in particular the influx of
nonliberal people into liberal states—would pose a threat to the survival
or perhaps simply to the flourishing and strengthening of liberal commitments and institutions where they exist. (*ibid.*)

The assumption here seems to be that some "others" are so different from "us"
that they cannot be persuaded by reason and experience to accept and support
our common purposes and our institutions, but rather will, if allowed to become
members of our political community in large number, subvert them.

Similar fears have been held in the past and have proven to be unfounded.
For example, Karen Slawner has pointed out that it was "strongly held
beliefs about personhood, rationality and moral capacity" (or rather the lack
thereof) that made it such a long, hard struggle to achieve political enfran-
chisement for women and African Americans in the USA (Slawner 1998: 83–
4). Notwithstanding that women and African Americans finally won their
struggle for the vote, America's liberal values and institutions survived.

It may be argued that the issue is not one of inherent difference but difference in acculturation. For example, Liz Fekete points out that, post-September
11, governments across Europe are increasingly dealing with minority communities, particularly Muslim ones, as if they represent collective threats to
the nation's "core values". The implicit assumption is always that the very
worst elements within minority communities are representative of the whole
and that their behaviour is entirely ascribable to "culture" rather than, for
example, socio-economic exclusion or individual pathology (Fekete 2004: 18–
21). Such cultural stereotyping is little different from racial stereotyping, and
policy based on unthinking ascription of all ills to cultural difference is as
little likely to address real problems as one based on an ascription of all ills
to racial difference.

There is, however, another argument for immigration control in defence
of our "way of life" that runs along different lines. For example, in 2003 the
Home Affairs Committee of the United Kingdom Parliament released a
report which warned that, if the numbers of people seeking asylum in developed countries was allowed to increase unchecked, "it could overwhelm the
capacity of the receiving countries to cope, leading inevitably to social
unrest" (Select Committee on Home Affairs 2003: para. 1). The Committee
accused those "who believe that there is no reason why a prosperous country
like Britain cannot afford to continue to absorb a growing number of
migrants" of failing "to recognise the social and political realities" (2003:
para. 3). In other words, when the Committee earlier referred to asylum-
seekers overwhelming a receiving country's capacity to cope, it was referring
not to economic but to social absorption capacity.

Irregular migration is often perceived in developed countries to be a threat
to standards of living, cultural identity and so on. Regardless of whether
these perceptions correspond to reality, they can be the cause of real problems.

Hostility towards irregular migrants has spilled over into racist violence and other forms of social instability in several European countries (Andrews 2001). In the face of extreme, widespread and continuing public disorder, it may indeed be necessary for a time to institute policies that bring immigration outcomes more closely into line with public expectations. The restoration of public order is in the interests of citizens and non-citizens alike, since a minimum level of public order is necessary to support the domestic rule of law (Walker 1988: 27–8). If the domestic rule of law breaks down, the country affected will no longer be capable of protecting either its own citizens or others (Coles 1995: 15). Naturally, any concessions to ill-informed public opinion could only be justified as a temporary measure, the longer-term solution being the better education of public opinion.

Protecting the economic and social rights of citizens

Ross Garnaut has observed that, historically, the Australian community's acceptance of immigration has risen and fallen in tandem with confidence in the domestic economy. Thus, "[a]s confidence in sustained growth strengthens, community attitudes become more supportive of high levels of immigration" (Garnaut et al. 2003: 8). Conversely, in times of high unemployment and recession, those advocating less immigration gain political ground because of the widespread perception that immigrants compete with Australians for jobs and/or welfare services. At the least, economic recession refocuses political attention on the composition of the immigration programme. In hard economic times, the immigrants most tolerated by most voters are those with capital to invest or with skills that are in short supply within the Australian community.

According to Ross Garnaut, the facts are that immigration "makes Australians richer on average" (Garnaut et al. 2003: 1). He attributes the increase in average incomes largely to scale effects arising from lower costs per person to provide Australians with many public and private goods and services, as well as to dynamic factors due to the increased attractiveness of the country to business leaders and "talented young people" (2003: 15). He goes on to observe, "[w]ho gains from immigration, and by how much, therefore depends to a considerable extent on how Governments use their increased budget capacity [arising from lower public sector per capita costs]" (2003: 2). If government budgets redistribute income from rich to poor (as they have tended to in the past), it will even be the case that immigration will benefit poor Australians more than rich ones (2003: 16).

The present Australian government makes much of the fact that it has rebalanced the immigration programme towards skilled migration (Ruddock 2002). Its assertion is that skilled migration increases Commonwealth budgetary capacity, while humanitarian and family migration "impact quite negatively on the budget", so that any increase in humanitarian migration, especially at the expense of skilled migration, would be fiscally irresponsible (House of Representatives 2002: 9754–5 [Mr Ruddock]). Yet economic forecasting carried out for the Australian Department of Immigration has indicated that *all* categories of permanent migrants, including the humanitarian and family categories, have an average positive net present value effect on Commonwealth and State budgets, due to the long-run benefits of increased tax revenues (Access Economics 2003: ii).[4]

While the specific economic impacts of immigration on developed countries other than Australia vary according to their individual labour market, fiscal and other policies, it appears that in developed countries generally the "net overall economic impact" of immigration (skilled and unskilled) is positive; albeit at present "relatively minor in comparison with the national incomes of the host economies" (UN Department of Economic and Social Affairs 2004: 96).

Interestingly, the governments of Western countries are now coming to realize that ageing, shrinking populations could spell the need for increasing immigration to stave off a bleak future "where jobs would go unfilled and services undelivered" (Annan 2004: 13; see also Prodi 2004). In response, European governments seem to be moving towards an Australian style of approach: trying to encourage the front door entry of immigrants who will very obviously deliver economic benefits (the highly skilled), while placating popular fears of immigration with the reassurance that other would-be immigrants will not be allowed to enter through either the front door or the back (Graff *et al.* 2001: 16; *Migration World Magazine* 2001: 8; Bennhold 2004: 2; Moulson 2004).

Yet should our own economic prosperity be all that matters to us? In the face of massive inequalities in the global distribution of resources, liberals should presumably not be countenancing *any* immigration controls, unless some mechanism other than immigration can be found for ensuring that all humans have equal access to global resources (Kymlicka 2001: 270–3). Nevertheless, the image dominating our minds, and dictating our attitude to unauthorized arrivals in particular, seems to be that of a "mass invasion" by the world's poor, attracted towards us by any perceived weakening in our determination to keep them out.

If indeed the world's poor were all to descend upon Australia—or any other Western country—the structures of the state would, of course, crumble under the weight of the demands placed upon them, with nobody at all better off as a result. If such a scenario were likely, we could thus be facing a situation in which "the consequences of a compromise in decision-making in public life (settling for the second best rather than the ideal) can result in a better outcome than that which would come from adopting the best abstract moral principle" (Hayden 1998: 54). The fact of the matter, however, is that such a scenario is not at all likely. No matter how easy it might be to do so, most of the nationals of poor countries do *not* migrate—or even wish to migrate—to wealthier countries (Sassen 1999: 141).

Giving meaning to democracy

The strongest argument in support of a nation's unconditional right to control immigration numbers and composition is the argument that anything else would compromise the practice of democracy. As far as states are concerned, an individual, who has not acquired automatic membership of the political community of a particular nation state on the basis of birth, cannot have it for the asking thereafter. In other words, as far as states are concerned, individuals cannot choose to be members of a different political community than that into which they are born, unless the political community of their choice chooses them in turn. As Whelan puts it (1988: 28–9):

> [T]he operation of democratic institutions should amount to "self determination", or control by the people over matters that affect their common interests. The admission of new members into the democratic group . . . would appear to be such a matter, one that could not only affect various private interests of the current members, but that could also, in the aggregate, affect the quality of their public life and the character of their community. If power over this matter lay elsewhere than in the hands of the members, or if the matter (concerning which a number of alternative choices seem possible) were permanently removed from the agenda, the democracy that existed would be seriously attenuated, it would not amount to self-determination.

The view that most people take is that there is an underlying tension between liberal values (including the belief in universal human rights) and democratic values, which surfaces in an irresolvable dilemma when liberal democratic societies are forced to confront the issue of how they should treat a *person* who is not also a *member* of their political community. However, there is a way out of the dilemma. It lies in thinking of democracy not as the practice of self-governance by a *pre-existing* political community, but rather as a political practice in which the question of who the (self-governing) people are is also and always in contestation. Bonnie Honig argues that "[t]he practice of taking rights and privileges rather than waiting for them to be granted by a sovereign power is . . . a quintessentially democratic practice" (Honig 2001: 99). She points out that the history of American democracy can be narrated as "a story of illegitimate demands made by people with no standing to make them . . . They make room for themselves by staging nonexistent rights, and by way of such stagings, sometimes, new rights, powers, and visions come into being" (2001: 101). Fiona Jenkins continues Honig's line of thought by suggesting that, rather than thinking of unauthorized immigration "as a threat to the maintenance of 'our' democracy" (Jenkins 2004: 92), we might instead "allow the demand for justice we encounter in the claims of refugees to play a critical role in reconceiving our own entitlements and the entitlements of others . . . as the problematic claims of the members of a democracy to come" (2004: 94).

The Limits of Control

As far as the governments of potential receiving countries in the West are concerned, the objective of immigration control is to facilitate the entry of immigrants who will deliver a net economic or other gain to the nation and to prevent the entry of all others. However, these governments are not the only players in the game. Governments of potential sending countries are also players. About a quarter of all countries think their emigration level is too high, and have in place policy measures to lower that level (UN Department of Economic and Social Affairs 2004: 87). These countries are particularly concerned by the emigration of highly skilled individuals (the brain drain) as their departure represents a loss both of past investment in education and training and future contributions to economic development (2004: xi). On the other hand, about 6 per cent of countries, many in the Asia-Pacific region, actively encourage labour emigration because the national economy benefits from remittances (the money sent back home by workers overseas) (2004: 87; Massey *et al.* 1998: 194). (Note that the money flowing into developing countries annually through remittances exceeds the official development assistance they receive from overseas by a considerable amount; Overbeek 2002: 77.)

Nor are sending country governments the only facilitators of migration. Social networks and the immigration industry also play a part. Many of the social networks spanning the world got their start in the age of the European empires. Many Chinese and Indian communities scattered through the world are there because their ancestors were encouraged or forced by colonial administrators to move to colonies in need of labour. Many European countries are host to communities of people from former colonies because postcolonial turmoil forced them there and/or they actually believed official narratives in which all the peoples of an empire were described as being one.

Once an expatriate community becomes established in a place, their presence makes it a more attractive destination for friends and relations "back home" who wish to emigrate or need to flee. This is because friends and relations can usually be counted upon for a helping hand, and helping hands are very necessary for both migrants and refugees in finding employment, housing and everything else necessary to make a new life (Massey *et al.* 1998: 186–7).

The last major group of migration facilitators consists of those who make a legal or illegal business of it. Moreover, like all good capitalists, members of the industry do not simply serve existing markets; they work at creating new ones. The immigration industry is thriving in Australia's region. Labour markets in Southeast Asia have long been facilitated by networks paying scant regard to borders or the laws intended to regulate movement across them (Human Rights Watch 2002: 30; Hugo 1999: 172–3). In relation to people-smuggling from the Middle East through Indonesia, Human Rights Watch notes that "[t]here is a long tradition of trading between the Arab world and Indonesians living in Batam and the north coast of Java, of which people-smuggling is only the modern manifestation" (Human Rights Watch 2002: 30 n.113). It is in fact quite usual for the inhabitants of postcolonial states the world over to ignore lines on maps that are devoid of social significance. In doing so, they may become illegal immigrants or smugglers from the perspective of states (Said 1993: 372–3), but whether their actions should necessarily attract moral opprobrium, let alone criminal sanction, is open to question.

Western countries are all for global free markets in goods and capital, but very much against a global free market in labour, for all that this opposition is inconsistent with both the political and economic versions of liberal doctrine (Hoffmann-Nowotny 1997: 104–5). Nevertheless, global capitalism is a package deal—like it or not. Once goods and capital are moving freely across national borders, it is impossible to exercise complete control over the movement of people (Stelzer 2001/2: 8). Moreover, if, as is often the case, transborder population movement is being driven by factors even more compelling than a convergence of interests between workers in one country and employers in another, the historical evidence suggests that not even the most draconian of border control policies will succeed in suppressing it.

In the foreword to a government publication entitled "Managing the Border: Immigration Compliance", the Australian minister for immigration laments: "With around 37,000 kilometres of coastline in Australia, the task of managing our borders is a significant challenge" (DIMIA 2004b: iii). Land borders are even more of a challenge to police than sea borders. The United States, which has unparalleled resources to devote to the task, has found it impossible to prevent large-scale and unauthorized inward movement across its border with Mexico. Then again, as James Graff points out, border control must be a still "tougher proposition for a poorly co-ordinated EU that has external land borders with 11 countries, not to mention the Mediterranean Sea" (Graff 2002). In fact, no matter how highly motivated and no matter the lengths to which it is prepared to go, no state has yet succeeded in exercising complete control over its borders (Miller 1999: 25).

The Australian government currently asserts that it is willing to spend whatever it takes to achieve the objective of complete border control (*Sydney Morning Herald* 2003). However, "spending whatever it takes" makes no economic sense for Australia or any other country, since the cost is certain to exceed the benefits gained (Stelzer 2001/2: 4; Griswold 2002). Thus, any government which stakes its political credibility on controlling borders is going to lose that credibility sooner or later; if not in one way (by being proven to have lost control of the border) then in another (by mismanaging the national economy). Thus it can actually make political sense for governments to step back from the language of control. Joanne van Selm, for instance, suggests it is far more constructive to speak of managing transborder population flows than of controlling them:

"Control" implies that the state can determine whether or not individuals arrive at its borders, and the fact that they are present therefore makes the state seem lacking somehow. "Management" implies rather that the state acknowledges that there is a situation with which it must deal to the generally mutual satisfaction of the various actors that depend on it to do so. (Van Selm 2003: 89)

Sharing Responsibility for Managing Transborder Movement

Bilateral, regional or global cooperation?

Given that transborder population movement is an inter-state phenomenon driven by powerful global forces, it is beyond the power of any one state acting unilaterally to either control or "manage" the phenomenon. Realizing this fact, the Australian government has entered into a great many bilateral arrangements intended to advance its immigration control objectives. These include interception arrangements such as the "regional cooperation arrangement" with Indonesia and the International Organization for Migration (IOM),[5] offshore processing arrangements with Nauru and Papua New Guinea (Senate Select Committee on a Certain Maritime Incident 2002: ch. 10), and readmission agreements with countries such as Afghanistan, Iran, the People's Republic of China and South Africa (Ruddock 2002b). Australia's pursuit of bilateral migration arrangements, in fact, conforms to a worldwide trend which has been gathering pace since the 1990s (UN Department of Economic and Social Affairs 2004: xvi). Bilateral arrangements are attractive to states because they can be negotiated with relative ease and rapidity in response to a particular problem faced at a particular time (*ibid.*). Naturally, it cannot be assumed that bilateral agreements advance the interests of both parties equally, since the malign effects of asymmetrical bargaining power manifest most acutely in such negotiations (Betts 2003: 18). Furthermore, even if a given bilateral arrangement does advance the interests of both participants, it may well do so at the expense of affected third parties whose interests are ignored.

As well as entering into bilateral arrangements, the Australian government actively promotes regional cooperation through such consultative mechanisms as the Bali Process on People Smuggling and Trafficking and the Asia Pacific Consultations on Refugees, Displaced Persons and Migrants (DIMIA 2004a: 64–5). As with bilateral migration arrangements, regional cooperation on migration has been on the rise since the 1990s and now exists in most parts of the world (UN Department of Economic and Social Affairs 2004: xvi). However, most of this "cooperation" takes the form of consultation. The European Union has made the most progress in achieving more substantial cooperation, though from a global perspective the desirability of the actual outcomes is open to question.

Article 63 of the Treaty Establishing the European Community, as amended by the Treaty of Amsterdam, required the Council of Europe to adopt by 1 May 2004 a legislative package setting minimum standards for the national asylum policies of member states.[6] Political agreement was reached on the last element of that package, the Asylum Procedures Directive, on 29 April 2004. Since unanimity among member states was required for adoption of each element of the package (Refugee Council 2004: 3), the minimum standards were, with some exceptions, driven down to the lowest common denominator of existing national standards. The EU's declared intention is to engage in a second stage of negotiations aimed at establishing a single asylum system for Europe (2004: 4). The ten new members of the EU will be full participants in these negotiations (*ibid.*). The UK's Refugee Council has observed that "[t]he length of time it has taken to negotiate stage one of the [Common European Asylum System], and the low level at which standards have been set, makes prospects bleak for stage two" (2004: 17).

In 2002, the European Commission commissioned a study on the feasibility of setting up a European resettlement scheme. The suggestion made by the authors of the study was that a European Resettlement Programme should be conceived of as an element of a Common European International

Protection System, the other elements being the Common European Asylum System and a programme for the delivery of humanitarian assistance in regions of origin (Van Selm *et al.* 2003: vi). The authors then discussed six possible models of European resettlement ranging from maintaining the existing situation of discretionary national schemes through to a "totally common programme" of resettlement by the European Union acting as a collective entity (2003: 154). In discussing the feasibility of a totally common programme, the authors observed that, while it was obvious that member states without existing resettlement programmes might lack the political will to introduce them, the tendency of those states with existing resettlement programmes would be to resist making any changes to the programmes they already had in place—especially if those programmes were perceived to be working well (2003: 143).

It seems a safe supposition that a Common European International Protection System is a long way from being realized. It seems an even safer supposition that a Common European Migration System is further still from being realized. At present, the European Commission is studying a proposal by Italy for a European programme of quotas for legal immigration from non-EU countries (*European Report no. 2802* 2003). The hope is that if the EU can offer an avenue of legal migration to the countries of nationality of illegal immigrants, it may have more success in procuring readmission agreements allowing for the return of those same illegal immigrants (*ibid.*). But the initial response to the proposal was largely negative (*BBC Monitoring International Reports* 2003b), and it was clear from the outset that the most that could be hoped for was Europe-wide coordination of immigration quotas set at the national level (*European Report no. 2802* 2003). The German Interior Minister, Otto Schily, was quoted as saying,

> Conditions in the various countries differ so widely, both economically and socially, that a single model for the entire union is not possible. It is up to Italy to decide whether or not the situation allows it to take in 40,000 Tunisians a year. In the same way we Germans have to be able to decide what our absorption capacity is . . . A system in which the EU Commission decides that one country has to accept a certain amount of immigrants, and another country yet another number, cannot function. Let us have no illusions, even a country that says it agrees with a given quota, will nevertheless have to be able to say who can and cannot enter. (*BBC Monitoring International Reports* 2003a)

The United Nations High Commissioner for Refugees has expressed the view that only global solutions to the problem of irregular population movement can adequately ensure that "people in need of international protection find it, people who wish to migrate have appropriate opportunities to do so, and abusive manipulation of entry possibilities is curtailed" (Lubbers 2003). This author agrees. Bilateral and regional cooperation arrangements are not necessarily a bad thing, but they are a bad thing if they operate at the expense of non-participants. This is exactly what tends to happen (Noll 2003: 299) and will continue to happen, until or unless states are obliged to ensure that any such arrangements are consistent with "an overarching, universally agreed and applied international framework" (UN Department of Economic and Social Affairs 2004: xxii).

Issues which have thus far been addressed through global agreements include refugee protection, people-smuggling, people-trafficking and the rights of migrant workers.[7] However, at present "there is no global institutional framework within which to address the full spectrum of international migration issues in a comprehensive and systematic manner" (UN Department of Economic and Social Affairs 2004: xvii). Negotiation of such a regime is far easier said than done.

Negotiating a global migration regime

International migration issues (including asylum-seeker issues) were included in the Programme of Action agreed upon at the United Nations International Conference on Population and Development held in Cairo in September 1994, and since then the Second Committee of the United Nations General Assembly has biennially considered whether an international conference on international migration and development ought to be convened (UN Department of Economic and Social Affairs 2004: 206). No consensus in favour of doing so has yet emerged, but the General Assembly has decided to hold a high-level dialogue on international migration and development in 2006 (2004: xxiii). Even more promisingly, an intergovernmental initiative— the Global Commission on International Migration—was launched in December 2003. Both developed and developing countries are represented in the core group of 12 states backing this Commission (Annan 2003) and, though independent of the United Nations, it has that organization's support (*UN Wire* 2003a, 2003d). The Commission's mandate is to do a gap analysis of current approaches to managing migration, including the institutional arrangements for so doing, and to make practical recommendations for improvement (*UN Wire* 2003a, 2003d). It was scheduled to present a final report to the UN Secretary-General in midsummer 2005 (*UN Wire* 2003a, 2003d). Meanwhile UNHCR, IOM, the International Labour Organization and other international organizations have also been attempting to encourage multilateral approaches to migration management through a range of separate and joint initiatives directed at inter-state dialogue and policy formation.

Similar efforts to achieve international cooperation in managing migration were made by international organizations in the 1970s and 1980s, to no avail (Lohrmann 1997: 317). However, these earlier efforts took place at a time when development of such a regime more obviously served the needs of developing countries than those of the West. Western countries now have greater incentive to participate in a global migration regime, because they are simultaneously discovering the limits of their individual ability to control back-door immigration *and* realizing that immigration could be necessary to their own future economic well-being. Developing countries have as much incentive as ever to participate, since their economies benefit (or can benefit) so substantially from remittances sent "home" from nationals living abroad. Nevertheless, the negotiation of such a regime will not be easy.

The greatest obstacle to be overcome in negotiating any cooperative regime is that of achieving goal congruence. As explained in an IOM background paper:

> While all States have a strong interest in better managed systems, the goal of managing migration may be quite different from State to State. For some, this management is focused on facilitating the freest possible movement of their nationals abroad for work and family reunification. For others, the management goal may be to limit this movement to the extent that it takes place outside normal channels. While this is but one example of disparate goals, there are others. Reaching shared goals or workable joint objectives for limited action and cooperation is a prerequisite for designing and carrying out joint capacity-building measures. (International Organization for Migration 2003b: para. 3)

If the construction of a truly global migration regime is attempted, the problems of achieving goal congruence will be even more acute than those faced in the attempt to construct regional regimes. Nevertheless, the problems need not be insurmountable, as long as participants are willing to focus on ultimate long-term objectives.

One example of a problem which need not be intractable is that of skilled versus unskilled migration. Developed countries are doing all they can to attract skilled immigrants while attempting with less than complete success to keep out unskilled immigrants. By contrast, developing countries generally consider their interests ill served by skilled emigration (brain drain), though advanced by unskilled emigration (Bhagwati 2004: 213). Nevertheless, the ultimate objective which developed countries are trying to achieve is the maintenance of their prosperity, while the ultimate objective for developing countries is an improvement in their own prosperity. Not only are these objectives compatible, they cannot in fact be separated. In a globalized and interdependent world, the best guarantee of Western prosperity is global prosperity. Thus, by designing a global migration regime to manage skilled and unskilled migration in a manner which promotes the development of the global South, the long-term interests of both developed and developing countries can be served. Developed countries might advance, or at the very least not jeopardize, their economic prosperity by officially allowing increased levels of unskilled immigration (perhaps in the form of temporary migration schemes in order to minimize social and political costs), at the same time as striving to limit the brain drain impact of skilled emigration by factoring the needs of the developing countries into their immigrant selection processes and making compensatory investment in the education and training programmes of those countries (UN Department of Economic and Social Affairs 2004: xiii, xviii–xix, xxi).

Nevertheless, the key problem of trying to negotiate a global migration regime in practice is that the short-term pains of adjustment likely to be experienced by some Western countries will tend to figure much more largely in political calculations than the long-term gains (Lohrmann 1997: 318). This is evidenced, for example, by the fact that developed countries have not permitted much progress to be made in World Trade Organization (WTO) negotiations on temporary movement of natural persons in the context of liberalizing trade in services (Mode 4 of the General Agreement of Trade in Services) (UN Department of Economic and Social Affairs 2004: 141). This is despite the expected gain for the global economy from liberalization of movement being "greater than the total gains expected from all of the other initiatives under discussion in the Doha work programme" (2004: 139).

Notwithstanding the unimpressive progress of Mode 4 negotiations, the best chance for success probably lies in following the GATT/WTO precedent and building up a global migration regime over many years through successive rounds of negotiation on specific issues (Doyle 2004: 4; Koslowski 2004: 15). To be sure, it will be no small feat to get governments even to come to the negotiating table in the first place. Most governments have thus far displayed a profound lack of interest, because they know that global migration agreements will be even more difficult to "sell" to their domestic constituencies than WTO agreements (Koslowski 2004: 2). Nevertheless, Rey Koslowski suggests that states, which have remained unmoved by the economic and human rights arguments for a global migration regime, may nevertheless be motivated to negotiate if cooperation on migration is clearly linked with cooperation in dealing with the "security implications of accelerating international mobility" (2004: 15).

It is not, of course, being argued that the WTO process is a perfect one, to be emulated in all respects in the negotiation of a global migration regime. Wealthy and powerful countries have been able to manipulate WTO processes to some degree (*UN Wire* 2003b, 2003c). It seems, however, naive to believe that a process which cannot be manipulated to some degree by the wealthy and powerful can be achieved in the real world. The fact that developing countries have successfully forced the USA and the EU to negotiate real reform of farm trade as part of the Doha Round (Wilson 2004: 14) seems proof that the WTO process works as well as any real-world process can be expected to work.

Protection issues

However well—or no—voluntary migration is managed, asylum-seeking will also continue for as long as its root causes remain unaddressed. The most significant international legal obligation at present owed by states to asylum-seekers is the obligation not to send them directly or indirectly to any place (including their country of nationality or former habitual residence) where their fundamental human rights would be in jeopardy (see Refugees Convention, article 33; Convention Against Torture and Other Inhuman or Degrading Treatment or Punishment, article 3; UN Human Rights Committee 2004: para. 12; Lauterpacht and Bethlehem 2001). However, not even the Refugees Convention places a duty on states actually to grant asylum (permission to live in their territory) to persons who cannot be returned to their country of nationality or former habitual residence. As a result, asylum-seekers can find themselves consigned to the limbo of permanently temporary immigration status within a state or, worse yet, in perpetual orbit between states which all insist that protection should be sought elsewhere. There is, therefore, a need to negotiate a global regime through which responsibility for the provision of durable and meaningful protection to those in need of it can be equitably shared by states.

As part of its Convention Plus initiative,[8] the UNHCR is seeking to "facilitate the resolution of refugee problems through multilateral special agreements" (UNHCR 2004b). It is working with groups of interested states to develop "generic multilateral agreements" on three matters: "the strategic use of resettlement as a tool of protection, a durable solution and a tangible form of burden-sharing; more effective targeting of development assistance to support durable solutions for refugees . . . and clarification of the responsibilities of States in the event of irregular secondary movements" (*ibid.*). These generic multilateral agreements are intended to serve as templates for "situation-specific multilateral agreements designed to resolve a particular refugee situation" (*ibid.*).

The problem with relying on situation-specific agreements being negotiated on an *ad hoc* basis, as the need arises, is that success is made dependent on the existence of political will to undertake each specific exercise. Yet, as the Assistant High Commissioner for Refugees has noted, "comprehensive arrangements have not been always pursued even for refugee situations that warranted them" (Morjane 2004). From a long-term perspective, it makes more sense for international efforts to be directed towards the negotiation of a non-situation-specific general multilateral agreement on sharing responsibility for the provision of international protection. It also makes sense for such an agreement to be negotiated as part of a comprehensive global migration regime, since it is only conceptually that asylum-seeker movement and migratory movement are separate phenomena.

The total annual number of refugee/humanitarian resettlement places made available worldwide pursuant to a global migration and protection regime would have to be sufficient to ensure that all successful protection claimants could be offered a durable solution within a reasonable time. In short, the total annual number of places made available would have to be a great deal more than at present. The United Nations High Commissioner for Refugees' ambitious "dream for the future" is for every developed country to provide an annual resettlement quota of 0.1 per cent of their existing population (which in Australia's case would be 20,000 places). This quota is well within the absorption capacities of the countries concerned and would make resettlement a genuinely available solution for those who need it most (Mares 2002: 242–3).

The size of Australia's annual Humanitarian Programme[9] makes it the third most generous resettlement country in the world at the present time. But even Australia has been far more generous with resettlement places in the past and can easily afford to be so again (Senate Legal and Constitutional References Committee 2002: paras 6.13–6.14). In 2003/4 there were 78,971 applicants for the 12,000 resettlement places that Australia provided under its Offshore Humanitarian Programme (DIMIA 2004a: 67). Officially, Australia's allocation of places gives "priority to people who are in the most vulnerable situations, and have the greatest need for resettlement places"

(Ruddock 2003)—and it is true that Australia's present allocation of places to *regions* accords with UNHCR's assessment of relative need (DIMIA 2004a: 68). However, the same cannot be said of Australia's allocation of places to *persons*. What makes the difference between selection and non-selection here is not the applicant's degree of need but Australia's preference for minimizing the cost to itself of resettlement.

In order to be granted any Offshore Humanitarian Programme visa, applicants must satisfy several public interest criteria including character, security and health requirements at the time of decision. Thus, for example, a person with a "disease or condition", the management of which would be likely to result in a "significant cost" to the Australian community, will probably[10] have their visa application refused (*Migration Regulations* Schedule 4, public interest criterion 4007; Maley 2003: 197). This is despite the fact that the sorts of circumstances which result in individuals meeting the core criteria of the Offshore Humanitarian Programme visa categories are also the sorts of circumstances which tend to produce medical needs in those individuals—and that those who do develop such medical needs are obviously more "in need" of Australia's assistance than those who do not (Refugee Council of Australia 2003: 55–6).

It is a further requirement for the grant of permanent visas in the Offshore Humanitarian Programme that the Minister be satisfied at the time of decision that "there are compelling reasons for giving special consideration to granting the applicant a permanent visa having regard not merely to the degree of need and lack of alternative durable solutions", but also to "the extent of the applicant's connection with Australia" and "the capacity of the Australian community to provide for the permanent settlement of persons such as the applicant in Australia" (*Migration Regulations* Schedule 2, clauses 200.222, 201.222, 203.222, 204.224). A similar requirement is imposed on the grant of temporary visas in the Offshore Humanitarian Programme, though the wording of the requirement has been tweaked to reflect the temporary nature of the visas. Among other things, what this requirement means in practice is that a Special Humanitarian Programme visa applicant needs to have a sponsor in the Australian community willing to meet the cost of airfares to Australia and so on and to provide support after arrival (DIMIA 2003: 11).[11]

As William Maley has observed (2003: 197): the cumulative effect of applying all the above criteria in the selection process is that Australia's Offshore Humanitarian Programme places are quite definitely not allocated to those in greatest need. This example indicates that, for a global resettlement programme to be truly effective, states should not retain the discretion to apply their own immigration criteria over and above the agreed protection criteria, when choosing which particular individuals to accept as part of their resettlement quota. But this, of course, may be asking for the politically impossible.

The problem of compliance

There is little point negotiating a global migration and protection regime which will unravel when put to the test of requiring governments to act contrary to their immediate political interests. Such an unravelling is almost guaranteed, unless the regime is strongly institutionalized. Importantly, the regime will have to include robust mechanisms for monitoring and enforcing compliance and for sanctioning non-compliance. An obvious means of institutionalization is the creation of a World Migration Organization (WMO) to play a similar role in relation to migration that the WTO plays in relation to trade (see e.g. Bhagwati 1998: 315–17; Martin 1997: 26). The WTO model may be far from ideal, yet it is at least "the most successful system for [settling] international disputes that the world has ever seen" (Stern 2004, quoting former WTO appellate judge James Bacchus). To the extent that lessons have been learned about how the WTO model can be improved, those lessons should, of course, be drawn upon in designing the WMO.

Conclusion

The opportunities at present available for authorized migration to Western countries are extremely limited and distributed according to criteria in which the needs of the countries providing the opportunities figure to a far greater extent than the needs of the individuals seeking them. This article considered the justifications usually proffered by Western countries for restrictive immigration policies and concluded that they were far from convincing. It then explained why endeavouring to achieve complete enforcement of restrictive and unilaterally determined immigration policies is, in any event, an exercise in futility. After establishing that Western countries need not, should not and cannot *control* immigration in the manner attempted until now, the article considered how states can instead *manage* mixed asylum-migration movement effectively "so that people in need of international protection find it, people who wish to migrate have appropriate opportunities to do so, and abusive manipulation of entry possibilities is curtailed" (Lubbers 2003). In summary, the only sort of management regime with a chance of succeeding in the long run is a global migration and protection regime. The negotiation of such a regime ought, therefore, to be attempted, for all that the challenges of doing so are impossible to overstate.

Acknowledgements

The author would like to thank Bruce Taylor for his research assistance, and Nic MacLellan and Tony Burke for their helpful comments on earlier versions of this article.

Notes

1. The United States has other minor immigration categories which together accounted for the remaining 9 per cent of its programme.
2. The more stringent security requirements imposed by resettlement countries post-September 11 have greatly increased processing times as well as making it more difficult for individuals to qualify for resettlement places (UNHCR 2002: para. 11; Troeller 2002: 86). In 2002, for example, the United States filled only 26,800 of its annual quota of 70,000 resettlement places (UNHCR 2003b: 16).

3. Benin, Brazil, Burkina Faso, Chile and Iceland do not appear to have made a resettlement quota available for 2003/4 (UNHCR 2004a). Argentina and Spain used to be included in UNHCR's list of resettlement quota countries but have now been removed (Van Selm *et al.* 2003: 14).

4. The research shows that this benefit is generally greater for young adult migrants (Access Economics 2003: ii).

5. Under this arrangement potential irregular movers who are prevented from leaving Indonesia are provided with accommodation, food and emergency medical care by IOM (at Australia's expense). IOM notifies UNHCR of any individuals who indicate that they are asylum-seekers. Although UNHCR is not a formal participant in the regional cooperation arrangement, it does assess the protection claims of asylum seekers referred to it in Indonesia as part of its normal mandate activities. Australia has similar arrangements with Cambodia and East Timor, which again rely on the cooperation of IOM and UNHCR.

6. It should be noted that under the Treaty of Amsterdam, EU asylum and immigration measures do not as a general rule apply to Denmark, and apply to the UK and Ireland only if they decide to opt in to the measures (Refugee Council 2004: 3).

7. See Convention relating to the Status of Refugees, 28 July 1951 (Refugees Convention); Protocol relating to the Status of Refugees, 31 January 1967; Protocol against the Smuggling of Migrants by Land, Sea and Air, 15 November 2002; Protocol to Prevent, Suppress and Punish Trafficking in Persons, especially Women and Children, 15 November 2000; and International Convention on the Protection of the Rights of All Migrant Workers and Members of Their Families, 18 November 1990.

8. For an explanation of the Convention Plus initiative, see the UNHCR website at http://www.unhcr.ch/cgi-bin/texis/vtx/protect?id=406d21802.

9. Between 1996/7 and 2003/4, Australia's annual Humanitarian Programme was set at 12,000 places. Some 4,000 of these places were for applicants granted Refugee category or Secondary Movement category visas (Ruddock 2003; Refugee Council of Australia 2002). The remaining 8,000 places (less any places taken by onshore protection visa applicants) (Ruddock 2003) were for applicants granted Special Humanitarian Programme category visas. Australia's Humanitarian Programme was increased to 13,000 places for the financial year 2004/5, with 6,000 of these places allocated to Refugee and Secondary Movement category visas (Vanstone 2004).

10. The Minister for Immigration has a discretion to waive the health requirement if satisfied that grant of the visa would be unlikely to result in "undue" cost to the Australian community.

11. Australia usually meets the costs of travel and so on for applicants accepted under the refugee category (DIMIA 2003: 9).

References

Abernethy, D. (2000), *The Dynamics of Global Dominance: European Overseas Empires, 1415–1980*, New Haven, CT and London: Yale University Press.

Access Economics (2003), *The Importance of Age in Migrants' Fiscal Impact*, Research Project Report, Canberra: DIMIA.

Andrews, J. (2001), A qualified welcome: how the EU treats its guests, most uninvited, *Europe* (November): 6–9.

Annan, K. (2003), Win–win outcome is possible if approach to migration is rational, compassionate, Secretary-General Annan tells new global commission, press release SG/SM/9064. Available at: http://www.un.org/News/Press/docs/2003/sgsm9064.doc.htm (accessed 30 December 2004).

Annan, K. (2004), Don't demonise migrants, encourage them, *The Australian*, (29 January): 13.

BBC Monitoring International Reports (2003a), German Interior Minister opposes EU immigration quotas (27 October) (accessed on the Lexis-Nexis Academic database).

BBC Monitoring International Reports (2003b), Belgian Interior Minister backs introduction of EU labor immigration quota (28 November) (accessed on the Lexis-Nexis Academic database).

Bennhold, K. (2004), Attacks in Spain put migrants in spotlight, *International Herald Tribune* (30 March): 2.

Betts, A. (2003), *The Political Economy of Extra-territorial Processing: Separating "Purchaser" from "Provider" in Asylum Policy*, Working Paper no. 91, Geneva: UNHCR.

Bhagwati, J. (1998), *A Stream of Windows: Unsettling Reflections on Trade, Immigration and Democracy*, Cambridge, MA: MIT Press.

Bhagwati, J. (2004), *In Defense of Globalization*, New York: Oxford University Press.

Carens, J. (1988), Nationalism and the exclusion of immigrants: lessons from Australian immigration policy. In M. Gibney (ed.), *Open Borders? Closed Societies? The Ethical and Political Issues*, New York: Greenwood Press, pp. 41–60.

Chimni, B. S. (2002), Aid, relief and containment: the first asylum country and beyond, *International Migration*, 40, 2: 75–94.

Coles, G. (1995), UNHCR and the political dimension of protection. Paper, UNHCR.

Crawford, G. (2001), *Foreign Aid and Political Reform: A Comparative Analysis of Democracy Assistance and Political Conditionality*, New York: Palgrave.

DIMIA (2003), *Refugee and Humanitarian Issues: Australia's Response*, Canberra: DIMIA. Available at: http://www.immi.gov.au/refugee/publications/refhumiss_03.pdf (accessed 29 December 2004).

DIMIA (2004a), Annual report 2003–4. Available at: http://www.immi.gov.au/annual_report/annrep04/index.htm (accessed 27 December 2004).

DIMIA (2004b), Managing the border: immigration compliance. Available at: http://www.immi.gov.au/illegals/mtb/index.htm (accessed 27 December 2004).

Doyle, M. (2004), The challenge of worldwide migration, *Journal of International Affairs*, 57, 2: 1–5.

Espiner, C. (2004), National identity key to migrant worries, *The Christchurch Press* (26 June): 17.

European Report no. 2802 (2003), Justice and Home Affairs Council: ministers mandate study into quotas of legal immigrants (13 September) (accessed on Lexis-Nexis Academic database).

Fagen, P. W. (2003), The long-term challenges of reconstruction and reintegration: case studies of Haiti and Bosnia-Herzegovina. In E. Newman and J. van Selm (eds), *Refugees and Forced Displacement: International Security, Human Vulnerability, and the State*, Tokyo, New York and Paris: United Nations University Press, pp. 221–49.

Fekete, L. (2004), Anti-Muslim racism and the European security state, *Race and Class*, 46, 1: 3–30.

Feller, E. (2001), Address given at the International Conference on the Reception and Integration of Resettled Refugees, Sweden, 25 April.

Garnaut, R., Ganguly, R. and Kang, J. (2003), *Migration to Australia and Comparisons with the United States: Who Benefits?* Research Project Report, Canberra: DIMIA.

Gledhill, J. (1994), *Power and Its Disguises: Anthropological Perspectives on Politics*, London and Boulder, CO: Pluto Press.

Graff, J. (2002), Across the new frontier: governments across the EU are cracking down on immigration, *Time International*, 159, 25. Available at: http://www.time.

com/time/europe/magazine/2002/0624/immigration/story.html (accessed 30 December 2004).

Graff, J., McAllister, J. F. O., Penner, M. and Walker, J. (2001), Sea of promise: Europe's governments want to crack down on human trafficking and stiffen asylum laws. But their economies can't afford to turn back the tide, *Time International*, 157, 7: 16.

Griswold, D. (2002), Willing workers: fixing the problem of illegal Mexican immigration to the United States, Trade Policy Analysis no. 19: Centre for Trade Policy Studies. Available at: http://www.freetrade.org/pubs/pas/tpa-019es.html (accessed 30 December 2004).

Habermas, J. (1998), *The Inclusion of the Other: Studies in Political Theory*, Cambridge, MA: MIT Press.

Hayden, W. (1998), Politics, public responsibility and the ethical imperative. In N. Preston and C. Samford (eds), *Ethics and Political Practice: Perspectives on Legislative Ethics*, Leichhardt, NSW: Federation Press, pp. 52–65.

Hoffmann-Nowotny, H.-J. (1997), World society and the future of international migration: a theoretical perspective. In E. Ucarer and D. Puchala (eds), *Immigration into Western Societies: Problems and Policies*, London and Washington: Pinter, pp. 95–117.

Honig, B. (2001), *Democracy and the Foreigner*, Princeton, NJ: Princeton University Press.

House of Representatives (Australian Parliament) (2002), *Parliamentary Debates*, 5 December.

Hugo, G. (1999), Managing mobilisation and migration of South-East Asia's population. In W. Tai-Chee and M. Singh (eds), *Development and Challenge: South-East Asia in the New Millennium*, Singapore: Times Academic Press, pp. 171–214.

Human Rights Watch (2002), By invitation only: Australian asylum policy. Available at: http://www.hrw.org/reports/2002/australia/ (accessed 30 December 2004).

International Organization for Migration (2003a), *World Migration 2003: Managing Migration Challenges and Responses for People on the Move*, Geneva: IOM.

International Organization for Migration (2003b), Workshops for policy makers: background document capacity-building in migration management, MC/INF/265 (5 November).

Jenkins, F. (2004), Bare life: asylum seekers, Australian politics and Agamben's critique of violence, *Australian Journal of Human Rights*, 10, 1: 72–95.

Juss, S. (2004), Free movement and world order, *International Journal of Refugee Law*, 16, 3: 289–335.

Koslowski, R. (2004), Possible steps towards an international regime for mobility and security. Paper given at the *Workshop on Global Mobility Regimes*, Stockholm, 11–12 June.

Kymlicka, W. (2001), Territorial boundaries: a liberal egalitarian perspective. In D. Miller and S. Hashmi (eds), *Boundaries and Justice: Diverse Ethical Perspectives*, Princeton, NJ: Princeton University Press, pp. 249–75.

Lauterpacht, E. and Bethlehem, D. (2001), *The Scope and Content of the Principle of Non-refoulement*, Background Paper for Expert Roundtable Series, Geneva: UNHCR.

Lohrmann, R. (1997), Immigration in the twentieth century: which framework for policy response? In E. Ucarer and D. Puchala (eds), *Immigration into Western Societies: Problems and Policies*, London and Washington: Pinter, pp. 310–22.

Lubbers, R. (2003), Statement made at the 59th Session of the United Nations High Commission for Human Rights, Geneva, 18 March. Available at: http://www.unhcr.ch/cgi-bin/texis/vtx/home/opendoc.htm?tbl=ADMIN&id=3e784cb14&page=admin (accessed 30 December 2004).

Lucas, R. (1999), International trade, capital flows and migration: economic policies towards countries of origin as a means of stemming migration. In A. Bernstein and

M. Weiner (eds), *Migration and Refugee Policies: An Overview*, London and New York: Pinter, pp. 119–41.

Maley, W. (2003), Asylum-seekers in Australia's international relations, *Australian Journal of International Affairs*, 57, 1: 187–202.

Mares, P. (2002), *Borderline: Australia's Response to Refugees and Asylum Seekers in the Wake of the Tampa*, Sydney: UNSW Press.

Marr, D. and Wilkinson, M. (2003), *Dark Victory*, Crow's Nest, NSW: Allen and Unwin.

Martin, P. (1997), The impacts of immigration on receiving countries. In E. Ucarer and D. Puchala (eds), *Immigration into Western Societies: Problems and Policies*, London and Washington: Pinter, pp. 17–27.

Massey, D., Arango, J., Hugo, G., Kouaouci, A., Pellegrino, A. and Taylor, E. (1998), *Worlds in Motion: Understanding International Migration at the End of the Millennium*, Oxford: Clarendon Press.

Migration World Magazine (2001), Europe's love hate affair with its immigrants, 8 (Jan.).

Miller, M. (1999), The prevention of unauthorized migration. In A. Bernstein and M. Weiner (eds), *Migration and Refugee Policies: An Overview*, London and New York: Pinter, pp. 20–44.

Morjane, K. (2004), Statement made at the High Commissioner's Forum, Geneva, 12 March.

Moulson, G. (2004), Landmark German immigration law passes final legislative hurdle, *Associated Press*, 9 July (accessed on the Lexis-Nexis Academic database).

Noll, G. (2003), Securitizing sovereignty? States, refugees and the regionalization of international law. In E. Newman and J. van Selm (eds), *Refugees and Forced Displacement: International Security, Human Vulnerability, and the State*, Tokyo, New York and Paris: United Nations University Press, pp. 277–305.

Overbeek, H. (2002), Neoliberalism and the regulation of labor mobility, *Annals of the American Academy of Political Social Science*, 581: 74–90.

Prodi, R. (2004), The future of the Union of 25. Paper given at the Semaines Sociales de France, Lille, 23 September.

Puchala, D. (1997), Conclusions. In E. Ucarer and D. Puchala (eds), *Immigration into Western Societies: Problems and Policies*, London and Washington: Pinter, pp. 338–44.

Refugee Council (2004), Briefing on the Common European Asylum System. Available at: http://www.refugeecouncil.org.uk/downloads/briefings/intl/common_euro.pdf (accessed 30 December 2004).

Refugee Council of Australia (2002), Australia cuts back its commitment to UNHCR, 7 May. Available at: http://www.refugeecouncil.org.au/html/news_and_events/media/2002/media07052002.html (accessed 11 January 2004).

Refugee Council of Australia (2003), Australia's refugee and special humanitarian programme: current issues and future direction. RCOA submission to the Australian Government.

Reynolds, H. (1998), Hanson and Queensland's political culture. In R. Manne (ed.), *Two Nations: The Causes and Effects of the Rise of the One Nation Party in Australia*, Melbourne: Bookman Press, pp. 141–50.

Roberts, G. (2005), "Racist" professor cautioned, but launches new attack, *The Australian*, 21 July: 7.

Rotberg, R. (2002), Failed states in a world of terror, *Foreign Affairs*, 81, 4: 127–40.

Ruddock, P. (2002a), Minister announces 2002–03 migration (non-humanitarian programme, MPS 30/2002, 7 May. Available at: http://www.minister.immi.gov.au/media_releases/ruddock_media02/r02030.htm (accessed 11 January 2004).

Ruddock, P. (2002b), Agreement with South Africa on people smuggling, MPS 073/2002, 2 August. Available at: http://www.minister.immi.gov.au/media_releases/ruddock_media02/r02073.htm (accessed 30 December 2004).

Ruddock, P. (2003), Humanitarian programme intake for 2003–04, MPS 19/2003. Available at: http://www.minister.immi.gov.au/media_releases/ruddock_media03/r03019.htm (accessed 29 December 2004).

Said, E. (1993), *Culture and Imperialism*, London: Chatto and Windus.

Sassen, S. (1999), *Guests and Aliens*, New York: New Press.

Select Committee on Home Affairs (United Kingdom Parliament) (2003), Fourth report: asylum removals. Available at: http://www.parliament.the-stationery-office.co.uk/pa/cm200203/cmselect/cmhaff/654/65403.htm (accessed 30 December 2004).

Senate Legal and Constitutional References Committee (Australian Parliament) (2002), Migration zone excision: an examination of the Migration Legislation Amendment (Further Border Protection Measures) Bill 2002 and related matters. Available at: http://www.aph.gov.au/senate/committee/legcon_ctte/completed_inquiries/2002-04/mig_bp/report/contents.htm (accessed 29 December 2004).

Senate Select Committee on a Certain Maritime Incident (Australian Parliament) (2002), Main report. Available at: http://www.aph.gov.au/senate/committee/maritime_incident_ctte/report/index.htm (accessed 30 December 2004).

Sheridan, G. (1998), Pauline Hanson and the destruction of the Australian dream. In R. Manne (ed.), *Two Nations: The Causes and Effects of the Rise of the One Nation Party in Australia*, Melbourne: Bookman Press, pp. 169–77.

Slawner, K. (1998), Uncivil society: liberalism, hermeneutics and "good citizenship". In K. Slawner and M. Denham (eds), *Citizenship after Liberalism*, New York: Lang Publishing, pp. 81–102.

Sorensen, N. N., Van Hear, N. and Engberg-Pedersen, P. (2003), Migration development and conflict: state-of-the-art overview. In N. Van Hear and N. N. Sorensen (eds), *The Migration-Development Nexus*, Geneva: IOM and UNHCR, pp. 5–50.

Special Rapporteur of the Commission on Human Rights on the Human Rights of Migrants (2000), First report submitted pursuant to Commission on Human Rights Resolution 1999/44, UN Doc E/CN.4/2000/82.

Stelzer, I. (2001/2), Immigration policy for an age of mass movement, *Policy*, 17, 4: 3–16.

Stern, A. (2004), Former WTO judge calls for more US engagement at WTO, *UN Wire*, 19 March. Available at: http://www.unwire.org/UNWire/20040319/449_14190.asp (accessed 30 December 2004).

Suhrke, A. and Zolberg, A. (1999), Issues in contemporary refugee policies. In A. Bernstein and M. Weiner (eds), *Migration and Refugee Policies: An Overview*, London and New York: Pinter, pp. 142–82.

Sydney Morning Herald (2003), Keeping boat people away worth any amount, says PM (8 July). Available at: http://www.smh.com.au/articles/2003/07/08/1057430181117.html (accessed 24 December 2004).

Troeller, G. (2002), UNHCR resettlement: evolution and future direction, *International Journal of Refugee Law*, 14, 1: 85–95.

UN Department of Economic and Social Affairs (2004), *World Economic and Social Survey 2004: International Migration*, New York: United Nations.

UNHCR (2002), Strengthening and expanding resettlement today: dilemmas, challenges and opportunities, global consultations on refugee protection, 4th Meeting (25 April), UN Doc EC/GC/02/7.

UNHCR (2003a), Easy guide to refugee resettlement schemes (15 June), Geneva: UNHCR.

UNHCR (2003b), *Refugees by Numbers 2003*, Geneva: UNHCR.

UNHCR (2004a), Easy guide on refugee resettlement programmes 2003/2004 (February), Geneva: UNHCR.

UNHCR (2004b), Convention Plus at a glance (15 October), Geneva: UNHCR.

UN Human Rights Committee (2004), General comment no. 31 [80]: the nature of the general legal obligation imposed on state parties to the covenant. Available at:

http://www.unhchr.ch/tbs/doc.nsf/(Symbol)/c92ce711179ccab1c1256c480038394a? Opendocument (accessed 30 December 2004).

UN Wire (2003a), Annan welcomes new global migration commission (24 November). Available at: http://www.unwire.org/UNWire/20031124/449_10708.asp (accessed 27 December 2004).

UN Wire (2003b), NGOs accuse WTO of favouring rich countries (23 July). Available at: http://www.unwire.org/UNWire/20030723/449_6855.asp (accessed on 27 December 2004).

UN Wire (2003c), Trade experts say WTO is marginalizing Africa (19 June). Available at: http://www.unwire.org/UNWire/20030619/449_5311.asp (accessed 30 December 2004).

UN Wire (2003d), UN-backed commission to examine migrant flows (10 December). Available at: http://www.unwire.org/UNWire/20031210/449_11183.asp (accessed 30 December 2004).

Van Selm, J. (2003), Refugee protection policies and security issues. In E. Newman and J. van Selm (eds), *Refugees and Forced Displacement: International Security, Human Vulnerability, and the State*, Tokyo, New York and Paris: United Nations University Press, pp. 66–92.

Van Selm, J., Woroby, T. and Patrick, E. (2003), Study on the feasibility of setting up resettlement schemes in EU member states or at EU level, against the background of the Common European Asylum System and the goal of a Common Asylum Procedure, study carried out by the Migration Policy Institute on behalf of the European Commission (Directorate General for Justice and Home Affairs). Available at: http://europa.eu.int/comm/justice_home/doc_centre/asylum/studies/docs/resettlement-study-full_2003_en.pdf (accessed 29 December 2004).

Vanstone, A. (2004), Border control pays: Australia to accept more refugees, VPS 56/04, 23 March. Available at: http://www.minister.immi.gov.au/media_releases/media04/v04056.htm (accessed 29 December 2004).

Walker, G. (1988), *The Rule of Law: Foundation of Constitutional Democracy*, Melbourne: Melbourne University Press.

Whelan, F. (1988), Citizenship and freedom of movement: an open admission policy? In M. Gibney (ed.), *Open Borders? Closed Societies? The Ethical and Political Issues*, New York: Greenwood Press, pp. 3–39.

Widgren, J. and Martin, P. (2002), Managing migration: the role of economic instruments, *International Migration*, 40, 5: 213–29.

Wilson, P. (2004), Poor nations flex trade muscles, *The Australian* (2 August): 14.

3
European Union Policy on Asylum and Immigration. Addressing the Root Causes of Forced Migration: A Justice and Home Affairs Policy of Freedom, Security and Justice?

Channe Lindstrøm

Introduction

On 1 May 2004, the European Union expanded to 25 countries, with a combined population of more than 450 million people and a GDP of almost €10,000 billion. The EU in the making and the creation of its multisectoral *acquis* is, to say the least, an ambitious undertaking. The EU Asylum and Migration Policy, as first formulated at the 1999 Tampere European Council, is a case in point: its comprehensive nature spans the areas of Justice and Home Affairs, Development and Humanitarian Assistance, as well as the Common Foreign and Security policy.

This paper will argue that the objective convergence of the EU migration and internal security regimes, coupled with increased populist pressures, has consolidated existing restrictive national asylum practices in an effort to curb unregulated migration into the Union. The EU cannot, as of now, be said to have devised a "partnership strategy" in which policies that impact on asylum and migration pressures are coordinated to ensure the maximum impact is achieved, i.e. by successfully addressing the "root causes" of migration. While it is recognized that the effects of policies aimed at addressing root causes can be visible only in the longer term, current policy methods and instruments work to establish legitimacy for the denial of protection and the conclusion of readmission agreements, with a view to shifting responsibility away from the European territorial core.

Furthermore, the institutional structure of the Union with its multiple overlapping layers of competence and governance poses significant challenges to the effective and coherent coordination and implementation of asylum, immigration and development/humanitarian policies. While the EU is a less than perfect democratic entity, it seeks to respond to *perceived* democratic pressures—in particular to the xenophobic tendencies present in European welfare states. However, one of the challenges facing mature democratic societies is precisely to resist the temptation to respond to populist pressures. European demographic patterns increasingly point to the necessity of recruiting labour from outside the Union in order to support a European population characterized by negative population growth and an increasing life expectancy. Politicians must safeguard the interests and welfare not merely of present but also of future welfare societies. Europe must also be seen as living up to the international legal standards asked of its partnership countries, for the channelling of trade and other development assistance. If Europe is lax on granting rights to asylum-seekers, as embedded in international human rights and refugee law, there are no particular incentives for other countries not to try to bend rules for themselves. In other words, European partnerships must be normatively grounded: they must primarily seek to improve conditions in the countries of origin, not to lessen migration pressures into the EU.

Asylum and Immigration as a Threat to the EU Security Regime

From the postwar period of unprecedented economic growth until today, three distinct structural cycles of migration into the European Union can be discerned. The first phase of European migration was characterized by massive foreign labour recruitment of low-skilled workers from the southern periphery to benefit the northern core, and the second phase reunited the families that had been unsettled in the earlier decades. The third phase has been characterized by a significant increase in asylum migration, the east to west movement of people following the 1989 collapse of the East European planned economies, as well as by an increasing conflation of immigration and asylum issues.

With the end to the European postwar economic boom, and with the end to the Cold War a few decades later, the immigrant worker and the refugee increasingly ceased to be regarded as economic, political or ideological assets in the receiving states of Western Europe. Indeed, as walls broke down and the four freedoms of movement (goods, services, capital—and people) began to be realized, the perception of asylum-seekers as individuals in need of humanitarian assistance and protection—as well as the sound economic basis upon which labour migrants were admitted—has given way to a perception of the entry of refugees and immigrants as a threat, not only to the national economy and its welfare distribution, but to the entire existing social order (see Cayhan 1999; Bigo 2000). In consequence, a fundamentally exclusive and defensive approach to European security has been predominant since the mid-1980s, as embodied in partly overlapping intergovernmental cooperative frameworks (Trevi, Schengen, Maastricht's third pillar on Police and Judicial Cooperation). Such frameworks constituted a "very peculiar, homogeneous and (in spite of its institutional clumsiness) cohesive 'internal security regime'" (Monar 2000: 12).

The 1992 Maastricht Treaty on European Union divided Community matters into three pillars. While the first pillar sought to consolidate the European Economic Area via *supranational* cooperation, matters of asylum and immigration were brought into the remit of EU competence within a securitized policy frame in the third pillar on "Police and Judicial Cooperation". Addressing the root causes of migration as a policy objective started only in response to the perceived threat of migration from Central and Eastern Europe; it was also to add impetus to the development of the EU Common Foreign and Security Policy in the second pillar. EU actions in the area of asylum and immigration have thus spanned multiple overlapping areas of competence from the start: post-Maastricht policies are characterized by intergovernmental cooperation and non-binding instruments, which widens their democratic deficit. They are widely criticized for the emphasis placed on the "lowest common denominator" (Geddes 2000).

For analytical clarity, the impact of these restriction-oriented policies of control can be divided into "internal" and "external". Internal policies include *non-arrival* measures consisting of preventative measures that directly impede the entry of asylum-seekers, such as visa regimes, carrier sanctions, airport liaison officers, interdiction at sea; together with *deterrence* policies (such as detention, temporary protection status, limitations in employment, welfare, residence and accommodation) intended to remove any incentives towards mobility. This paper confines its attention to the external aspects of migration control policies. Here it is important to distinguish between *diversion* policies such as readmission agreements, that shift the responsibility for the granting of asylum and the provision of protection, from *containment* policies that, by addressing the root causes of migration, seek to prevent the conditions that either force people to flee or encourage them to move in the first place.

In spite of the establishment of an internal working party to facilitate the coordination of policy, proposals on asylum and immigration continued to be developed within the third pillar, while the policy instruments for executing them were located within the first and second pillars, which in turn were subject to different legislative procedures (Myers 1996). The proposed Treaty establishing a Constitution for Europe, in its present form, does away with the pillar structure, yet seems set to retain the institutional inhibitions imposed by long-existing tensions between national and community administrations and the "inter-pillar" battles between the foreign policy, humanitarian and development dimensions of the EU apparatus.

The 1998 Vienna Action Plan manifests the securitized line of thinking on matters of asylum and immigration. The Austrian Presidency envisaged an EU migration regime based on a model of concentric circles, whereby the EU represents the inner circle; neighbours (associated states and the Mediterranean area) represent the second circle "gradually being linked into a similar system . . . increasingly in line with the first circle's [migration] standards". Relations with a third circle of states (Commonwealth of Independent States (CIS), Turkey, North Africa) will concentrate "primarily on transit checks and combating facilitator networks", thereby treating these as buffer zones to divert population movements prior to arrival on EU territory. Finally, EU cooperation with the fourth circle (Middle East, China, sub-Saharan Africa and Horn of Africa) would focus on eliminating push factors by way of financial assistance (CEU 1998a, 1998b; Thouez 2000: 9). This concentric structure has been replicated in the internal security regime (Brochman and Hammar 1999). Both regimes have employed strategies of control and diversion in order to achieve objective convergence, i.e. reducing threats to security and stability by preventing and diverting population movement into the EU.

The concentric structure is further evident in the European Commission's Country and Regional Strategy Papers, which in effect define three degrees of European engagement pertaining to cooperation on asylum and migration. Countries of *transit* may be divided into those that enjoy "accession negotiation" status (first degree), i.e. Bulgaria, Croatia, Romania, Turkey and the remaining Western Balkan countries, and those that do not (second degree), e.g. the CIS and North Africa. The EU has managed, in true protectionist fashion, to postpone the free movement of people from and within the new Accession States; and accession negotiations with the Republic of Turkey are currently pointing in the same direction. Significant funds are granted for Turkey to set up an asylum system that would, to all intents and purposes, make Turkey the last stop for many an asylum-seeker seeking to enter European Union territory (CEC 2000a: Part 4). The third degree of engagement is to be found with countries of *origin* that do not border the European Union.

The EU expanded its security regime prior to the 2004 accession of the new member states, in order to reduce the likelihood of importing specific internal security risks, such as organized crime and "uncontrolled population movement". The 1998 Pre-Accession Pact on Organized Crime with the ten Central and Eastern European countries and Cyprus provided for the candidate countries to adopt in their domestic legislation and practices, *inter alia*, the existing EU *acquis* on the fight against illegal immigration, which implied full acceptance of the Schengen *acquis* as stated in Article 8 of the Schengen Protocol. The 1999 Stability Pact for South-eastern Europe was also conceived in a reactionary manner following the break-up of the Former Republic of Yugoslavia. Although the Pact provided a framework for discussing issues of human rights, economy and security, asylum and migration policies were actually—and not surprisingly—discussed mainly in the context of security.

In security discourse, Weiner argues, an issue is dramatized and presented as of supreme priority. An agent claims the need and right to treat such an issue by extraordinary means (Weiner 1995). Not only is this a failure to deal with asylum and immigration as a matter of normal politics (by moving the issue into the realm of discretionary *high* politics), it leaves little room for democracy and the constraints that the democratic process, per intent, imposes upon decision-making. Note that responsibility for the safeguarding of internal security rests with the member states. This poses challenges of implementation since, while welfare and security concerns remain nationalized, migration issues are increasingly being "communitarized". In this context, it is worth noting that the European Court of Justice currently possesses no executive authority to rule on matters relating to internal security and the Common Foreign and Security Policy (CEU 1997: Art. 68.2).

Developing the Common European Asylum and Migration *Policy*

The entry into force of the 1997 Amsterdam Treaty on the European Union in 1999 provided for the establishment of a "[European] Area of Freedom, Security and Justice" and the creation of a Directorate-General for Justice and Home Affairs (CEU 1999b: Art. 2). This new integration of the security and judicial branches of the Union was strengthened through the communitarization of domains that had hitherto belonged to the third pillar. For example, the development of EU policies in the areas of "visa, asylum, immigration and other policies related to the free movement of persons" was transformed into a fundamental Treaty objective under the first pillar (Art. 2).

On the one hand, Guiraudon (1998) has argued that EU member states have found their sovereignty to be internally constrained by domestic political goals and bureaucratic processes—rather than *externally* constrained by European or otherwise international legal standards. Thus the processes by which immigration and asylum policies have been *externalized* through policy cooperation at EU level have allowed member states to pursue their domestic policy objectives by other means. Partly due to these institutional inhibitions, the decision-making processes set up by the Amsterdam Treaty continued to allow for the "worst practices" of individual states to be transposed into both EU legislation and framework decisions, thereby allowing for their *export* to other EU member states. What may currently best be characterized as the European "asylum regime of minimum standards" is a result of states being bound into restricting their borders, in order to prevent a disproportionate influx of refugees and immigrants in comparison with their neighbours. The Basic Law of Germany, for example, contained asylum provisions that were liberal by European standards. The 1993 asylum compromise brought German practices in line with common European measures, such as the definition of safe third countries and the fast-track rejection of "manifestly unfounded" asylum applications (Marx and Lumpp 1996). The Schengen Agreement is yet another example of extraterritorial control. It has helped set up buffer states, and to "shift the burdens and dilemmas of control outside the jurisdiction of liberal states in Western Europe" (Hollifield 2000: 110). European intergovernmental cooperation on asylum and security has, in many ways, had the effect of *rescuing* the European nation states (Milward 1999).

On the other hand, Geddes suggests that the EU should not be regarded solely as an external venue to which member states escape, without also considering the scope for EU competencies to feed back into domestic contexts in a deeper and increasingly wider EU (Geddes 2001: 65). He sees the EU as a potential corrective to lowest-common-denominator intergovernmental decision-making. It is a view echoed by transnational advocacy networks, such as ECRE, who call for more power to the European Commission, the Court and the Parliament and thus argue for more, not less, European integration. Such involvement creates opportunities—in terms both of strengthening national, inter- and non-governmental consultation fora, and of establishing greater transparency and accessibility with regard to information—which themselves may enhance normative exertions of influence in decision-making processes (Niessen and Rowlands 2000).

Nevertheless, EU and member state relations with most third countries in the field of asylum and migration have in practice been focused on migration controls and law enforcement concerns. Specifically, they have dealt with readmission, irregular emigration and transit flow controls, as well as police and judicial cooperation against human trafficking: all this to such an extent that migration control and law enforcement may be described as having been *outsourced* to third countries in exchange for intensified trade and development cooperation.

Instruments of diversion: return and readmission policies

Readmission agreements have traditionally been perceived as a measure of immigration control, in that they provide for the return of nationals of the contracting states who have illegally entered the territory of the other contracting state. However, these agreements have become increasingly instrumental as a pretext for the return of asylum-seekers as well. Readmission texts have repeatedly failed to guarantee the fundamental principle of refugee protection, that of *non-refoulement*, which grants everyone the right not to be returned back to a country where they may face persecution. The practice of inserting a compulsory readmission clause in agreements with third countries denies asylum-seekers access to a substantive asylum procedure whenever they can be demonstrated either to originate from a country deemed as safe (safe country of origin), or to have transited through other countries where they have had the opportunity to request asylum (safe third country).[1]

This systematic and generalized readmission policy has led to an expanded "buffer zone" around the EU (cf. the concentric circles of the EU migration and internal security regimes). In the absence of any procedure in the EU for examining the human rights record of a country prior to the agreement (or during the operation of such a readmission agreement), the risk of *refoulement* is greatly increased. For example, despite considerable protection gaps with regard to the treatment of refugees in countries such as Libya and Syria (which are notably not signatories to the 1951 Refugee Convention), the EU has sought intensified cooperation with them. Further, the EU has not been shy of using its political muscle to force through many agreements, as in the case of current readmission negotiations with Morocco. Such a policy of "threats and/or punishment" is, apart from its morally dubious nature, internally inconsistent. If the EU cuts off or reduces trade, aid, investment or diplomatic relations with a developing country, that country will have fewer resources to control onward migration and no reason to do so. Furthermore, if that country becomes poorer and/or more troubled as a result of the EU's sanctioned behaviour, its population is increasingly likely to migrate to the EU (ECRE 2004: 5–7).

Instruments of containment: root causes and partnership policies of the third degree

Tackling the root causes to prevent migration flows is an umbrella expression, consisting of actions directed at both attenuating causes of departure and reducing cross-border movements. "Source control" measures, such as conflict prevention, development assistance, trade partnerships and political dialogue are increasingly deployed in order to lessen the migration pressure towards the EU. Given the lack of analytical consensus with regard to both the nature and scope of root causes, this is a dangerously all-encompassing project: it involves actions in the social, economic and political spheres, in terms of both domestic and foreign policies. Or, in the words of the 1999 Tampere European Council:

> The European Union needs a comprehensive approach to migration addressing political, human rights and development issues in countries and regions of origin and transit. This requires combating poverty . . . preventing conflicts and consolidating democratic states and ensuring respect for human rights . . . [and] a greater coherence of internal and external policies of the Union. (CEU 1999b: para. 11)

As a consequence of what some have termed a "global migration crisis" (Weiner 1995), matters of asylum and migration have been increasingly conflated. The issue of asylum-seekers and refugees has been inflated in the European context and, in consequence, perceived within the framework of illegal immigration (see CEC 2000a, 2002b). Given that the causes of refugee flows often overlap with—or may themselves be provoked or aggravated by—economic marginalization and poverty, massive unemployment, environmental degradation, population pressure and poor governance, the conflation between asylum and immigration may be compared to the policy tensions existing between humanitarian aid (emergency crisis management) and development assistance (generation of sustainable livelihoods).

EU development assistance has, since Maastricht, been based on an uneasy balance between its intergovernmental (€3 billion a year European Development Fund) and Community character (€6 billion a year) (Simon 2003: 5). The EU provides some 55 per cent of Official Development Assistance and more than two-thirds of grant aid. Having both humanitarian and development aid at its disposal, the EU is well placed to ensure sound management of the transition between emergency aid, rehabilitation and development. Furthermore, aid is the only measure over which governments have complete control. It can therefore be tailored to serve any ends, ranging from the implementation of human rights clauses in cooperation agreements, to strategic security objectives (Martin 1994).

The reorganization of the Council that took place in 2002, in Seville, resulted in the creation of a General Affairs and External Relations Council (GAERC), responsible for key EU external relations policies: "common foreign and security policy, European security and defence policy, foreign trade, development cooperation and humanitarian aid" (CEU 2002a). This institutional integration resulted in the abolition of the EU Development Council. There might be an opportunity here to improve the effectiveness, coordination and coherence of European development cooperation to CFSP geostrategic approaches and for issues of immigration and asylum to "be incorporated more specifically into Community programmes with third-countries, both in the area of trade and of development" (CEC 2000a: 8). Yet there is a real risk that priorities and goals of the EU's external/foreign policy might come to override development and human rights concerns. For example, it is a matter of concern that the analysis and assessments of the ACP Country Strategy Papers will be discussed with the partner country, but not negotiated (CEC 2000b), even though political dialogue with the state in question may be crucial for the successful implementation of these agreements. As such "risk countries" are outside the anticipated realm of European enlargement, they may not be placated into accepting development assistance in return for implementing exclusionary measures as defined and imposed by the EU—unlike the Central and Eastern European countries, which did so in return for EU membership (Lavenex 1999).

The increasing diversion of funds from development to relief reflects the fact that measures intended to address root causes prior to the occurrence of conflict have been diverted into elaborating strategies of containment once conflict has erupted. "Prevention" has assumed a new meaning: preventing the influx of refugees and immigrants into the EU. The prevalent paradigm of "aid in place of migration and protection" is thus limited by both current understandings of development, budget constraints, and institutional modes of governance (see Scholdan 2001). The questions emerge: as to whether the aid system has both the mandate and the capacity to implement the development agenda, and whether the current understanding of the nature of conflict—and hence existing models of development—are sufficient and appropriate to prevent conflict and generate development (Macrae 1999; CEU 2000).

The High Level Working Group on Asylum and Migration: bridging or minding a gap?

While the root causes and partnership policies outlined above have sought institutionally to integrate policy between different Directorates-General within the European Commission, the second path to developing a *migration prevention* policy is by way of the High Level Working Group on Asylum and Migration (HLWG), which acts under the auspices of the European Council.

The HLWG, set up in 1998, was initially charged with preparing cross-pillar Action Plans on six countries from which large numbers of refugees and migrants come to Europe, namely Morocco, Albania, Afghanistan, Sri Lanka, Somalia and Iraq (HLWG 1999). While the remit of the HLWG was expanded in 2002 to include China and Central Asia, as well as North and sub-Saharan Africa (CEU 2002b), analysis in this paper is concerned with the first batch of Action Plans as they, thus far, mark the most concrete manifestation of the attempt to institutionalize centralized responsibility and a concerted framework of action for all relevant EU institutions dealing with asylum and migration policies. The plans were to contain operational measures for cooperation with third countries regarding foreign policy, and development and trade, as well as migration and asylum.

The quality of the analysis of the reasons for departure—the core part of the HLWG reports—varies. With the exception of Iraq, the focus is on migration for economic reasons—even if preceding sections on the political and human rights situation list many deficiencies in the countries of origin. "The Action Plans and reports seem to be quite separate from one another: While a report will openly discuss the nature of human rights abuses in a given country, the Action Plans will suggest promoting readmission of rejected asylum-seekers, as if the two points might never coincide in abuse of the returnee" (Van Selm 2002: 16). The plans propose a non-innovative mix of diplomatic, humanitarian and development assistance as measures to eliminate the root causes of migration, which have already been enshrined in the areas of trade, external relations and development (HLWG 1999).

The most concrete ventures of the plans are into the realm of readmission agreements and securing protection in the conflict region by, for example, "regionalizing" Afghan refugees in Pakistan and Iran or "localizing" internally displaced Sri Lankans within presumed safe areas in Sri Lanka (HLWG 1999). But it is difficult to see how Action Plan measures, such as returning rejected Kurdish asylum-seekers from Iraq to Turkey or cooperation with the Central Asian republics with regard to the travel routes of Afghan nationals, could promote structural stability. The control element of migratory flows is stressed without parallel emphasis on building up structures that would allow e.g. Albania to deal successfully with the readmission of third-country nationals. The EU has put tremendous pressure on the former Yugoslav governments to introduce visas for all migrant-producing countries. It has made economic and humanitarian aid to Serbia and Montenegro contingent upon the country's sealing of its borders to Chinese immigrants, and is encouraging Morocco to use a "rigorous visa policy" towards nationals of all West African states (HLWG 1999: 16).

Scholdan (2001) further argues that the Action Plans do not strike the right balance between security and integration, since only a small proportion of the measures relate to integrating nationals of the target countries into society in the EU. In the Tampere framework, the European Council stressed the need for rapid decisions on "the approximation of national legislation on the conditions for admission and residence of third country nationals" (CEC 2000a: 3). However, the June 2003 deadline for this approximation has been missed.

While the new mandate of April 2002 grants the HLWG a more flexible geographical scope and allows it to focus on regional approaches to the management of migratory flows, seven out of the ten terms of reference relate to regionalization and containment.[2] Such a starting point marks no departure from the 1999 Action Plans. It is not clear, therefore, how the modification of the HLWG mandate is to bring about any real changes to its work: rather than institutionalizing centralized coordination, the proposed policy measures reinforce the diversification of responsibility for implementation. This is perhaps due to the fact that, despite the HLWG operating under the auspices of the Council, it is still subjected to the institutional logic governing the work of the Directorates-General of the Commission, when seeking to integrate policy initiatives targeted at migration with policies promoting development objectives. This collision of institutional logics was actually recognized by the HLWG at the Nice European Council meeting in December 2000 (HLWG 2000).

The revised mandate of the HLWG further grants the group a leading role in the EU's JHA external dimension to "promote the EU's role in the efforts of the international community aimed at addressing the main causes for migration" (CEU 2002b: part 4). Yet, the primary obstacle to policy cohesion derives from the fact that developing the JHA external dimension is not an objective in itself. The aim has never been to develop a "foreign policy" specific to JHA, although the number of different objectives involved in addressing immigration, asylum, external border controls, combating drug addiction, customs cooperation, police and judicial cooperation in criminal matters could certainly benefit from such a dimension. It is also not clear how the HLWG is expected to interact and coordinate issues with the GAERC. JHA is further constrained by the principle of subsidiarity, which requires that the EU should intervene only if its action provides added value to bilateral action by member states (EU DG External Relations 2000: 6).

Prior to any new Action Plans being adopted, it is necessary to understand why the first Action Plans have had so little effect. Such issues then need to be addressed in order to avoid any new Action Plans being dismissed as "obsolete" by the JHA Commissioner himself and as "abstract EU-desire-oriented plans" (Van Selm 2002: 16).

Instruments of containment: neighbourhood policies of the first and second degree

As opposed to the ACP partnership model described above and other third-country relationships of the third degree, the EU's relations with the countries and regions to her south and east are based on a proximity policy, which recognizes their political and strategic importance, in terms both of trade and of acting as European buffer zones (Vachudová 2000).

The contrast between relationships of the first and second degree is stark. While the EMP under the MEDA and AENEAS regulations retains an almost exclusive focus on migration control as outlined above, the partnership of the first degree with countries in the Western Balkans is the first of its kind to go beyond traditional migration control measures in its discussions of social inclusion and *sustainable* return.

The European Commission's European Neighbourhood and Partnership Instrument (ENPI) sets out programmes and activities for increasing cooperation with states in the Mediterranean basin and Middle East, as well as states to the east of the enlarged EU and in the Caucasus.

The EU has particularly increased funding for intervention sectors related to asylum and migration; particularly for the TACIS, CARDS, EMP and MARRI programmes, where migration issues increasingly form part of the dialogue. For the period 2002–6, some €450 million were allocated to finance actions directly linked to migration. Such actions have included, *inter alia*, institutional capacity-building, improving external border control, combating illegal immigration and trafficking in human beings, the return and reintegration of refugees and displaced persons, and setting up reception policies and infrastructure for refugees (see CEC 2000a: 18).

A regulation providing for a five-year programme for financial and technical assistance to third countries in the areas of migration and asylum (AENEAS), was established in March 2004 with a total reference amount of €370 million. Article 1 of the regulation provides that AENEAS is "particularly, but not exclusively, intended for those third countries actively engaged in preparing or implementing a readmission agreement initialled, signed or concluded with the European Community" (CEC 2000c: Art. 1). Pastore (2004) has identified, in the transition from the B7–667 budget line to the AENEAS programme, the beginning of a process likely to transfer certain management competencies from the JHA Directorate-General to the RELEX Directorate-General and EuropeAid.

As the Commission is negotiating a readmission agreement with Morocco and has already negotiated directives for Algeria, these two countries have been granted priority as regards their eligibility under the AENEAS programme. Previously, budget-heading B7–667 has financed pilot projects in Morocco and Algeria (reducing illegal African migratory pressure). In 2005–6 Algeria will benefit from a €10 million programme to train air and border police in order to improve management of migratory flows. For the MASHREQ countries, measures to support the social and immigration components of the Association Agreements are planned for 2005–6. For Egypt, the focus will be on pursuing cooperation on illegal immigration issues (institutional capacity-building, information campaigns, facilitating the return of migrants and their reincorporation in the labour market). In Lebanon, assistance will be provided to enhance external border control.

In contrast to this focus on external border control of illegal immigration, the Migration, Asylum, Refugees Regional Initiative (MARRI) in the Western Balkans has a proactive agenda. It was formed in 2003 by the merger of two Stability Pacts for South-eastern Europe programmes. MARRI complements the broader SAP and coordinates its efforts with associated EU-sponsored activities. MARRI's agenda takes in a very comprehensive set of issues, including sustainable return, the development of asylum procedures, irregular migration, visa policies, border control (primarily regarding reception of asylum-seekers) and information systems interoperability. MARRI plays an advisory, information-sharing and coordination role, with the eventual goal of having the associated states develop European-level standards of legislation, training and processes. The approach to individual issues is also comprehensive. In a region where some 1 million refugees and displaced people are still thought to be awaiting return or a settlement solution—and which still is a top source of asylum-seekers and irregular migrants in other European states—MARRI has gone beyond traditional refugee issues and focused on access to rights and citizenship and on the social and economic conditions necessary for sustainable return or integration (see Pastore 2004).

The Migration Subcommittees and Working Groups described above (in the framework of the Stabilization and Association Agreements for the Western Balkans) have created workable models for bilateral EU–third-country migration dialogue and decision-making. These can be strengthened and expanded, if the EU is committed to doing so. In short, the partnership of the first degree with countries in the Western Balkans is the first of its kind to carry with it possibilities for more freedom, security and justice—for all.

Developing a Common European Asylum *System*

Although the 1999 Tampere European Council called for a Common European Policy on Asylum and Migration to be formulated by 1 May 2004, no such policy has come into existence as yet.

The key EU directives and regulations in the area of asylum and migration—representing state-of-the-art progress in the approximation of national legislation—are as listed in box 1. They were complemented by the Proposal for a Council Decision establishing the European Refugee Fund for the period 2005–10. But, taken all together, this can hardly be hailed a *comprehensive* and *common* European Policy on Asylum and Migration.

However, in the autumn of 2004, the development of the EU Asylum and Migration Policy took two interesting turns. First, the Justice and Home Affairs Council in Luxembourg adopted a regulation establishing the

---

Box 1

Key EU directives and regulations pertaining to asylum and migration

Temporary Protection Directive: Council Directive 2001/55/EC of 20 July 2001 on minimum standards for giving temporary protection in the event of a mass influx of displaced persons and on the measures promoting a balance of efforts between member states in receiving such persons and bearing the consequences thereof.

Reception Directive: Council Directive 2003/9/EC of 27 January 2003 on laying down minimum standards for the reception of asylum-seekers.

Dublin II Regulation: Council Regulation (EC) No 343/2003 of 18 February 2003 establishing the criteria and mechanisms for determining the member state responsible for examining an asylum application lodged in one of the member states by a third-country national.

Family Reunification Directive: Council Directive 2003/86/EC of 22 September 2003 on the right to family reunification.

Qualification Directive: Council Directive 8043/04, Asile 23 of 27 April 2004 on minimum standards for the qualification and status of third-country nationals and stateless persons as refugees or as persons who otherwise need international protection and the content of the protection granted.

The Procedures Directive: Draft Council Directive 14203/04, Asile 64 of 9 November 2004 on minimum standards on procedures in member states for granting and withdrawing refugee status.

European Agency for the Management of Operational Cooperation at the External Borders on 1 May 2005. Second, the European Council developed the Hague Programme, in November 2004 in Brussels, to "strengthen Freedom, Security and Justice in the European Union". The European Council called for "a strategy covering all external aspects of the Union policy on freedom, security and justice, based on the measures developed in this programme to the Council". The draft Hague Programme, however, fails to repeat the Tampere Conclusions' reference to a status "valid throughout the Union" and the obligations of *non-refoulement*, though it institutionally contains a commitment to abolish the requirement of unanimous voting in the Council on all EU immigration and asylum law. This would also mean co-decision powers for the European Parliament. The Programme itself would not abolish the voting requirements (as the Programme is not legally binding); it would simply indicate a political commitment to act. A change in the decision-making rules will require the adoption of a Council decision by unanimous vote following consultation of the European Parliament (Statewatch 2004: 4).

The Hague Programme provides for the launching of pilot regional refugee protection programmes before the end of 2005 (CEU 2004a: 20). The Protection "Tool Box" is envisaged to comprise the following: action to enhance protection capacity; a Registration Scheme; an EU-wide Resettlement Scheme; assistance for improving the local infrastructure; assistance in regard to local integration of persons in need of international protection in the third country; cooperation on legal migration; and "action" on migration management (CEC 2004b). Novel in the Hague Programme is that the European Council calls for the Commission to produce regular progress reports, according to the "Hague Action Plan Timetable"—and has thus developed a method to ensure implementation of JHA measures in member states (Statewatch 2004: 7).

While Tampere asked for a Common European Union Asylum and Migration *Policy* to enter into force on 1 May 2004, Hague envisages that "second-phase" instruments and measures of the Common European Asylum *System* should be submitted to the Council and the European Parliament with a view to their adoption before the end of 2010. "In this framework, the European Council invites the Commission to present a study on the appropriateness, the possibilities and the difficulties, as well as the legal and practical implications of *joint processing of asylum applications within the Union*" (CEU 2004a; added emphasis). The Hague Programme further envisages the creation of a European (asylum) office to assist all forms of cooperation between member states relating to the Common European Asylum *System*, which would include looking into the merits, appropriateness and feasibility of the joint processing of asylum applications outside EU territory (CEU 2004a).

Conclusion

As yet, the EU cannot be said to have devised a root causes strategy in which policies impacting on asylum and migration pressures are coordinated to ensure that the maximum impact is achieved. Although some neighbourhood policies of the first degree have the potential to develop into an increasingly normative framework, the EU is currently executing a two-pronged approach to contain the movement of those persons in need of protection within their regions of origin. Firstly, by conflating matters of asylum and immigration in the formulation of migration control measures (as illustrated by the CARDS, TACIS, ACP and MEDA partnership programmes), these policies of diversion and containment have "served to seriously undermine the foundations of the refugee protection regime" (UNHCR 2001: 7). Secondly, while development policy and other cooperation programmes provide the most powerful instruments at the Community's disposal for addressing the root causes of conflict, this paper has shown that these instruments lose in effectiveness and credibility when engulfed in institutional battles over "turf", with a consequent emphasis on the containment of population movement.

While it is recognized that the effects of root causes policies may only be visible over the longer term, immediate engagement in addressing these causes must be grounded in a normative discourse that primarily seeks to improve conditions in the countries of origin, rather than lessening migration pressures into the EU. Aid cannot act in place of protection and immigration. Making readmission and repatriation the priorities of the EU Action Plans on Asylum and Migration, and of the Hague Programme, is hardly the way to build peace and prevent future conflicts.

The retention of the EU pillar structure, in matters related to the Common Foreign and Security Policy, places serious constraints on the effective execution of asylum and migration policies. Root causes policies still find themselves in a double bind whereby, while matters of asylum and immigration are increasingly communitarized, the lenses through which these matters are perceived—as a threat to internal security and stability—are located within the national executive framework of individual member states. Within the EU apparatus, further institutional difficulties are encountered as different bodies are mandated to act on root causes without any elaborate coordination, objective convergence or pooling of funds. The HLWG was created in an attempt to redress the lack of prioritization within the JHA directorate itself, but its proposed policy measures are curiously decentralizing responsibility for implementation, rather than acting as a focal point for information, communication and coordination. The extent to which the Hague Programme will address these institutional shortcomings remains to be seen.

This paper calls not only for a shift away from conceptualizing asylum and immigration as matters of internal security but also for institutional reform, one crucial component being the establishment of a compliance and enforcement mechanism on asylum and immigration. Without an overarching supervisory mechanism, it will be impossible to oversee supranational cooperation between states, or to ensure the legitimate implementation of root causes policies. (In this respect, UNHCR has put forward a three-pronged approach to the future of the institution of asylum in Europe, whose implementation is proposed to be monitored by a European Advisory Board to ensure that current divergences in national practices are gradually eliminated.)

The EU possesses the potential means and authority to produce a real and positive impact along the relief–development continuum, if institutional competence is coordinated and funds are made available to carry out the implementation of various policy instruments. However, the problems that population movement and displacement pose will only be resolved—rather than shifted—if a more coherent approach to migration takes up a triple challenge. First, to manage population movements in a way that upholds basic human rights and the institution of asylum. Second, to safeguard the legitimate interests of the states and communities affected by these movements. Third, to invest the necessary political resources in preventing and reversing the causes of involuntary migration, including engaging in partnerships in real terms with the countries in question. Without the political will to address and improve the shortcomings that this paper has identified, the EU may justifiably be regarded as paying mere lip service to fashionable calls for partnership and sustainable development, while in reality acting on root causes in order to substitute the institution of asylum with the infusion of development aid. It will thereby merely consolidate existing national practices: executing measures perceived as instrumental for curbing immigration into the EU, by way of defensive exclusion, reactive diversion, and containment.

Appendix: List of Acronyms

ACP   African Caribbean and Pacific states.
AENEAS   Financial and technical assistance to third countries in the areas of migration and asylum.
CARDS   Community Assistance for Reconstruction, Development and Stabilization in the Western Balkans.
CEC   Commission of the European Communities.
CEU   Council of the European Union.
CFSP   Common Foreign and Security Policy.
CIS   Commonwealth of Independent States.
DG   European Union Directorate-General.
ECRE   European Council on Refugees and Exiles.
EMP   European Mediterranean Partnership.
ENPI   European Neighbourhood and Partnership Instrument.
ERF   European Refugee Fund.
EU   European Union.
GAERC   General Affairs and External Relations Council.
HLWG   High Level Working Group on Asylum and Migration.
JHA   Justice and Home Affairs Directorate-General.
MARRI   Migration, Asylum, Refugees Regional Initiative in the Western Balkans.
MASHREQ   Bahrain, Egypt, Iraq, Jordan, Kuwait, Lebanon, Oman, Palestine, Qatar, Saudi Arabia, Syria, United Arab Emirates, and Yemen.
MEDA   Financial and technical measures to accompany the reform of economic and social structures in the framework of the Euro-Mediterranean partnership.
RELEX   External Relations Directorate-General.
SAP   Stabilization and Association process.
TACIS   Grant-financed technical assistance to Eastern Europe and Central Asia.

Notes

1. At the time of writing, the Council has authorized the European Commission to negotiate Community readmission agreements with 13 third countries/entities (Morocco, Sri Lanka, Russia, Pakistan, Hong Kong, Macao, Ukraine, Albania, Algeria, China, Turkey, Libya and Syria). The Commission has successfully concluded negotiations with Sri Lanka, Hong Kong, Macao and Syria while the 2000 Cotonou Agreement with the ACP countries also contains a standard readmission clause (CEU 1999c: Art. 13). Negotiations with Russia, Ukraine and Morocco are well under way.
2. Namely, "Preventing economic migration (ii); assistance in the reception of displaced persons in the region (iii); readmission (v); reception and protection in the region (vii); illegal immigration (ix); voluntary repatriation (x)" (CEU 2002b: part 2).

Bibliography

Bigo, D. (2000), When two become one—internal and external securitisations in Europe. In M. Kelstrup, and M. C. Williams, *International Relations Theory and the Politics of European Integration: Power, Security and Community*, London and New York: Routledge.

Brochman, G. and Hammar, T. (1999), *Mechanisms of Immigration Control*, Oxford: Berger Books.

Castles, S. *et al.* (2003), *States of Conflict: Causes and Patterns of Forced Migration to the EU and Policy Responses*, London: Institute for Public Policy Research.

Cayhan, A. (1999), Migrants as a threat: a comparative analysis of securitarian discourse. In V. Gray (ed.), *A European Dilemma, Citizenship and Identity in Western Europe*, Oxford: Bergham Books.

Commission of the European Communities (CEC) (1995), *On the inclusion of respect for democratic principles and human rights in agreements between the Community and third countries*, Communication from the Commission to the Council and the European Parliament, COM (95), 216 of 23 May, Brussels: CEC.

Commission of the European Communities (CEC) (2000a), *On a Community Immigration Policy*, Communication from the Commission to the Council and the European Parliament, COM (2000), 757 final, 22 November, Brussels: CEC.

Commission of the European Communities (CEC) (2000b), *Community cooperation: framework for country strategy papers*, Working Document of the Commission, SEC (2000), 1049, Brussels: CEC.

Commission of the European Communities (CEC) (2000c), *On the implementation of measures intended to promote observance of human rights and democratic principles in external relations for 1996–1999*, Report from the Commission, COM (2000), 726 final, 14 November, Brussels: CEC.

Commission of the European Communities (CEC) (2001), *On a common policy on illegal immigration*, Communication from the Commission to the Council and the European Parliament, COM (2001), 672 final, 15 November, Brussels: CEC.

Commission of the European Communities (CEC) (2002), *Integrating migration issues in the European Union's relations with third countries*, Communication from the Commission to the Council and the European Parliament, COM (2002), 703 Final, 3 December, Brussels: CEC.

Commission of the European Communities (CEC) (2003a), *Turkish National Programme for the Adoption of the Acquis*, Brussels: CEC.

Commission of the European Communities (CEC) (2003b), *Wider Europe—Neighbourhood: a new framework for relations with our Eastern and Southern Neighbours*, Communication from the Commission to the Council and the European Parliament, COM (2003), 104 Final, 11 March, Brussels: CEC.

Commission of the European Communities (CEC) (2003c), *Towards more accessible, equitable and managed asylum systems*, Communication from the Commission to the Council and the European Parliament, COM (2003), 315 Final, 3 June, Brussels: CEC.

Commission of the European Communities (CEC) (2004a), *Area of freedom, security and justice: assessment of the Tampere Programme and future orientations {SEC (2004), 680 and SEC (2004), 693}*, Communication from the Commission to the Council and the European Parliament, COM (2004), 410 final, 2 June, Brussels: CEC.

Commission of the European Communities (CEC) (2004b), *On the managed entry in the EU of persons in need of international protection and the enhancement of the protection capacity of the regions of origin "improving access to durable solutions"*, Communication from the Commission to the Council and the European Parliament, COM (2004), 410 final, 4 June, Brussels: CEC.

Commission of the European Communities (CEC) (2004c), *Reference document for financial and technical assistance to third countries in the area of migration and asylum: the AENEAS Programme 2004–2006*, Brussels: CEC.

Council of the European Union (CEU) (1997), *Amsterdam Treaty on European Union*, 2 October, Brussels: CEU.

Council of the European Union (CEU) (1998a), *Vienna European Council Conclusions*, Brussels: CEU.

Council of the European Union (CEU) (1998b), *Strategy Paper on Immigration and Asylum, from the Austrian Presidency to the K4 Committee*, 13 July, Doc. no. 9809/98, Brussels: CEU.

Council of the European Union (CEU) (1999a), *Action Plan of the Council and the Commission on How Best to Implement the Provisions of the Treaty of Amsterdam on an Area of Freedom, Security and Justice*, 3 December 1998, Brussels: CEU.

Council of the European Union (CEU) (1999b), *Presidency Conclusions*, Tampere European Council, 15 and 16 October, Brussels: CEU.

Council of the European Union (CEU) (1999c), *ACP–EU Partnership Agreement*, signed in Cotonou 23 June 2000, *Official Journal of the European Communities*, L 317, 15 December 2000, Brussels: CEU.

Council of the European Union (CEU) (2000), *The European Community's Development Policy*, Joint Statement by the Council and the Commission, Doc. 13458/00, 10 November, Brussels: CEU.

Council of the European Union (CEU) (2001), *Council Conclusions on the European Union's Role in Promoting Human Rights and Democratisation in Third Countries*, Luxembourg European Council, 25 June, Brussels: CEU.

Council of the European Union (CEU) (2002a), *Seville European Council Conclusions*, Brussels: CEU.

Council of the European Union (CEU) (2002b), Modification of the terms of references of the High Level Working Group on Asylum and Migration (HLWG), "A" Item Note from Permanent Representatives' Committee to the Council, 30 May, Doc. no. 9433/02, Brussels: CEU.

Council of the European Union (CEU) (2004a), *Presidency Conclusions—Brussels*. Annex I: *The Hague Programme: Strengthening Freedom, Security and Justice in the European Union*, 4 and 5 November, Brussels: CEU.

Council of the European Union (CEU) (2004b), *Preliminary draft Constitutional Treaty, Cover Note from the Presidium to the Convention*, European Convention, The Secretariat, Doc. CONV 369/02, 28 October 2002, Brussels: CEU.

European Council on Refugees and Exiles (2004), *Broken Promises—Forgotten Principles: an ECRE Evaluation of the Development of EU Minimum Standards for Refugee Protection Tampere 1999*, Brussels 2004, London: ECRE.

European Union Directorate General of External Relations (DG External Relations) (2000), *European Union priorities and policy objectives for external relations in the fields of justice and home affairs*, Communication from COREPER to the General Affairs Council/ European Council, DG External Relations, 6 June, 7653/00 JAI 35, Brussels: CEC.

Geddes, A. (2000), *Immigration and European Integration: Towards Fortress Europe?* Manchester: Manchester University Press.

Geddes, A. (2001), Asylum in Europe: states, the European Union and the international system, *Refugee Survey Quarterly*, 20, 2: 59–72.

Guiraudon, V. (1998), *International Human Rights Norms and their Incorporation: the Protection of Aliens in Europe*, European Forum Working Paper EUF no. 98/4, Florence: European University Institute.

High Level Working Group on Asylum and Immigration of the European Union (HLWG) (1999), *Final Report of the High Level Working Group on Asylum and Migration*, 18 October, Brussels: CEU.

High Level Working Group on Asylum and Immigration of the European Union (HLWG) (2000), *High-Level Working Party on Asylum and Migration: Adoption of the report to the Nice European Council*, Note to the Council/European Council, Doc. 13993/00 JAI 152 AG 76, 29 November 2000, Brussels: CEU.

Hollifield, J. (2000), Immigration and the politics of rights: the French case in comparative perspective. In M. Bommes and A. Geddes (eds), *Immigration and Welfare: Challenging the Borders of the Welfare State*, London: Routledge, pp. 103–35.

Lavenex, S. (1999), *Safe Third Countries: Extending the EU Asylum and Immigration Policies to East and Central Europe*, Budapest: Central European University Press.

Macrae, J. (1999), *Aiding Peace . . . and War: UNHCR Returnee Reintegration, and the Relief-development Debate*, New Issues in Refugee Research, UNHCR Working Paper 14, Geneva: UNHCR.

Martin, P. L. (1994), Reducing emigration pressure: what role can foreign aid play? In W. R. Böhning and M.-L. Scholeter-Paredes (eds), *Aid in Place of Migration: Selected Contributions to an ILO-UNHCR Meeting*, Geneva: International Labour Organization.

Marx, R. and Lumpp, K. (1996), The German Constitutional Court's Decision of 14 May 1996 on the concept of "Safe Third Countries": a basis for burden sharing in Europe? *International Journal of Refugee Law*, 8, 3: 419–39.

Milward, A. S. (1999), *The European Rescue of the Nation State*, New York: Routledge.

Monar, J. (2000), *Justice and Home Affairs in a Wider Europe: The Dynamics of Inclusion and Exclusion*, ESRC "One Europe or Several?" Programme Working Paper 07/00, Sussex: ESRC.

Myers, P. (1996), *The European Union's Structure, Powers and Policy-making Process in Relation to the Root Causes Approach*, London: Institute for Public Policy Research.

Niessen, J. and Rowlands, S. (eds) (2000), *The Amsterdam Proposals or How to Influence Policy Debates on Asylum and Immigration*, Brussels: European Network against Racism/London: ILPA.

Pastore, F. (2001), Reconciling the prince's two arms: internal–external security policy coordination in the European Union. Occasional Paper 30 for *The Institute for Security Studies of the Western European Union* (October).

Pastore, F. (2004), Cooperation with sending and transit countries: beyond sticks and carrots? Conference paper, Dutch Presidency Conference on Asylum, Migration and Frontiers, September, Washington, DC: Migration Policy Institute.

Philippart, E. (1998), Deconstruction and reconstruction of EU pillars: the Euro-Mediterranean Partnership and the Middle East Peace Process. Paper presented at the Third Pan-European International Relations Conference ECPR-ISA, 16–19 September, Vienna: ECPR-ISA.

Scholdan, B. (2000), Addressing the root causes: relief and development assistance between peace building and preventing refugee flows, *Journal of Humanitarian Assistance*. Available at: http://www.jha.ac/articles/a058.htm (accessed July 2005).

Simon, A. (2003), The New Organization of the Council of the European Union: Setback or Opportunity for EU Development Cooperation? European Centre for Development Policy Management Discussion Paper no. 46, January, Maastricht: ECDPM.

Statewatch (2004), *The "Hague Programme", Annotation of Final Version*, by Professor Steve Peers, University of Essex, November, London: Statewatch.

Thouez, C. (2000), *Towards a Common European Migration and Asylum Policy?* New Issues in Refugee Research UNHCR Working Paper no. 27, August, Evaluation and Policy Analysis Unit, Geneva: UNHCR.

United Nations High Commissioner for Refugees (UNHCR) (2001), Revisiting the Dublin Convention: some reflections by UNHCR in response to the Commission staff working paper. Unpublished ms.

UNHCR Working Group on Migration and Asylum (UNHCR-WG) (2000a), *The Interface between Internal Migration and Asylum*, Geneva: UNHCR.

UNHCR Working Group on Migration and Asylum (UNHCR-WG) (2000b), *Reconciling Migration Control and Refugee Protection in the European Union: A UNHCR Perspective*, Discussion paper, Geneva: UNHCR.

Vachudová, M. A. (2000), Eastern Europe as gatekeeper: the immigration and asylum policies of an enlarged European union. In P. Andreas and T. Snyder (eds), *The Wall Around the West: State Borders and Immigration Control in North America and Europe*, Lanham, MD: Rowman and Littlefield, pp. 153–71.

Van Selm, J. (2002), The High Level Working Group: can foreign policy, development policy and asylum and immigration policy really be mixed? Conference paper, WIDER United Nations University Conference, September, Tampere: UNU.

Van Selm, J. (2004), *The Hague Program Reflects New European Realities*, in Migration Information Source online, 1 January. Available at: www.migrationinformation.org/Feature/display.cfm?id=276 (accessed January 2005).

Weiner, M. (ed.) (1993), *International Migration and Security*, Boulder, CO: Westview Press.

Weiner, M. (ed.) (1995), *The Global Migration Crisis: Challenge for States and for Human Rights*, New York: HarperCollins.

4
A Sledgehammer to Crack a Nut: Deportation, Detention and Dispersal in Europe

Liza Schuster

Background and Context

During the 1990s the position of Europe in the global refugee system changed from a region receiving few asylum-seekers to one faced with suddenly increasing numbers (Robinson 2003a). There were several reasons for this: the fall of the Berlin Wall in 1989 and the collapse of the Soviet Union, the crisis in the former Yugoslavia in the early 1990s, the continuing conflicts—some of them post-colonial—in Africa, Asia and the Middle East, together with cheaper air travel and more direct flights to European cities. The result was an increase in mobility generally, and in the movement of refugees from Africa and Asia to Europe and the EU, in particular. Up until the later part of the 1980s, the numbers of spontaneous asylum-seekers arriving in western and northern Europe was small and reasonably consistent, with Germany and France receiving the majority of them, followed by Sweden. Countries in the Mediterranean basin, as well as Ireland, had traditionally been countries of emigration and received far fewer asylum-seekers, in some cases just a few dozen annually.

By 1991 numbers had increased across Europe, especially in Germany, which hosted 75 per cent of those from the former Yugoslavia. In 1991, more than a quarter of a million asylum-seekers arrived in Germany (compared with 73,400 in the UK and 47,380 in France) and this increased to 438,191 in 1992. By contrast, Italy has consistently received fewer asylum-seekers than the other three countries—though the crisis in the former Yugoslavia and then Kosovo resulted in larger numbers of arrivals in 1991 (23,317) and 1999 (33,364) respectively (http://www.ecre.org.factfile/). This last was due to Italy's proximity to the former Yugoslavia and also because, for many, it acts as a gateway to Europe for those coming from other countries to the South and East.

Figure 1 shows the pattern of asylum-seeking in European Union member states between 1992 and 2003. It clearly demonstrates the peaks in terms of numbers in the early 1990s in response to the disintegration of the former Yugoslavia and then again in the late 1990s as a result of the crisis in Kosovo.

Figure 1

Total number of asylum applications reveived in EU 1992–2004*

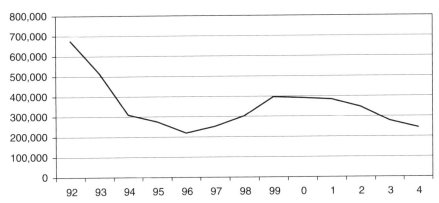

*To facilitate comparison, only the applications in the "15" were counted for 2004.

Ostensibly in response to the increase in numbers, a policy debate began to develop at EU level as European states sought to equalize the "burden" of asylum-seekers. Although it was agreed that harmonization of asylum policy across the Union was necessary, throughout the 1990s this objective met with insurmountable opposition. Nevertheless, a consensus did emerge about the nature of the "problem" (numbers), and the solution (greater controls). Although the numbers have fallen consistently since 2000, this consensus has not been challenged, and the drive towards even greater restrictions has not been reduced. In the absence of a European asylum policy, individual European states had already begun to introduce broadly comparable measures in the 1980s: visa restrictions, carriers' liability (fining airlines— then later shipping, road and rail carriers—if they carried anyone without the correct documentation) and fingerprinting. The 1990s saw the introduction of lists of safe countries and the third safe country rule: to ensure that asylum-seekers' cases were assessed by only one European country. By 2004, the deadline set at Tampere for the creation of a common European asylum policy, many of these measures had become institutionalized at national level, although few EU directives relating to asylum had been implemented (ECRE 2005).

Furthermore, measures targeting asylum-seekers were introduced not just at the border, but within states. This paper is concerned with responses to asylum-seekers at this national level and is particularly concerned to provide an analysis of the ways in which legislative developments have worked incrementally to exclude asylum-seekers from any opportunities for integration and to impose restrictions on various aspects of their lives—including mobility within the asylum state—while their claim is being considered.

In the next section, we explain what is meant by deportation, detention and dispersal in relation to asylum-seekers, before exploring the way in which these measures are used by national governments (in this case chiefly the UK, France, Germany and Italy) as part of their everyday regimes to control migration generally, and asylum in particular. Following an evaluation of these measures in terms of their efficacy and expense, we conclude with some reflections on their ethics in the light of the current global turbulence.

Deportation, Detention and Dispersal

Deportation, detention, dispersal and destitution have historically been used in different combinations and at different times when thought necessary to control or manage immigrants. What links all four strategies is their exclusionary nature. Deportation is the physical removal, and therefore the ultimate exclusion, of individuals or groups from the territory of the state. Detention is enclosure in a camp or prison and consequently the exclusion from the receiving society. Dispersal is the distribution of asylum-seekers to areas around a country. The rationale put forward for this last, in the case of the UK and Germany, is to spread the costs of reception and in particular housing between different local authority areas (Boswell 2003), and to avoid high concentrations of asylum-seekers in particular places, such as could provoke hostility from local populations (Schönwalder 1999; Institute of Race Relations 1999; Schuster 2003a). The consequence of dispersal, however, is the exclusion of asylum-seekers from social and kinship networks hitherto so important in the early settlement of asylum-seekers and refugees (Koser 1997; Bloch 2002).

Deportation

Deportation,[1] or at least the right to deport those thought to be undesirable from the country or exclude them from entry, is the right of a state and is entrenched in the asylum system. Significantly, Gibney and Hansen (2003: 2) note that "deportation is, from the state's point of view, both ineffectual and essential". They go on to argue that is necessary for states to be able to deport those without the right to remain for three reasons: first, it "assuage[s] public opinion, which would not view the state's incapacity in this area with equanimity"; second, deportation acts as a disincentive to other potential migrants; third and finally, it allows the state to apply pressure on migrants to return voluntarily if they are not to be deported (2003: 15). Deportations clearly act as a signal to the electorate that something is being done about people who do not have a legal right to remain. However, it is difficult to judge whether or not they also act as a disincentive to potential migrants or as an effective means of persuading people to return "voluntarily".

In strictly legal terms, states that deport asylum-seekers are not contravening their obligations under Article 33 of the 1951 Convention, which states that:

> No Contracting state shall expel or return (*refouler*) a refugee . . . to the frontiers of territories where his life or freedom would be threatened on

account of his race, religion, nationality, membership of a particular social group or political opinion.

This is because, in theory at least, deportation *should* only occur after the courts have satisfied themselves that the life or freedom of the applicant is not in danger. However, one of the risks of deportation is the fallibility of the asylum determination process—as demonstrated by a successful appeal rate of one in five in the UK, for example (National Audit Commission 2004: 9; UNHCR 2005b), and the lack of information on those who have been deported. Let us first consider the numbers and then go on to consider the potential human cost, together with the actual cost, of deportation in the EU context.

Deportation is difficult to achieve, especially in instances where migrants do not have travel or identity documents, or their country of origin is unknown, or they are unwilling to cooperate or the deportation is contested. Nevertheless, deportations are increasing—though meaningful comparisons are difficult, since statistics are not compiled systematically and are often incomplete. Furthermore, in some cases it is not clear what or who is being counted nor what their migration status is. The UK, for instance, is the only country that disaggregates statistics and for which it is possible to ascertain the number of actual asylum-seekers being deported. (In 2003, for instance, 17,040 asylum-seekers were deported from the UK, while the number of asylum applicants was 61,025, including dependants.) Therefore the following figures are indicative only.

For Germany, France and Italy, the aggregated categories indicate the extent to which deportation is used—that is, the extent to which people are physically removed from the territory of the state—but not the proportion of deportees who are asylum-seekers.

Germany does not publish data on deportations, so this information has been derived from responses to questions asked by MPs in the Bundestag. At the prompting of a representative of the Berlin Refugee Council, Petra Pau, an independent MP, asked how many people had been deported by air from German airports in 2003. The answer was 23,944, while in 2002 it was 26,286. Information on the numbers removed using other modes of transport (for example by bus to Germany's neighbouring states of the Czech Republic and Poland) is not available, but the Berlin Refugee Council estimates that the annual total for all deportations is about 30,000.[2] This is in the context of there being only 50,000 asylum-seekers in 2003.

In France, where the numbers of asylum applications have increased over the five years (from 44,500 in 2000 to 61,600 in 2004; UNHCR 2005a), statistics used to be difficult to come by. However in 2003 the Interior Minister, Nicholas Sarkozy, began issuing targets and putting pressure on the prefectures to increase the numbers they deport (Lochak 2004). As a result, the number of removal orders executed increased from 21,200 in 2002 to over 35,000 in 2003 (ANAFÉ 2004). However, these figures include undocumented migrants as well as asylum-seekers, and also include those refused admission at the border, as well as those deported to another EU country under the terms of the Dublin Convention (now Dublin II) that assigns responsibility for examining a claim to the first EU state entered.[3]

Italy is particularly efficient at removing people from its territory and, thanks in particular to Caritas, there are statistics available on its deportations. Once again, however, the figures are not disaggregated for asylum-seekers and not particularly reliable for the purposes of comparison (Coslovi and Piperno 2005). Furthermore, since Italy continues to return some people without even permitting them to make claims, such figures would be unreliable in themselves. Be this as it may, for 2003, total expulsions numbered over 65,000, including 18,844 people who were accompanied to the border and forcibly expelled and a further 24,202 who had been refused entry at the border. This marked a decrease from the previous year when a total of 88,500 had been expelled; a drop which Coslovi and Piperno attribute to a sharp fall in the number of irregular migrants in Italy (thanks to a regularization programme) and to a decrease in the number of attempted landings (2005: 13–14).

Such as they are, these statistical portraits reveal little about the reality of deportation or its human and social costs. There is a glaring lack of information about deportees after their expulsion. Pro Asyl, a German umbrella organization, has carried out a study of Turkish Kurds whose claims for asylum in Germany had been rejected and who were returned to Turkey (Pro Asyl 2002a, 2002b). More recently, Liz Fekete of the Institute of Race Relations has pulled together information from across Europe on 200 cases—including deportations from the UK to Zimbabwe, Somalia and the Democratic Republic of Congo (DRC); and from some German states to Chechnya and Afghanistan. Her report includes detailed histories of a number of individuals, such as Mr Reyes Prado. He was deported from the UK to Colombia even though four members of his family had been assassinated. Within a month of being returned, he too was the victim of an assassination attempt. Fekete also outlines the case of a Syrian asylum-seeker expelled to Syria, where he was detained and executed three months later. In addition, a Cologne lawyer has detailed the cases of Togolese asylum-seekers who managed to return to Germany, having been tortured and detained when deported (Fekete 2005).

In all of the cases documented (approximately forty) in the German studies (Pro Asyl 2002a, 2002b), the men and women had arrived in Germany and claimed asylum on the basis of alleged detention and torture by the Turkish authorities. Their claims were rejected because the German authorities argued that safe internal flight alternatives were available (to other parts of Turkey) or because their stories were not found to be credible. In each case, on return to Turkey, the people involved were arrested, detained and in some cases again tortured before managing to return to Germany, this time bringing with them sufficient documentary evidence of detention and/ or torture. As a result, they were granted, not refugee status, but leave to remain on humanitarian grounds.

European governments frequently claim that assurances were sought and received, from the countries to which people are expelled, that torture will not be used. However, a report in the *Guardian* last year demonstrated the extent to which such assurances are sought *not* in order to assure the safety of the person to be deported, but rather to facilitate the deportation. The paper detailed Tony Blair's attempts to push through four deportations to

Egypt, against the advice of the Foreign Secretary and senior Home Office officials to the effect that Egypt would never promise not to detain or torture—and if it did, would be even less likely to honour such promises (*Guardian*, 16 November 2004). The *Guardian* cited a letter from Prime Minister Blair's private office saying he "believes we should use whatever assurances the Egyptians are willing to offer, to build a case to initiate the deportation procedure and to take our chances in the courts".

The Coslovi and Piperno study (2005, cited above) focuses on another consequence of deportation for the many who are neither killed nor detained on return: exclusion from their communities of origin. In order to leave, some may have incurred debts that have little prospect of being paid off, and so they remain a burden on their families. Others are regarded with suspicion, since their communities may see them at best as failures, if not as criminals. European migration law is frequently little-understood, and there is often an assumption that the person deported must have done something wrong to get sent back (*ibid.*).

In addition to any dangers and difficulties to be faced on return to the country of origin, the conditions under which people are deported can be inhumane and degrading—and have led to a number of deaths in recent years (Fekete 2005). Details of violence and excessive force being used to compel people to board aircraft have been in circulation for over 10 years, but are only now beginning to receive more publicity. Aside from the reports in France by ANAFÉ (2003a, 2003b) and De Loisy's exposé (2005), a BBC documentary uncovered evidence of the treatment of people being transported to airports in the UK, and Fekete's report (2005) includes a catalogue of violence and gratuitous force leading to death and injury, associated with deportations from European countries.

On occasion, this treatment of people—who are often shackled, who may have their mouths and bodies encased in packing tape, or who may be sedated (Fekete 2005)—provokes distress and anger among other passengers, some of whom have felt compelled to intervene. In order to halt such interventions—which have on occasion prevented deportations taking place—the French government, for example, has brought charges against the passengers who intervened; the most high-profile case being that of an Italian anthropologist who wrote of his experiences in the French newspaper *Libération* (23 December 2004) and in the Italian *Corriere della Sera* (7 February 2005). Governments are also increasingly avoiding public confrontations by chartering aircraft to deport people (Fekete 2005; Lochak 2004).

In addition, European governments are now engaging in joint deportations. These began in early 2003 and initially developed outside the structures of the EU. The European Parliament was subsequently consulted, but the Council of Ministers preferred not to wait for its approval before signing an accord at the end of January 2004, allocating €30 million to facilitate joint deportations. The first of the joint charter flights took place on 9 March 2004. An Airbus from the Belgian Air Force left Melsbroek airfield carrying 40 asylum-seekers and undocumented migrants—36 from Belgium, 3 from the Netherlands and 1 from Luxembourg—for Pristina (Kosovo) and Tirana (Albania) (Communiqué de Presse, Ligue de Droits de l'Homme Belgique;

see also Fekete 2005). In July 2005, France, Germany, Italy, Spain and the UK (the G5) announced that they were going ahead with joint expulsions and planned the first to Afghanistan. Joint expulsions, and the pooling of resources this implies, may seem a cost-effective way of carrying out deportations, yet the organization and personnel involved is intense and expensive,[4] and the destinations far from safe.

In short, deportation is an expensive and inefficient practice (Schuster 2003a). Furthermore, in the specific context of asylum-seekers, there are also specific human costs, as detailed above. This, together with evidence from the UK of the mistakes made in the determination process (National Audit Commission 2004), indicates the risk that deportations can lead to people being returned to face torture, detention and death. Nevertheless, in the context of asylum policy in EU member states, deportation has become what Gibney and Hansen (2003: 2) call "the noble lie" and therefore a necessity for all governments who need to be seen to be in control of migration and of borders.

Detention

Detention is now used by most European countries to facilitate removals, and its use is defended by governments on the grounds that deportation without detention would be almost impossible and that, since those detained are subject to removal, it is not in fact arbitrary. However, in Britain, France, Germany and Italy some asylum-seekers are detained on arrival and some after an initial rejection of their claim and before their appeal has been heard. Thus detention is not only being used at the end of the asylum process prior to deportation, as is claimed by governments. The majority of those held in detention centres or "removal centres" are eventually released; either because they cannot be removed because of conditions in the country of origin, or because travel documents for the persons to be removed cannot be issued, or because they are allowed to appeal, or because they are granted leave to remain on compassionate grounds, or, finally, because their claim for asylum is allowed. Governments detain people who are at different stages of the asylum process, including people whose appeals have not yet been heard, and those who have just arrived and claimed asylum. This means that some people who are subsequently recognized as refugees—and who may have been subject to imprisonment, torture and degrading treatment in their countries of origin— are held in detention centres in their country of hoped-for refuge (JRS 2004).

Most EU countries have limits on the amount of time people can be detained—although these limits vary widely—but in the UK,[5] Ireland, Denmark and Greece there is no maximum. In France, it has recently been increased to 32 days, in Italy it is 60, while in Germany it is up to 6 months, and in very exceptional cases as much as 18 months. Although France has the strictest limits on the length of time a person may be held in detention, conditions there, especially in the *zones d'attente*, are among the worst in Europe, with people being held in overcrowded quarters, without access to sanitation or adequate food (ANAFÉ 2003a; De Loisy 2005). The violence perpetrated by the border police against asylum-seekers in the *zones d'attente*— particularly at Roissy (Charles de Gaulle airport) where the overwhelming majority of people (95 per cent) who spend time in *zones d'attente* are held and where 96–8 per cent of asylum claims are lodged—is now well-documented (ANAFÉ 2003b; De Loisy 2005).

Among concerns listed in a second report by the organization are the repeated and manifest refusals to register claims for asylum, the failure to provide information on their rights to those detained (particularly to non-Francophones), the refusal to permit the disembarkation of undocumented passengers from boats when they reach port, the *refoulement* of people to countries considered safe without allowing them to apply for asylum, and the restriction and obstruction of access to concerned NGOs to the centres (ANAFÉ 2003a). (Authorized associations may visit each centre a maximum of eight times in any one year.)

In Germany, chaplains from the Jesuit Refugee Service have access to all parts of the centres, but they are overwhelmed by the numbers in their care and deeply concerned by conditions in the detention centres. Dieter Müller, a chaplain visiting Köpernick detention centre, noted it was the African detainees who were held longest, in part because of difficulties establishing identity.[6] The Köpernick centre is a former prison, and the structure itself reflects this. The noise levels 24 hours a day are very high, a characteristic common to detention centres across Europe. This adds to the problems of visiting. Visitors are separated from detainees by thick Perspex, which means that communication necessitates shouting—rendering privacy impossible. Detainees have also complained about lights being left on 24 hours a day in rooms, or switched on in the early hours of the morning so that the guards can carry out a head count.

In Italy there are 15 centres where migrants, including those who may wish to claim asylum, are held while identity and travel documents are sought to facilitate their deportations. It is difficult to estimate how many are held in the centres at any one time or for how long, since turnover is relatively rapid and Italy has expelled people within days—before NGOs could make contact with the new arrivals or advise them of their rights. A recent report published by *Medici Senza Frontieri* (MSF), the only NGO allowed to enter the CPTs (*Centri di Permanenza Temporanea*) in Italy, examined the conditions and the treatment of detainees. It was critical of all the centres and called for the immediate closure of at least three of them (which led to its own exclusion from the centres!) (MSF 2004). Some of the centres housed the detainees in containers, similar to those used to house builders on building sites though more basic: rarely containing more than beds, a chair and possibly a locker.[7] In winter these are freezing cold and in summer boiling hot. At Trapani and Lamezia Terme, the accommodation is overcrowded and detainees are forced to spend most of the day in their sleeping area because of a lack of alternative space. Aside from this inadequate infrastructure, MSF also found evidence of minimal contact with social services (health/welfare), insufficient legal and psychological aid, the use of drugs to sedate detainees, and excessive force by the police within the centres (MSF 2004).

In the UK, asylum detainees are now held mostly in purpose-built or adapted detention centres. The government refuses to make statistics available on how many people are detained each year, their age, stage of immigration or asylum case, or the outcome of their detention; yet some facts are available. There is currently capacity for 2,700 detainees, though the Labour government has declared its intention to increase this to 4,000 (http://www.biduk.org/immigration/factsd.htm). There are ten immigration removal centres (IRCs) in the UK. Most are run by private companies contracted to the Immigration and Nationality Directorate (IND), but three are run by the Prison Service (BID 2005).

The involvement of private, profit-making companies in the detention process is a worrying development, especially in the light of abuses recently documented. The Medical Foundation for the Care of Victims of Torture examined 14 cases of alleged abuse by guards/wardens and found that, in 12 out of those 14 investigated, "gratuitous or excessive force was used" and that at least 4 detainees had been tortured in their countries of origin (Medical Foundation 2004). Some months later, the BBC carried out an undercover investigation which documented the racist behaviour and attitudes of some staff, and filmed some of them advising on how "control and restraint" methods could be used inappropriately. A number of campaigning organizations (CARF, SADY and NCADC 2005) have compiled a report on 35 detainees who have suffered physical and sexual abuse while in detention—including cuts, bruises and swelling (the majority of cases), nerve damage (from handcuffs), sexual assault, urethra/groin damage, cracked shoulder, fractured finger, exacerbation of psychological problems and serious head injury (NCADC electronic newsletter, 23 March 2005). These cases were reported by volunteer visitors who see a maximum of 10 per cent of the detainees, raising the possibility that the practice is much more widespread.

In the reports cited above, the psychological damage inflicted by this form of exclusion is manifested in suicide attempts, some of which are successful. Indeed self-harm seems to be relatively common in Italy, Germany and the UK (Fekete 2005). While the UK was for a time exceptional in detaining even small children, this practice is increasing across continental Europe, although children tend not to be detained for the prolonged periods seen in the UK (up to 13 months in the case of the Ay children aged 7, 11, 12 and 14, see www.ncadc.org.uk; see also www.biduk.org).

Moreover, the damage done by detention does not end when people are released—as the majority are (MSF 2005). Detention is extremely expensive not merely in real costs but in terms of the future integration of those who are given leave to remain in the country of asylum. Delays experienced by asylum-seekers in terms of making social contacts, learning the language of the country of asylum and accessing the labour market all impact on their longer-term integration—and can result in deskilling, a loss of confidence and lowered self-esteem (Bloch 2004).

Dispersal

Dispersal is a strategy used less routinely than deportation or detention in European countries of asylum. It is most developed in the UK, Germany, the Netherlands and Sweden, and is also used in the Republic of Ireland to distribute asylum-seekers in areas around a country.

Historically, dispersal was a mechanism for either concentrating or dispersing ethnic minorities, according to the prevalent ideology. Germany and the Netherlands were the two countries using these strategies as a means of controlling—or trying to control—the settlement patterns of migrants in the postwar period (Arnoldus *et al.* 2003; Boswell 2003). In the UK, migrant families were clustered "spontaneously" in districts within major industrial cities in the postwar period and this led to some white parents complaining about "black-majority" schools. Local Education Authorities (LEAs), with the sanction of a Department for Education and Science Circular in 1965 (Circular 7/65), were advised to restrict the proportion of immigrant children in any school to 30 per cent. This resulted in a system of removing black children from their local school and bussing them to other schools in the same LEA (Grosvenor 1997). It was argued that bussing black children to predominately white schools would facilitate assimilation and enhance education. However, as Troyna and Williams note (1986: 20): "dispersal was neither a legitimate nor a logical response to perceived educational needs. It was a policy of surrender to racism", and was ultimately abandoned.

Among the countries featured in this paper, it is Germany and the UK that use dispersal as a strategy in the asylum process. Germany introduced the dispersal of asylum-seekers in 1974, and it was codified in 1982. Britain did not follow suit until 2000, though dispersal had already been used in Britain on an *ad hoc* basis, in response to particular cohorts of programme refugees, that is, refugees arriving with refugee status as part of an organized programme. This included Ugandan Asians and Vietnamese refugees in the 1970s and 1980s (Boswell 2003). Bosnians and Kosovans were also dispersed in the 1990s, though they had been admitted to the UK under a Temporary Protection scheme and not as refugees (see Koser and Black 1999; Van Selm 2000).

Under the German system, asylum-seekers are dispersed to *Länder* on a quota basis. Asylum-seekers have little say in their placement to a particular area and local authorities only have to take into account the closest family members—parents, children, spouse—when allocating the district to which they are sent. This means that it can be difficult for family members who arrive separately to be accommodated in the same area. Germany takes the geographical control of asylum-seekers to the extreme by imposing a *Residenzpflicht* (a duty to reside in a particular area) on them and fining those who breach its regulations. In one case in Thüringen, the only public telephone from which asylum-seekers can call their solicitors, friends or family is fifty metres from an asylum hostel and across the border between one area and another. Consequently, the *Residenzpflicht* is regularly breached, creating the opportunity for the local police, or the BGS (*Bundesgrenzschutz*—the federal police charged with protecting Germany's borders and ports), to intimidate the asylum-seekers at will.[8] Those caught and charged with breaching this regulation are fined approximately £20 each time they do so, and concerns have been expressed by refugee advocates that such breaches can prejudice adjudicators making decisions on asylum claims.[9] Osarin Igbinoba of Karawane, who encourages asylum-seekers to draw attention to the *Residenzpflicht* by breaching it, Volker Hügel of Pro Asyl and Georg Classen of the Berlin Refugee Council all confirm that the *Residenzpflicht* offers abundant opportunities for abuse.[10]

In the UK, dispersal was introduced as an integral, rather than exceptional, element of the asylum system by the New Labour government in the 1999 Immigration and Asylum Act. Under this legislation, implemented in 2000, eligibility for support with accommodation costs for new asylum-seekers arriving in Britain was linked to dispersal. This means that in cases where asylum-seekers opt out of the dispersal system, they receive no assistance with housing costs and must depend instead on their family and friends for accommodation. Data on the support of asylum-seekers, from March 2004, showed that 36 per cent of them had opted for subsistence-only support. The majority of these were living in London (http://www.homeoffice.gov.uk/rds/pdfs04/asylumq104.pdf), reflecting the presence there of refugee and other minority ethnic communities.

Previous attempts to disperse programme refugees, of which the Vietnamese refugees in the 1970s are the best-known example, led to secondary migration to urban areas within already established communities. This was because dispersed refugees experienced isolation. In some of the dispersal areas there were few opportunities to find employment and local authorities were unable to provide appropriate services for the new arrivals (Duke *et al.* 1999). The result was the movement of dispersed refugees to areas where relevant communities already existed (Robinson and Hale 1989; Robinson 2003b).

The rationale for the dispersal of asylum-seekers turns on the costs of increasing numbers and the need to "burden-share" between areas and regions. Boswell (2003) also notes that, in the German case, there was a goal of deterrence behind the dispersal, since it was designed to make Germany a less attractive asylum destination. Some policy-makers have also justified dispersal on the grounds that clusters of asylum-seekers can have a negative effect on social cohesion.

Recent research, however, has emphasized the negative effects that dispersal can have on asylum-seekers. Historically, on arrival in a new country, asylum-seekers clustered together sharing important resources such as accommodation, money and information. Among the first acts of arriving migrants who have family or friends in Europe is the attempt to contact them. While asylum-seekers often have little influence over their country of asylum—relying instead on the networks and route provided by smugglers and agents—once *within* a country, kinship and social networks were key in deciding where to live (Bloch 2002). Where there are large enough numbers of people from a particular country of origin, community formation and maintenance occurs and, with this, community organizations become established to provide not merely information and advice but also a range of other activities—social, cultural, political and educational.

Secondly, dispersal is either quota-led (Germany) or housing-led (UK). In the UK this means that asylum-seekers are sent to areas where low-cost housing is available and these are often inner-city areas with high levels of unemployment and few employment opportunities. This can create competition for already scarce resources in economically and socially deprived areas, the result of which has been an increase in racism and racist attacks (Boswell 2003; Robinson 2003b, 2003c). This clashes with one of the foundations on which dispersal is based: that spreading minorities helps to ensure positive social interaction and therefore promotes social cohesion. The emerging literature on rural racism and racist attacks on asylum-seekers in dispersal areas shows the thesis to be ill-founded. Some asylum-seekers have found themselves in ethnically homogeneous areas outside the urban centres, where there is a shortage of support services, where the asylum-seekers are often the only visibly different foreigners around, and where they become targets for abuse and violence (Schönwalder 1999; Institute of Race Relations 1999; Schuster 2003a). Dispersal also raises moral and ethical issues concerning choice as a basic right of citizenship in both Germany and the UK. This further exclusion of asylum-seekers from the social norms and rights associated with liberalism must, in itself, adversely affect social cohesion

Conclusion

Deportation, detention and dispersal programmes are not new, any more than are the abuses being committed by European states (Bloch and Schuster 2005) in executing them. Until recently, however, they were used only occasionally in response to particular crises. They would usually be discontinued once the "crisis" had passed though, importantly, the enabling legislation would be left in place. What is particularly disquieting about current practices across Europe is their normalization—the way in which it has become acceptable to treat certain categories of children, women and men as less deserving of dignity and as less entitled to respect of their human rights. Currently, there is no war in Europe, the numbers of asylum-seekers are falling across the continent, and Britain, France, Germany and Italy all accept that further migration is needed for economic and demographic reasons. There is no asylum "crisis" and it is contentious whether there is an undocumented migration crisis. Nonetheless, governments, civil servants and officials are able to conceive of and implement policies and practices that lead directly and indirectly to thousands of deaths, to the deprivation of their liberty of people who have not committed any crime—including children and babes in arms—and to serious injury and psychological damage.

The harm that these practices do extends beyond the people targeted to the societies that tolerate forced deportation, detention and forced dispersal. That they have a corrosive impact on those who implement them can be seen from the abuses perpetrated by some of the staff in detention centres. But they also have a corrosive impact on a society that tolerates them.

Acknowledgements

I owe the title and much more in this article to Alice Bloch of City University. My thanks also to Catherine Jones Finer.

Notes

1. European governments prefer to use euphemisms such as "removal" or "return" rather than "deportation", which awakes to varying degrees in different countries memories of the deportations to camps and across Europe during the Second World War.

2. Interview by Liza Schuster in 2003.
3. Dublin II has altered this somewhat, so that now responsibility lies with the state that permitted either entry or residence.
4. Data from the Netherlands put the cost of deporting 14,590 people by plane in 2002 at €120.7 million.
5. While most people detained in the UK are held for an average of two months, there have been a number of cases of prolonged periods of detention.
6. Interview with Dieter Müller, Berlin, 28 October 2002.
7. In Hamburg, containers are also used as housing for asylum-seekers.
8. Interview with Sandra Jesse, Thüringen Refugee Council, Erfurt, 10 September 2002.
9. *Ibid.*
10. Interviews with Osarin Igbinoba, Weimar, 9 September 2002; Georg Classen, Berlin, 25 October 2002; Volker Hügel, Berlin, 28 October 2002.

Bibliography

ANAFÉ (2003a), *Zone d'attente: 10 ans après, les difficultés persistent*, Paris: ANAFÉ.

ANAFÉ (2003b), *Violences policières en zone d'attente*, Paris: ANAFÉ.

ANAFÉ (2004), *La frontière et le droit: la zone d'attente de Roissy sous le regard de l'ANAFÉ—bilan de six mois d'observation associative (avril–octobre 2004)*. Paris: ANAFÉ.

Arnoldus, M., Dukes, T. and Musterd, S. (2003), Dispersal policies in the Netherlands. In V. Robinson, R. Andersson and S. Musterd, *Spreading the "Burden"? A Review of Policies to Disperse Asylum-Seekers and Refugees*, ch. 3, Bristol: Policy Press.

BID (2005), *About Detention*. Available at: http://www.biduk.org/immigration/facts.htm

Bloch, A. (2000), A new era or more of the same? Asylum policy in the UK, *Journal of Refugee Studies*, 13, 1: 29–42.

Bloch, A. (2002), *The Migration and Settlement of Refugees in Britain*, Basingstoke: Palgrave Macmillan.

Bloch, A. (2004), *Making it Work: Refugee Employment in the UK*, Asylum and Migration Working Paper 2, London: Institute for Public Policy Research.

Bloch, A. and Schuster, L. (2005), At the extremes of exclusion: deportation, detention and dispersal, *Ethnic and Racial Studies* 28, 3: 491–512.

Boswell, C. (2003), Burden-sharing in the European Union: lessons from the German and UK experience, *Journal of Refugee Studies*, 16, 3: 316–35.

CARF, SADY and NCADC (2005), *The Use of Unlawful Force against Immigration Detainees*. Available at: http://www.ncadc.org.uk/resources/library.htm (accessed 2 June 2005).

Castles, S., Crawley, H., and Loughna, S. (2003), *States of Conflict: Causes and Patterns of Forced Migration to the EU and Policy Responses*, London: Institute for Public Policy Research.

Castles, S. and Miller, M. (2003), *The Age of Migration: International Population Movements in the Modern World*, 3rd edn, Basingstoke: Macmillan.

Colic-Peisker, V. (2003), Bosnian refugees in Australia: Identity, community and labour market integration, *New Issues in Refugee Research*, Working Paper 97, Geneva: UNHCR.

Coslovi, L. and Piperno, F. (2005), Rimpatrio forzato e poi? Analisi dell'impatto delle espulsioni di differenti categorie di migranti: un confronto tra Albania, Marocco e Nigeria, Rapporto finale di ricerca prodotto nell'ambito del progetto ALNIMA (2002/HLWG/26). Available at: http://www.cespi.it/PASTORE/Rapporto%20ALNIMA-IT.pdf

De Loisy, A. (2005), *Bienvenue en France! Six mois d'enquête clandestine dans la zone d'attente de Roissy*, Paris: Le cherche midi.

Duke, K., Sales, R. and Gregory, J. (1999), Refugee resettlement in Europe. In A. Bloch and C. Levy (eds.), *Refugees, Citizenship and Social Policy in Europe*, ch. 6, Basingstoke: Macmillan.

ECRE (2005), Key EU policy documents and legislation. Available at: http://www.ecre.org/eu_developments/eu_docs.shtml#apa (accessed 12 April 2005).

Fekete, L. (2005), *The Deportation Machine: Europe, Asylum and Human Rights*, London: Institute of Race Relations.

Gibney, M. and Hansen, R. (2003), Deportation and the liberal state: the forcible return of asylum-seekers and unlawful migrants in Canada, Germany and the United Kingdom, *New Issues in Refugee Research*, Working Paper 77, Geneva: UNHCR EPAU.

Gilbert, A. and Koser, K. (2004), *Information Dissemination to Potential Asylum-seekers in Countries of Origin and/or Transit*, Findings 220, London: Home Office.

Grosvenor, I. (1997), *Assimilating Identities: Racism and Educational Policy in Post 1945 Britain*, London: Lawrence and Wishart.

Heath, T., Jefferies, R. and Lloyd, A. (2003), *Asylum Statistics: United Kingdom*, London: Home Office.

Holmes, C. (1988), *John Bull's Island: Immigration and British Society, 1871–1971* London: Macmillan.

Institute of Race Relations (1999), Lessons from Europe: How the UK government's asylum proposals will create racism and social exclusion, *European Race Bulletin*, 30: 1–3.

Joly, D. (1996), *Haven or Hell? Asylum Policies and Refugees in Europe*, London: Macmillan.

JRS (2004), *Detention in Europe: JRS-Europe Observation and Position Paper 2004*, Jesuit Refugee Service Europe. Available at: http://www.detention-in-europe.org/

Koser, K. (1997), Social networks and the asylum circle: the case of Iranians in the Netherlands, *International Migration Review*, 31, 3: 591–611.

Koser, K. and Black. R. (1999), Limits to harmonisation: the temporary protection of refugees in the European Union, *International Migration*, 37, 3: 521–43.

Liebaut, F. (ed.) (2000), *Legal and Social Conditions for Asylum-seekers and Refugees in Western Europe*, Copenhagen: Danish Refugee Council.

Lochak, D. (2004), Éloigner: Une tâche comme une autre, *Plein Droit*, 62.

Medical Foundation (2004), *Harm on Removal: Excessive Force against Failed Asylum-seekers*, London: Medical Foundation for the Care of Victims of Torture.

Miles, R. and Clearly, P. (1993), Migration to Britain: racism, state regulation and employment. In V. Robinson (ed.), *The International Refugee Crisis: British and Canadian Responses*, Basingstoke: Macmillan, in association with the Refugee Studies Programme, Oxford University.

MSF (2004), *Rapporto sui Centri di Permanenza Temporanea e Assistenza*, Medici Senza Frontiere. Available at: http://www.sgbergamo.it/com/gennaio2004/CPT_FINALE.pdf

National Audit Commission (2004), *Improving the Speed and Quality of Asylum Decisions*, London: Audit Office. Available at: http://www.nao.org.uk/publications.nao_reports/03-04/0304535.pdf (accessed 12 April 2005).

Pro Asyl (2002a), *Fluchtland Türkei—Inländische Vertreibung—Asyl—Festung Europa*, Frankfurt: Pro Asyl.

Pro Asyl (2002b), *Von Deutschland in den Türkischen Folterkeller*, Frankfurt: Pro Asyl.

Robinson, V. (2003a), Defining the "problem". In V. Robinson, R. Andersson and S. Musterd, *Spreading the "Burden"? A Review of Policies to Disperse Asylum-seekers and Refugees*, ch. 2, Bristol: Policy Press.

Robinson, V. (2003b), Dispersal policies in the UK. In V. Robinson, R. Andersson and S. Musterd, *Spreading the "Burden"? A Review of Policies to Disperse Asylum-seekers and Refugees*, ch. 5, Bristol: Policy Press.

Robinson, V. (2003c), Exploring myths about rural racism: a Welsh case study. In C. Williams and N. Evans (eds.), *Exploring Ethnic Diversity in Wales*, Cardiff: University of Wales Press.

Robinson, V. and Hale, S. (1989), *The Geography of Vietnamese Secondary Migration in the UK*, Warwick: ESRC Centre for Research in Ethnic Relations.

Robinson, V. and Segrott, J. (2003), *Understanding the Decision Making of Asylum-seekers*, London: Home Office.

Sales, R. (2002), The deserving and the undeserving: refugees, asylum-seekers and welfare in Britain, *Critical Social Policy*, 22, 3: 456–78.

Schönwälder, K. (1999), Persons persecuted on political grounds shall enjoy the right to asylum—but not in our country: asylum policy and debates about refugees in the Federal Republic of Germany. In A. Bloch and C. Levy (eds.), *Refugees, Citizenship and Social Policy in Europe*, ch. 4, Basingstoke: Macmillan.

Schuster, L. (2003a), Common sense or racism? The treatment of asylum-seekers in Europe, *Patterns of Prejudice*, 37, 3: 233–56.

Schuster, L. (2003b), *The Use and Abuse of Political Asylum in Britain and Germany*, London: Frank Cass.

Seifert, W. (1997), Admission policy, patterns of migration and integration: the German and French case compared, *New Community*, 23, 4: 441–60.

Silverman, M. (1992), *Deconstructing the Nation: Immigration, Racism and Citizenship in Modern France*, London: Routledge.

Troyna, B. and Williams, J. (1986), *Racism, Education and the State: The Racialisation of Education Policy*, London: Croom Helm.

UNHCR (2005a), *Asylum Levels and Trends in Industrialized Countries, 2004: Overview of Asylum Applications Lodged in Europe and non-European Industrialized Countries in 2004*, Geneva: UNHCR.

UNHCR (2005b), *Quality Initiative Project: Key Observations and Recommendations March 2004–January 2005* (March). Available at: http://www.unhcr.org.uk/press/press_releases2005/pr11March05.htm

Valtonen, K. (2004), From the margin to the mainstream: conceptualising refugee settlement processes, *Journal of Refugee Studies*, 17, 1: 70–96.

Van Selm, J. (ed.) (2000), *Kosovo's Refugees in the EU*, London: Continuum.

Walker, A. and Walker, C. (1997), Introduction: the strategy of inequality. In *Britain Divided: The Growth of Social Exclusion in the 1980s and 1990s*, London: Child Poverty Action Group.

5
Governance, Forced Migration and Welfare

Peter Dwyer

Introduction

This paper discusses the emergent supranational asylum policy of the European Union (EU) before moving on to review recent policy changes at nation state level (i.e. within EU member states). As increasing numbers of forced migrants[1] look to enter Europe certain common themes are evident in the policy responses of member states. Many national governments have attempted to reduce the welfare rights enjoyed by forced migrants and have simultaneously removed such migrants from the jurisdiction of mainstream welfare systems. An essential characteristic of policy at the member state level has been a reduction in the direct role of the state in meeting the basic needs of forced migrants. This has been accompanied by a willingness on the part of the state to devolve responsibility for the provision of forced migrants' welfare to an array of public, private and voluntary actors at regional and local levels. It is argued that, in seeking to manage forced migration, the "dispersed state" (Clarke 2004; Clarke and Newman 1997) has become involved in complex networks of governance both within and beyond its own borders. The third section of the paper draws on a recently completed qualitative study in the city of Leeds (UK) to consider how such devolved networks of governance operate and the impact they have on forced migrants' welfare.

A basic assumption underpinning the Keynesian welfare national state model—that welfare states were relatively homogonous and concerned to deliver welfare only to a closed national population—is being undermined by increasing migration. Indeed, the rising numbers seeking asylum in Western Europe are often presented by the popular media as indicating the failure of national states to govern their own territories authoritatively. Jessop's discussion of the "hollowing out" of the nation state as powers are delegated upwards, sideways and downwards is highly relevant here (Jessop 1999). Increasingly national governments are becoming involved in complex multilevel networks of governance to keep forced migrants out and/or to provide meagre levels of welfare for those who enter their territory. Jessop points out, however, that much political power still remains with the nation state and that policy related to the entry and welfare of forced migrants remains very much the prerogative of nation states. The current network of governance around forced migration is thus best characterized as a reworking of state power in changed circumstances. The nation state remains a key player and "the most significant site of struggle among competing global, triadic, supranational, national, regional and local forces" (Jessop 1994: 27). Many of the "partners" involved in policy are subordinate to the aims and ambitions of national governments driving a particular policy agenda (Clarke and Glendinning 2002).

Welfare of Forced Migrants in the European Union: Upwards, Sideways and Downwards?

The international agreements of the past (e.g. Schengen, 1985) paved the way for the cautious development of an immigration policy within the EU institutions. The elevation of aspects of asylum policy to the supranational level has been accompanied by a series of reforms within many member states which have seen national governments adopt policies that move responsibility for the welfare of forced migrants out of mainstream systems while simultaneously reducing levels of provision. In many instances the nation state's responsibility for the welfare of forced migrants is effectively being devolved downwards to a complex network of regional and local actors that includes local authorities, private companies and voluntary and charitable agencies. In addition member states are keen to deflect the problem of forced migration sideways on to other states.

Upwards and sideways: towards a common European asylum system?

Following the European Council declaration in favour of promoting greater cooperation between member states on migration in Amsterdam (1997) and an agreement at Tampere in 1999, member states have sought to develop a common EU asylum policy (Caviedes 2004; Veenkamp *et al.* 2003; Moraes 2003; Geddes 2001). As part of this process national governments have been keen to agree common minimum standards for the care of forced migrants in order to curb "asylum shopping" and to reduce the possibility of certain states with more "generous" welfare provisions attracting larger numbers of asylum claims (Refugee Council 2004a). When policing national borders member states can no longer act unilaterally. Restrictive entry policies in one state may have a knock-on effect in pushing people to try and enter another EU state (Caviedes 2004). Faced with these considerations, in May 2004 member states agreed shared procedures for the processing of asylum claims and the reception, care and removal of forced migrants (Black 2004). The details of this policy are laid out in a number of EU Regulations and Directives.

Council Directive 2003/9/EC sets out minimum standards for the reception of asylum-seekers and is concerned with rights to work, training and welfare. Highly conditional subsistence-level benefits and shelter are to be made available to those who do not have the means to support themselves. Under pressure from the UK government, member states have agreed to the inclusion of Article 16, which outlines powers for states to withdraw the right to social support from individuals who are deemed to be abusing the system. Article 11 states that asylum-seekers shall be allowed to work if a decision on their claim has not been reached within a twelve-month period, in cases where the delay is due to institutional failure on the part of the state. Agreement on a common definition of "refugee" and a subsidiary humanitarian protection status has also been reached (Directive COM (2000) 578).

Two other legislative devices are at the heart of developing supranational EU asylum policy. Regulation 343/2003, the so-called Dublin II regulation (in force since September 2003), is a system of rules concerned with establishing responsibility for individual asylum-seekers. Effectively the member state who first allowed a particular forced migrant to enter its borders, legally or illegally, has a duty to examine the claim for asylum and support the migrant during that process. Directive COM (2000) 578, finally, is concerned with establishing EU-wide standards and procedures for the processing of asylum claims, and the granting and withdrawal of refugee status. This Directive expands the definition of "unfounded cases" to include those forced migrants who arrive with insufficient or false documentation, as well as those arriving from an agreed list of "safe countries of origin". Migrants whose claims are deemed to be "unfounded" will be subject to removal to a "safe third country" (outside the EU), prior to any appeal (ECRE 2004a; Refugee Council 2004a). An attempt to deflect responsibility for the care of forced migrants sideways on to other nation states, preferably "third country" states, is clearly part of future "Europeanized" asylum policy.

Emergent EU asylum policy has been heavily criticized. The United Nations Commissioner for Refugees has condemned member states for pandering to populist pressures in bringing the worst elements of national policy into EU law (see also Kjaerum 2002). Furthermore, the new grounds for excluding certain individuals from refugee status may be in breach of the UN Refugee Convention. Others argue that seeking asylum in Europe has effectively been criminalized and that destitution remains a real possibility for forced migrants resident in EU states (ECRE 2004a, 2004b).

Cooperation at the supranational EU level has given member states a policy arena in which to legitimize and extend exclusive elements of national policy and keep forced migrants out (Geddes 2001). Additionally, those seeking asylum are increasingly constructed as unwanted, "undeserving" economic migrants and a potential drain on national resources. In some other areas of migration policy, it may be appropriate to describe EU member states as semi-sovereign actors, but in matters related to the entry, residence and support of forced migrants, they are keen to keep a tight grip on policy, albeit within a changed institutional framework (Del'Olio 2004; Dwyer 2004b; Geddes 2003; Sales 2002). The emergence of a common policy at the EU level does not signal a loss of state control,

> rather it can be argued that states are seeking to reassert control over forms of migration that their policies define as unwanted. This allows them to resolve problems of international regulatory failure in European forums that strengthen the role of executive actors. (Geddes 2001: 29)

Contemporary forced migration is a global phenomenon (Castles 2003, 2004), but policy changes related to forced migrants' social welfare are being played out against the backdrop of national welfare states, many of which are currently undergoing restructuring and retrenchment (Geddes 2003; Düvell and Jordan 2002). As part of that process many European states have looked to separate out and reduce the social rights of forced migrants.

Downwards: the dispersal of forced migrants' welfare rights within EU member states

As the numbers of forced migrants entering the EU have risen, restrictive immigration and asylum legislation has been introduced in individual member states (Sales 2002). Stringent efforts to keep forced migrants out have been combined with attempts to reduce the welfare entitlements of those who enter to seek asylum (Bloch and Schuster 2002). Such legislative changes have consolidated the link between immigration/residency status and welfare entitlement (Cohen 2002a).

In the United Kingdom the welfare rights of forced migrants have been systematically reduced by five pieces of legislation in the past eleven years. All persons seeking asylum are now subject to a distinct system of welfare provision under the management of the National Asylum Support System (NASS), which is responsible for the coordination and funding of accommodation and financial support. NASS meets its housing responsibilities by subcontracting to a mixture of accommodation providers, including local authorities and private landlords (Sales 2002). Following an induction period spent in emergency accommodation, NASS permits individuals to choose one of two support options: accommodation and subsistence or subsistence only. However, the right to NASS support is highly conditional. Individuals must be destitute, accommodation is offered on a "no choice" basis and clients have to agree to be dispersed to an allocated cluster area. If any of the above, or certain other specified, conditions are broken the right to housing and financial support can be withdrawn (Zetter and Pearl 2000). Section 55 of the Nationality, Immigration and Asylum Act 2002 states that migrants must apply for asylum status "as soon as is reasonably practicable" (i.e. within three days of entering the UK) or face disqualification from public support. This policy has pushed thousands of forced migrants into extreme poverty or destitution, has been roundly condemned, and is subject to challenge in the courts (GLA 2004; IAP 2004; Refugee Council 2004b). Although Section 55 is currently under review, the limited welfare rights of forced migrants in the UK have recently been further reduced in the Asylum and Immigration (Treatment of Claimants etc.) Act 2004 (Dwyer and Brown 2005).

Work reviewing the welfare of forced migrants across EU member states illustrates that the UK's exclusionary approach is far from unique. Schuster's (2000) review of the welfare provided to asylum-seekers in seven states concluded that, while differences which reflect specific national approaches remain, states look to provide meagre subsistence-level benefits/support and cheap accommodation, often in hostels cut off from the main populace (see also Schuster's paper in the present collection). A consideration of forced migration and welfare policy in specific EU member states highlights a number of points salient to this discussion of governance.

First, the notion of the "dispersed state" (Clarke 2004; Clarke and Newman 1997), in which

"Dispersal" has fragmented service provision, multiplying the number of agents and agencies involved, increasing the number of (micro) decision-making settings and generating new problems of coordination, regulation and scrutiny (Clarke 2004: 37)

is particularly pertinent when considering the welfare of forced migrants. The regional and local networks of public, private voluntary/charitable providers that are now charged with meeting the basic needs of forced migrants in many states across the EU are a classic example of the complex patterns of devolved governance that characterize the dispersed state. (For relevant discussions and details of Germany, Italy, the UK and Scandinavian countries, see Del'Olio 2004; Geddes 2003; Liedtke 2002; Morris 2001. For Greece, Sitaropoulos 2002. For Spain, Jubany-Baucells 2002.) Furthermore, dispersal of forced migrants, in the literal sense, is now a non-negotiable principle underpinning welfare provision in a number of EU states (Robinson *et al.* 2003; Morris 2001).

Second, it remains the case that, regardless of the myriad potential providers, individual member states (in exercising their power to define the specific sociolegal status of each forced migrant) retain the ultimate power of determining the welfare provisions that may, or may not, accrue to specific categories of forced migrant. This is a good example of individual member states retaining effective power within changed institutional circumstances. As previously noted, member states now have to recognize supranational (EU) definitions of "refugee", etc., as outlined in Directive COM (2000) 578. Nonetheless, the process of examining forced migrants' asylum claims and the allocation of a particular sociolegal category (and any derived rights to welfare) remain with the individual member states. Individuals whose asylum claim is rejected by a member state, and who are routinely denied the right to paid work, often find they either have to somehow fend for themselves and/or rely on charity. Such stark choices have previously been a feature of less developed Southern European welfare states but, as member states look to restrict and reduce the rights of certain categories of forced migrants, the latter's need to rely on illegal work and/or charity is becoming more commonplace (Dwyer and Brown 2005; Bloch and Schuster 2002).

Third, involving a range of public and private, voluntary actors in the local and regional delivery of welfare can be characterized, somewhat optimistically, as a "joined-up" network of governance. A more sceptical analysis of the situation *vis-à-vis* the dispersal of forced migrants' welfare, however, is likely to emphasize the symbiosis at the heart of such "partnerships". For example, Cohen (2002a, 2002b) notes the recognition on the part of UK local authorities (LAs) that cooperation with NASS dispersal policies would provide potential tenants for empty properties. He also believes certain voluntary, nongovernmental organizations (NGOs) have compromised their independence

67

and critical capacity by entering into Home Office-funded contracts to supply regional support services. However, while LAs and NGOs may now need NASS, the state's power relative to its *private* partners may be somewhat weaker. Public/private partnerships will only be of interest to the private sector for as long as they remain profitable (Rummery 2002).

An interest in meeting the basic human needs of forced migrants does not appear to be a central focus of developing EU asylum policy (Kjaerum 2002; Boswell 2000). Indeed, greater emphasis has been placed on ensuring that a tough line on asylum and forced migration is extended to the ten accession countries (Lavenex 2003). Overall, such supranational harmonization as has occurred is, at best, to be characterized as part of a general levelling-down of standards (Düvell and Jordan 2002). Within individual member states, national governments have deliberately sought to separate out and simultaneously reduce and/or remove the welfare entitlements of forced migrants. As part of this process the state has increasingly involved a complex array of agencies in the regional and localized delivery of welfare.

The Dispersed State in Action: Forced Migrants and Welfare in Leeds

Leeds (population 700,000), is the biggest city in the Yorkshire and Humberside region of England, an area which has the highest regional population of NASS-accommodated asylum-seekers (20 per cent of the UK total). The largest population within the region is resident in Leeds (Home Office 2004a). Statistics show 2,574 asylum-seekers living in Leeds on 1 September 2004. This figure does not include "failed asylum-seekers", those opting for "subsistence only" support, or those denied provision under Section 55. It does include unaccompanied minors cared for by the social services (LRAS 2004).

The Yorkshire and Humberside Consortium for Asylum-seekers and Refugees (established in 2000) consists of ten local authorities. As a member of the consortium, Leeds City Council is contracted to NASS to provide 336 properties until October 2005. In June 2003 the council also negotiated a separate contract to provide 65 spaces in the "Hillside" induction centre for newly dispersed asylum-seekers (LCC 2004). Three other agencies, the Angel Group, Clearsprings (both private companies) and Safehaven Yorkshire (a not-for-profit organization), are also contracted to supply accommodation for dispersed asylum-seekers. These landlords provide the bulk of asylum-seekers' accommodation in Leeds, some of which they procure through subletting arrangements with other local private landlords (Wilson 2001).

Some informal welfare services are also provided by various charitable and voluntary agencies across the city. A key aim of the Leeds research was to explore the roles of formal and informal welfare agencies and actors in meeting the basic needs of forced migrants.

The Leeds study: method and sampling

In total, 34 respondents took part in the study. Semi-structured qualitative interviews were conducted with 23 forced migrants and 11 key respondents involved in the delivery of welfare services. A purposive non-random sampling technique was used and 5 refugees, 7 asylum-seekers, 6 people with subsidiary humanitarian protection status and 5 failed asylum-seekers/"overstayers" were interviewed. Some 14 of the forced migrants were male and 10 were female. Ages ranged between 21 and 57 years. Migrants identified 9 countries of origin: Afghanistan, Democratic Republic of Congo, Iran, Iraq, Iraqi Kurdistan, Kosovo, Pakistan, Somalia and Zimbabwe.

Interviews were conducted in Leeds between 30 January 2004 and 21 June 2004 and lasted on average 60 minutes. Two ethical principles underpinned the fieldwork: informed consent and confidentiality. Forced migrants who participated received a £20 supermarket voucher each. All migrants were offered the use of a suitable interpreter but the majority (21) chose to be interviewed in English. Interviews were recorded on audiotape and transcribed verbatim. Subsequent transcripts were anonymized, assigned a code number (FM1, KR2, etc.) and analysed using grid analysis and thematic coding techniques (Ritchie *et al.* 2003). A Nudist 6 computer software package was used to assist this process.

Sociolegal status and the hollowing out of forced migrants' welfare rights

Within the generic population of forced migrants dispersed across the UK four subcategories, each with widely differing rights, can be identified (CPAG 2002; Morris 2002; Sales 2002). *Refugees* have the same welfare rights as full citizens. They can work and enjoy rights to family reunion. *Asylum-seekers* are migrants who are making a claim for refugee status. Welfare rights for this group vary considerably, depending on their date of entry. Individuals lodging "in-country claims" more than 72 hours after entry effectively have no right to public support under "Section 55" rules. Since July 2002, asylum-seekers have not been allowed to work and they have no rights to family reunion. *Humanitarian protection/discretionary leave status* (previously known as exceptional leave to remain, i.e. ELR), is granted for periods of up to three years to certain migrants whom the government recognizes would be in danger if they were returned to their country of origin. They enjoy the same welfare rights as citizens and may work, but they lack rights to family reunion. *Failed asylum-seekers/overstayers* are asylum-seekers whose claims have been turned down and who thus have no right to remain and no recourse to social welfare or (legal) paid work.

The elaborate local networks of governance regulating the welfare of these four groups of forced migrants in Leeds are mapped out in figures 1 and 2. These diagrams summarize the various rights and options available to individuals, in respect of meeting their basic housing and financial needs (dependent on their particular sociolegal status), at any given time. Such complex arrangements are now often an established part of policy across Europe (Robinson *et al.* 2003). The negative impacts of these diverse arrangements on the day-to-day well-being of forced migrants are evidenced by the findings of the Leeds study.

The general inadequacy of the current social security and housing provisions available to many forced migrants and their routine experience of poverty

Figure 1

Forced migrants in Leeds meeting financial/day to day needs, rights and options

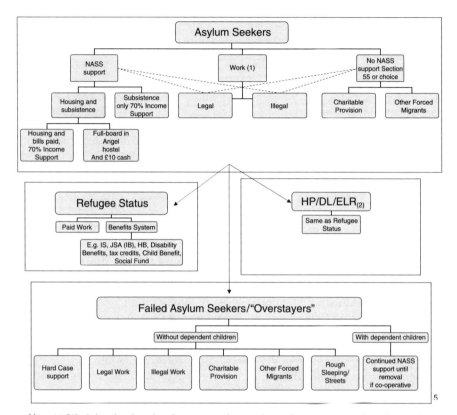

Notes: (1) Work is a legal option for some asylum seekers who were granted work permits pre 2002. The same option appears to be available to failed asylum seekers/overstayers who had previously acquired work permits but have not been removed from the UK. Our sample included such migrants. (2) HP = humanitarian protection status, DL = discretionary leave to remain, ELR = exceptional leave to remain.

and social exclusion has been discussed elsewhere (Dwyer and Brown 2005). However, it is important to note that the welfare rights of certain forced migrants may well have (to borrow Jessop's terminology) been "hollowed out" to extinction. The state's allocation of a specific sociolegal category is in itself an instrument of governance defining an individual forced migrant's welfare rights. Obviously, it is failed asylum-seekers/overstayers and those denied welfare under Section 55 rules who are the most disadvantaged.

Destitution is a real if largely hidden (from public view) problem for the latter. A recent Leeds City Council report notes that only 19 out of 120 asylum-seekers whose claims were rejected in 2003 have been removed from

Figure 2

Forced migrants in Leeds meeting housing needs, rights and options

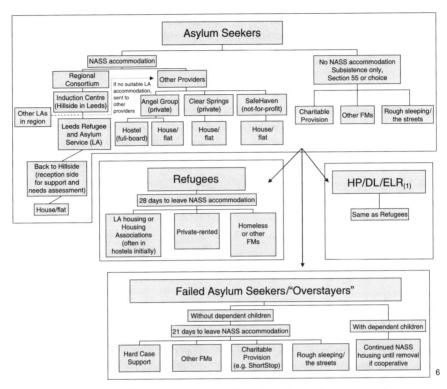

Notes: (1) HP = humanitarian protection status, DL = discretionary leave to remain, ELR = exceptional leave to remain.

the UK (LCC 2004). The whereabouts and means of support of the remainder are unknown. An accurate estimate of the number of destitute forced migrants in the UK is unattainable, owing to the clandestine nature of the problem. However, Brangwyn (2004) notes that the London boroughs supported 34,818 destitute asylum-seekers in April 2004. One respondent (FM1), who is involved with a Leeds-based Refugee Community Organization (RCO), stated that their organization had a list of 40 destitute people. A Section 55 respondent, devoid of access to social welfare provision, was entirely reliant on charity for his day-to-day survival.

> *"Look at me you're looking at a pauper ... let me use the word we're scrounging, just scrounging, there is no structure of survival. We are merely existing and I don't know why in the first world people are allowed to go like that ... We have been having food from this couple they support us, some other times well-wishers just throw you a food parcel ... Once or twice I've got a food parcel from St George's*

Crypt . . . Things need to change. It's inhuman for this kind of treatment especially for close to one year." (FM18, Section 55 asylum-seeker)

Two other respondents who were destitute were almost nostalgic about their previous "asylum-seeker" status, which had afforded them accommodation and limited financial support under NASS rules. Such sentiments reflect their current plight: a situation in which they are devoid of any rights to welfare, rather than the generosity of NASS provision.

FM6: *"At first it was good since we were living in a supported [NASS] house and everything was well. We were living in a nice way and getting our money from the post office. But when it came to the end of the tribunal, we were told to move out of the house. That's when the problems started."* (Failed asylum-seeker/overstayer [FM5 nodding in agreement])

FM5: *"That's why we are now facing problems. Since we are not allowed to work, this leaves us destitute. It's not easy being destitute because there's nothing you can do, you've got nothing to eat, you have no more support, nowhere to stay, no work. Destitution, that's why we have problems."* (Failed asylum-seeker/overstayer)

Another graphic account of the impact of a specific sociolegal status came from a key informant.

"With Section 55 we're seeing some people who are not eligible for support when they apply. A couple of weeks ago I had an eight-month pregnant woman who was destitute. She couldn't get social services to take her on as a pregnant woman, in relation to the unborn child, and NASS were saying that she'd not applied for support in enough time. So obviously that had massive implications for her. At the other end there are destitute people who have come to the end of the process who go home to find their bags on the doorstep. There's been no move to deport them and they have got nowhere to go." (KR1, a nurse)

Forced migrants granted refugee status or leave to remain under humanitarian protection rules are, relatively speaking, better off than asylum-seekers and failed asylum-seekers/overstayers in terms of their welfare rights. However, there are still problems for these groups. Two key informants described how the development of a separate NASS welfare system for asylum-seekers left many successful asylum applicants unprepared for the harsh realities of life at the sharp end of the mainstream British social security system.

"I don't think there are as many issues for an asylum-seeker as for a refugee. For a refugee you get a decision and the period of notice that you're given to end one support system and start another support system is a big issue . . . It [the NASS system] makes people dependent. It institutionalizes people . . . Once they get a positive decision it is very difficult. They have no idea of the cost of living in terms of renting accommodation and paying bills." (KR5, manager of local authority asylum team)

The inadequacy of mainstream benefits was noted by five respondents who had humanitarian protection or refugee status. One individual was over £1,000 in arrears on their electricity bill and was struggling to cope. Another reflected that she was previously "better-off" as an asylum-seeker, rather than under her current refugee status.

> *"When I got £38 every week [as an asylum-seeker], I bought some food and every two or three weeks I saved some money and bought clothes. But now—£54 for one week it's not enough really . . . I need to account for gas, for electricity, for some food, for water—it's not enough."* (FM14, refugee)

A positive change of sociolegal status may bring access to the same social security rights as other citizens, but these are essentially rights to limited and increasingly conditional social assistance benefits (Dwyer 2004a, 2004b).

A "positive" transition across sociolegal statuses from asylum-seeker to humanitarian protection status or refugee also raises other, housing-related, issues. Several key respondents stated that the current transition period of 28 days, allowed for successful asylum applicants to move out of NASS accommodation, was insufficient. Delays and a lack of coordination between agencies often led to a much shorter period of notice to leave NASS support. Finding new accommodation in such a short period is often impossible (see also Craig *et al.* 2004; Carter and El-Hassan 2003). Four of our eleven respondents with refugee or humanitarian leave status lived in various hostels or slept on friends' floors before finding a new home. In 2003 Leeds Council received a total of 337 applications from people who recorded their cause of homelessness as being a refugee. In the same year 276 applications for rehousing were received from refugees (LCC 2004). Puckett (2003) also reports that SafeHaven refused to evict 300 tenants in Yorkshire because of fears that they would become homeless on leaving NASS accommodation.

Furthermore, the Leeds research suggests that hidden homelessness is widespread among migrants who have no right to apply to be housed. All of the failed asylum-seeker/overstayers and the Section 55 respondents were effectively homeless. Although the government now recognizes that more effective and personalized support is required in the transition period for those who achieve refugee status (Home Office 2004b), homelessness among forced migrants has become a national issue (Shelter 2004). Additionally, many failed asylum-seekers staying in the UK remain reliant on other forced migrants for shelter (see below). This factor, coupled with the high demand for social rented property in Leeds, ensures that homelessness among forced migrants will remain an issue for the immediate future.

Housing asylum-seekers: regulation, scrutiny and boundary disputes

Details about the contracts that NASS has signed with various agencies to provide accommodation for asylum-seekers are hard to access, since agreements are covered by the Official Secrets Act. However, NASS's inexperience in managing housing, and its willingness to devolve power to individual providers, has led to variable and, on occasions, substandard provision.

"NASS is certainly not very experienced yet . . . so the kind of housing management issues that a social housing provider or social landlord and local authority would be familiar with, overcrowding, transfers, those sorts of issues it's just not experienced in dealing with and therefore hasn't worked out its policies. It relies very much on providers to do the sensible thing . . . if they don't know what the sensible thing is there is no knowledge and experience base back at NASS to give them proper guidance." (KR10, NASS respondent)

Several other key respondents argued that, particularly in the early days of dispersal, the lack of central guidance from NASS allowed private companies to provide an inadequate or inappropriate service.

"Local authority housing tends to be reasonably good, ex-council houses in not particularly desirable areas that they will do up . . . they'll have all the basics and a fairly good standard. When the whole dispersal thing started off private housing providers were a different kettle of fish and they would, and still do [sub]contract to a another landlord. Who will contract to another landlord and you have a whole series of landlords going down to a person who might have one or two houses and there was no monitoring down there and some of the conditions were pretty much appalling . . . Things have improved over time . . . NASS have started to check on things." (KR2, national charity Leeds manager)

Even if standards have improved—though our study and others (Craig *et al.* 2004; Quilgars *et al.* 2003; Robinson *et al.* 2003) suggest that problems may persist—other housing issues remain. Respondents noted that there was not enough accommodation for families, that the NASS housing system was inflexible and, at times, slow in responding to requests for a change of address, even in cases where clients were suffering racial harassment. NASS's relative inexperience in housing management, coupled with the diversity of landlords involved in supplying accommodation (see figure 2), appear initially to have hindered the state's ability to regulate and inspect local providers and ensure the required quality of service.

NASS has been severely criticized for mismanagement and wasting public money (Noble *et al.* 2003). The initial accommodation contracts that NASS negotiated were set up on the basis that contractors would be paid for beds supplied, rather than occupied. The recent fall in asylum applications means that, nationally, NASS has been paying for empty accommodation. Keen to avoid future criticism, and with a stated aim of reducing costs, NASS began renegotiating new contracts early in 2005. Against this backdrop, the various agencies involved in supplying accommodation in Leeds are keen to protect and develop their own particular roles. Leeds City Council has made strong representations for LAs in the Regional Consortium to be given an enhanced provisory role and certain controls over the private sector (LCC 2004). Emergent "boundary disputes" (Clarke 2004) between the various agencies now involved in providing and managing asylum-seekers' accommodation seem all too likely.

Picking up the pieces: a role for NGOs, RCOs and other forced migrants

In the absence of state provision in certain Southern European welfare states, non-governmental organizations (NGOs) have long been key welfare providers for forced migrants. In many other European welfare states NGOs that were previously concerned with campaigning in support of migrants are having to play an increasing role in meeting basic needs. Increasingly these organizations are being drawn into complex and often competitive arrangements to support forced migrants (Düvell and Jordan 2002). In Leeds a range of informal welfare services is provided by an assortment of charitable and voluntary agencies across the city. In addition there are a growing number of Refugee Community Organizations (RCOs) which offer varying levels of advice, companionship and support. As the state erodes forced migrants' rights to public welfare, the voluntary/informal sector is often left to pick up the pieces.

RCOs differ from mainstream NGOs, in that they often lack paid staff and are not registered charities. The continued existence of many remains precarious. In spite of these facts, the UK government has stated that it wants to expand the welfare role of RCOs in the future provision of support for forced migrants (Zetter and Pearl 2000). Three of the forced migrants we interviewed (two asylum-seekers, one with ELR) ran Leeds-based RCOs. In spite of highly constrained personal circumstances, all were devoting substantial amounts of time to supporting other forced migrants. Their organizations provide a variety of cultural, social and sporting events for fellow nationals and also offer informal legal advice and links to more formal welfare providers and educational institutions. None of these organizations is more than a year old. Each individual is essential for the continuation of their particular RCO, which without their efforts, would cease to exist. The little funding that is available to RCOs has to be obtained via a system of local competitive tendering.

FM23: *"We don't have money . . . I'm living in NASS accommodation that is my office, I have that very small room. They* [migrants] *call me and we meet there."*

Interviewer: *"And do you get money?"*

FM22: *"I've asked* [The Community Chest fund] *for two lots of funding. The first for a cultural event and they gave us the money . . . On the second one I asked for £5,000 and they gave us £1,000 and you can't really do the work you want to do . . ."*

A key respondent with responsibility for community development in Leeds was dismayed at the assumption that marginalized communities were somehow expected to step in and offer support in instances where formal welfare rights had been removed.

"I think it's appalling to rely on RCOs. I think the whole idea of this system was that somehow there would not need to be a lot of provision because everybody's going to be looked after by RCOs informally . . . [Let] the community take care of

everybody on the basis that nobody will be just lying on the street, or freezing from cold. We are reverting back to a draconian system where people don't have any rights, especially asylum-seekers." (KR3, respondent from national refugee charity)

Leaving aside debates about the desirability of migrant communities taking on a greater role, the contingent and informal nature of many RCOs (Kelly 2003) and their limited funding indicate that many are ill-equipped to take on a greater role in meeting basic welfare needs (Zetter and Pearl 2004, 2000).

Self-help or no help?

The burden of providing emergency accommodation and basic day-to-day necessities for those who have limited, or no, recourse to social welfare is increasingly falling on other forced migrants who are themselves impoverished. Some 16 of the 23 migrants in our study spoke of reliance on other forced migrants for basic necessities (i.e. food, clothes, accommodation), at some time. All the "overstayers" in our study are reliant on other forced migrants for accommodation. Those who work illegally often rent a room from a "friend" (i.e. a fellow national) on a short-term basis. Usually this accommodation is offered for a reasonable charge. These arrangements are insecure, but clandestine failed asylum-seekers/overstayers have very few other options. FM15 had lodged with eight or nine different people at the time of interview.

> *"On the streets it's easy to talk to anyone, 'hi hi please if you know somebody with a room this is my telephone number, contact me please'. It depends, sometimes I'll live in one house two or three months. If we like each other I stay in the house, but if I get a problem with them I have to change."* (FM15, failed asylum-seeker/ overstayer)

Beyond emergency overnight accommodation, homeless forced migrants who lack the ability to pay are totally reliant on the charity of other forced migrants for shelter. Much is offered and little expected in return, but over-crowding is commonplace.

> *"I know of some houses where 10 people live together because one of them gets 4 years [ELR] and the council give him a house and another 9 people are refused. They don't have any other place to go they stay with a friend."* (FM11, ELR)

> *"What private providers have found . . . is a house that should accommodate 2 people has actually got 20 people staying in it because they've not let their friends sleep on the streets they've invited them into their own NASS accommodation, so there's a lot of overcrowding going on."* (KR5, manager of local authority asylum team)

The welfare rights of forced migrants are subject to the dual processes of separation and erosion. The setting up of localized networks of governance has done little to enhance the public welfare that forced migrants can call upon. The Leeds study reinforces Rummery's (2002) assertion that there is little evidence to suggest that such partnerships are enhancing the welfare of end users. The new networks of the dispersed state do not intrinsically provide solutions to the problem of who cares for forced migrants in a host state (Merrien 1998). Arguably they make their day-to-day living conditions worse.

Conclusions

This discussion of governance, welfare and forced migration has shown how nation states have used supranational and localized networks of governance to deter the entry of unwanted forced migrants. Simultaneously, national governments have exercised their authority in a variety of settings to reduce or eradicate the welfare rights of forced migrants. In some respects this paper can be seen as a descriptive account of the reconfiguration and exercise of state power in changed institutional circumstances (Clarke and Glendinning 2002; Jessop 1999). However, a focus on forced migration and welfare offers insights into why such changes have occurred. Contemporary forced migration is a global phenomenon, but in seeking asylum forced migrants are essentially looking to nation states for protection and support. As many European welfare states undergo the shift towards "active/Third Way" welfare regimes, a qualitative shift has occurred in the key principles underpinning access to national collective welfare rights. Notions of need and entitlement have become secondary to issues of claim and contribution. The concept of a social right is increasingly giving way to the idea of "conditional entitlement" (Dwyer 2004a). In a world where nation states are looking to do less for their own citizens we should not perhaps be too surprised if they choose to ignore the needs of those that are deemed to be outside the national jurisdiction. The "deserving" dissident fleeing the political persecution of the Cold War era is long gone. Instead, states today, ably assisted by the populist press (Statham 2003), have constructed forced migrants as "undeserving" economic immigrants who have made no prior contribution to their host state and should, therefore, expect little in return.

Acknowledgements

This research was supported by the ESRC under grant number 000-22-0377.

I would like to thank all the respondents who took part in the fieldwork that informs this paper. Thanks are also due to David Brown, the researcher on the study.

Note

1. In this paper the term *forced migrant* is used as general label to include the four groups of international migrants under discussion (i.e. refugees, asylum-seekers, those with humanitarian leave to remain, and "overstayers"). It is recognized that others, e.g. those displaced by development projects and people trafficked illegally for exploitative purposes, are also forced migrants (cf. Castles 2003).

References

Black, I. (2004), Last minute EU deal reached on asylum, *The Guardian*, 30 April 2004: 8.

Bloch, A. and Schuster, L. (2002), Asylum and welfare: contemporary debates, *Critical Social Policy*, 22, 3: 393–413.

Boswell, C. (2000), European values and the asylum crisis, *International Affairs*, 76, 3: 537–57.

Brangwyn, M. (2004), *Refugees and Asylum-seekers Item no 13: Report to the Leaders' Committee*, London: Association of London Government.

Carter, M. and El-Hassan, A. A. (2003), *Between NASS and a Hard Place*, London: The Housing Associations' Charitable Trust.

Castles, S. (2003), Towards a sociology of forced migration and social transformation, *Sociology*, 37, 1: 13–34.

Castles, S. (2004), Why migration policies fail, *Ethnic and Racial Studies*, 272: 205–27.

Caviedes, A. (2004), The open method of co-ordination in immigration policy: a tool for prying open fortress Europe? *Journal of European Public Policy*, 11, 2: 289–310.

Clarke, J. (2004), Dissolving the public realm? The logics and limits of neo-liberalism, *Journal of Social Policy*, 33, 1: 27–48.

Clarke, J. and Glendinning, C. (2002), Partnerships and the remaking of welfare governance. In C. Glendinning, M. Powell and K. Rummery (eds), *Partnerships, New Labour, and the Governance of Welfare*, Bristol: Policy Press, pp. 3–51.

Clarke, J. and Newman, J. (1997), *The Managerial State: Power, Politics and Ideology in the Remaking of Social Welfare*, London: Sage.

Cohen, S. (2002a), Dining with the devil: the 1999 Immigration and Asylum Act and the voluntary sector. In S. Cohen, B. Humphries and E. Mynott (eds), *From Immigration Controls to Welfare Controls*, London: Routledge, pp. 141–56.

Cohen, S. (2002b), The local state of immigration controls, *Critical Social Policy*, 22, 3: 518–43.

CPAG (2002), *Migration and Social Security Handbook*, London: Child Poverty Action Group.

Craig, G., Dawson, A., Hutton, S., Roberts, N. and Wilkinson, M. (2004), *Local Impacts of International Migration: The Information Base*, Social policy working paper, Hull: University of Hull.

Del'Olio, F. (2004), Immigration and immigrant policy in Italy and the UK: is housing policy a barrier to a common approach towards immigration in the EU?, *Journal of Ethnic and Migration Studies*, 30, 1: 107–28.

Düvell, F. and Jordan, B. (2002), Immigration, asylum and welfare: the European context, *Critical Social Policy*, 22, 3: 498–517.

Dwyer, P. (2004a), Creeping conditionality in the UK: from welfare rights to conditional entitlements, *Canadian Journal of Sociology*, 29, 2: 265–87.

Dwyer P. (2004b), *Understanding Social Citizenship: Themes and Perspectives for Policy and Practice*, Bristol: Policy Press.

Dwyer, P. and Brown, D. (2005), Meeting basic needs? The survival strategies of forced migrants, *Social Policy and Society*, 4, 4: 1–12.

ECRE (2004a), *Broken Promises—Forgotten Principles*, London: European Council on Refugees and Exiles.

ECRE (2004b), *Refugee and Human Rights Organizations across Europe Express Their Deep Concern at the Expected Agreement on Asylum Measures in Breach of International Law*, Press Release, 28 April, London: European Council on Refugees and Exiles.

Geddes, A. (2001), International migration and state sovereignty in an integrating Europe, *International Migration*, 39, 6: 21–42.

Geddes, A. (2003), Migration and the welfare state in Europe. In S. Spencer (ed.), *The Politics of Migration: Managing Opportunity, Conflict and Change*, London: Blackwell, pp. 150–62.

GLA (2004), *Destitution by Design: Withdrawal of Support from In-country Asylum Applicants: An Impact Assessment for London*, London: GLA.

Home Office (2004a), *Asylum Statistics 1st Quarter 2004*, London: Home Office.

Home Office (2004b), *Strength in Diversity: Towards a Community Cohesion and Race Equality Strategy*, London: Home Office Communications Directorate.

IAP (2004), *The Impact of Section 55 on the Inter-agency Partnership and the Asylum-seekers it Supports*, IAP. Available at: http://www.refugeecouncil.org.uk/downloads/rc_reports/iap_s55_feb04.pdf (accessed 10 June 2004).

Jessop, B. (1994), The transition to post-Fordism and the Schumpeterian workfare state. In R. Burrows and B. Loader (eds), *Towards a Post-Fordist Welfare State*, London: Routledge.

Jessop, B. (1999), The changing governance of welfare: recent trends in its primary functions, scale and modes of coordination, *Social Policy & Administration*, 33, 4: 348–59.

Jubany-Baucells, O. (2002), The state of welfare for asylum-seekers and refugees in Spain, *Critical Social Policy*, 22, 3: 415–35.

Kelly, L. (2003), Bosnian refugees in Britain: questioning community, *Sociology*, 37, 1: 35–50.

Kjaerum, M. (2002), Refugee protection between state interests and human rights: where is Europe heading, *Human Rights Quarterly*, 24: 513–36.

Lavenex, S. (2003), EU enlargement and the challenge of policy transfer: the case of refugee policy, *Journal of Ethnic and Migration Studies*, 28, 4: 701–21.

LCC (2004), *Report of Scrutiny Board (Neighbourhoods and Housing): Asylum-seekers*, May, Leeds: Leeds City Council.

Liedtke, M. (2002), National welfare and asylum in Germany, *Critical Social Policy*, 22, 1: 479–97.

LRAS (2004), *Statistics Bulletin*, Leeds: Leeds Refugee and Asylum Service.

Merrien, F. X. (1998), Governance and modern welfare states, *International Social Science Journal*, 50, 1: 58–67.

Moraes, C. (2003), The politics of European Union migration policy. In S. Spencer (ed.), *The Politics of Migration: Managing Opportunity, Conflict and Change*, London: Blackwell, pp. 116–31.

Morris, L. (2001), Stratified rights and the management of migration: national distinctiveness in Europe, *European Societies*, 3, 4: 387–411.

Morris, L. (2002), Britain's asylum and immigration regime: the shifting contours of rights, *Journal of Ethnic and Migration Studies*, 28, 3: 409–25.

Noble, G., Barnish, A., Finch, E. and Griffith, D. (2003), *Report of the Independent Review into the Operation of the National Asylum Support Service*, London: Home Office.

Puckett, K. (2003), The invisible thousands, *Housing Today* (7 November). Available at: http://www.housing-today.co.uk.asp?storycode=1031912&featureCode=&s (accessed on 15 April 2004).

Quilgars, D., Burrows, R. and Wright, K. (2003), *Refugee Housing and Neighbourhood Issues: a Scoping Review*, York: Centre for Housing Policy, University of York.

Refugee Council (2004a), *Refugee Council Briefing on the Common European Asylum System*, London: Refugee Council.

Refugee Council (2004b), *Hungry and Homeless: The Impact of the Withdrawal of State Support on Asylum-seekers, Refugee Communities and the Voluntary Sector*, London: Refugee Council.

Ritchie, J., Spencer, L. and O'Connor, W. (2003), Carrying out qualitative analysis. In J. Ritchie and L. Spencer (eds), *Qualitative Research Practice*, London: Sage, pp. 219–62.

Robinson, V., Andersson, R. and Musterd, S. (2003), *Spreading the Burden? A Review of Policies to Disperse Asylum-seekers and Refugees*, Bristol: Policy Press.

Rummery, K. (2002), Towards a theory of welfare partnerships. In C. Glendinning, M. Powell and K. Rummery (eds), *Partnerships, New Labour and the Governance of Welfare*, Bristol: Policy Press, pp. 229–47.

Sales, R. (2002), The deserving and the undeserving? Refugees, asylum-seekers and welfare in Britain, *Critical Social Policy*, 22, 3: 456–78.

Schuster, L. (2000), A comparative analysis of the asylum policy of seven European governments, *Journal of Refugee Studies*, 13, 1: 118–31.

Shelter (2004), *The black and ethnic minority housing crisis*, London: Shelter.

Sitaropoulos, N. (2002), Refugee welfare in Greece: towards a remodelling of the responsibility-shifting paradigm? *Critical Social Policy*, 22, 3: 436–55.

Statham, P. (2003), Understanding anti-asylum rhetoric: restrictive politics or racist publics? In S. Spencer (ed.), *The Politics of Migration: Managing Opportunity, Conflict and Change*, London: Blackwell, pp. 163–77.

Veenkamp, T., Bentley, T. and Buonfino, A. (2003), *People Flow: Managing Migration in a New European Commonwealth*, London: Demos.

Wilson, R. (2001), *Dispersed: A Study of Services for Asylum-seekers in West Yorkshire December 1999–March 2001*, York: Joseph Rowntree Foundation.

Zetter, R. and Pearl, M. (2000), The minority within the minority: refugee community-based organizations in the UK and the impact of restrictionism on asylum-seekers, *Journal of Ethnic and Migration Studies*, 26, 4: 657–97.

Zetter, R. and Pearl, M. (2004), Refugee community organizations, *Inexile*, 34: 11–12.

6

The Experiences of Frontline Staff Working with Children Seeking Asylum

D. Dunkerley, J. Scourfield, T. Maegusuku-Hewett and N. Smalley

Introduction

Bauman (2004) has argued, in characteristically pessimistic tone, that modernity requires the creation of superfluous populations, "human waste". He sees the current panics about asylum-seekers across the West as exemplifying late modern societies' preoccupation with the processing of human waste. The issue of asylum-seekers moved up the UK political agenda in early 2005 as a matter capable of capturing and fuelling electors' prejudices in anticipation of a general election. Indeed, the current social and political context is neatly summarized by Bauman's comment that

> the figure of the asylum seeker, once prompting human compassion and spurring an urge to help, has been sullied and defiled, while the very idea of "asylum", once a matter of civil and civilized pride, has been reclassified as a dreadful concoction of shameful naivety and criminal irresponsibility. (Bauman 2004: 57)

This paper focuses on the process of human waste management in discussing the experiences of frontline staff who work with asylum-seeking children.

Bloch and Schuster (2000) have observed that, although there are differences between different countries' responses to asylum, there is also much commonality, especially with regard to the tendency for asylum-seekers to be seen as recipients of welfare rather than contributors to it. As these same authors note, there is a strong connection between the hostility of political rhetoric on asylum and a rise in racist attacks.

Children come into the picture both when they travel with adult carers and when they seek asylum as unaccompanied minors. Much of the research into refugees within the UK has been undertaken in England and relates to adults. A great deal of the research that does exist on refugee children is often incorporated into material on children from minority ethnic or bilingual backgrounds. However, research specific to refugee children is beginning to emerge that highlights not only the vulnerable position of refugee children (see for example Dennis 2002; Russell 1999; Audit Commission 2000; Barnardo's 2000) but also their resilience (Kidane 2001). It is well established that the demographics and differences in practices between regions have impacted upon the development and quality of service provision for these children. Rutter (2003) has concisely summarized these disparities and highlights gaps in research knowledge. It seems clear, from the evidence available, that there is an increasing gulf between legislation developed to protect children in the UK and the reality of immigration policy and practice. Factors such as dispersal, uncertainty about one's future, living in poverty, detention of families, disrupted education and health care, racism and marginalization all impact detrimentally on children. There has been much criticism of the implications of the most recent UK asylum legislation for child welfare. Section 9 of the Immigration and Asylum (Treatment of Claimants, etc.) Act 2004 gives the Home Office powers to terminate all welfare support, except the accommodation of children in local authority care (under Section 20 of the Children Act 1989), for failed asylum-seeking families who are deemed to be in a position to leave the UK. Cunningham and Tomlinson (2005) argue that the potential for thus separating children from their families clashes with Britain's domestic and international human rights commitments and undermines the government's stated ambition to ensure that "every child matters" (DfES 2003).

Findings presented in this paper derive from a larger study commissioned by Save the Children, concerned with the experiences of asylum-seeking children in Wales (Hewett *et al.* 2005). Wales has four dispersal areas—Cardiff, Newport, Swansea and Wrexham—and it is to these locations that asylum-seekers are sent by the National Asylum Support Service (NASS), pending decisions on the right to remain and refugee status. The numbers of dispersed people are not great, compared with dispersal areas elsewhere in the UK. At the end of September 2004, some 2,280 asylum-seekers were dispersed and supported by NASS in Wales, compared with 41,475 in the whole of the UK (Home Office 2004a).

Robinson concluded (1999) that provision for refugees in Wales could only be understood with reference to cultures of "ignorance", "disbelief" and "denial". We found there had been changes since then. Democratic devolution in Wales has little impact on direct asylum *policy*, since the Home Office is the key player and its responsibilities are not devolved. Nevertheless, the majority of the *services* that asylum-seekers need and receive are the responsibility of the Welsh Assembly Government.

The relatively recent dispersal of asylum-seekers to Wales should have enabled services to learn from some of England's mistakes. Also, the relatively small numbers of asylum-seekers—and the small scale of Wales as a unit of administration—make coordination potentially easier to effect. That said, there was considerable continuity with research findings from England with regard to the negative effects of the dispersal system, untreated mental health problems arising from experience of trauma in countries of origin, difficulties over access to education and health care, dissatisfaction with some accommodation and some children being placed with foster carers "out of county". There is no scope for presenting our detailed findings on the children's experience in this paper. These are explained fully in Hewett *et al.* (2005).

This paper's concern is with the experiences of professionals working with asylum-seeking children. Of course, most of the difficulties that professionals face are primarily the children's difficulties. If social welfare staff experience frustration and ethical dilemmas, these are nothing compared with the pressures on adults and children seeking asylum. However, there are inevitable tensions for welfare professionals in the front line of the asylum system. To take one of the welfare professions as an example, the role of social workers in relation to asylum-seekers has been discussed by Christie (2002, 2003) and Humphries (2004) among others. Christie (2002: 196) draws attention to social workers' potentially "collusive role in the reproduction of national and other boundaries that contribute to the exclusion of particular groups and to the facilitation of others". In the context of the "social" being increasingly characterized by mobility as well as by "societies" within national boundaries (see Urry 2000), he argues for a "post-national social work" (Christie 2003). Humphries is less measured in tone, arguing that social workers are generally subservient to policies that cause further damage to vulnerable people and that their role in relation to immigration typifies this subservience:

> Social work has been drawn into implementing racist policy initiatives, whilst still maintaining its unreflective, self-deceiving, anti-oppressive belief systems. (Humphries 2004: 95)

She cites studies by herself and others that paint a bleak picture of social workers having little relevant knowledge and experience in relation to asylum-seekers; regarding the duty to check immigration status as another irritating bureaucratic procedure rather than an ethical dilemma—and protesting that they had no resources to deal with post-traumatic stress disorder in asylum-seekers. She concludes that "it is no wonder they [social workers] are despised and feared by the people they purport to help" (2004: 104).

While Humphries writes specifically with regard to social work, that particular profession has no monopoly on ethical standards, and much of what she argues may apply equally to other welfare professionals working as frontline staff in this context.

Research Design

We interviewed both children/young people and professionals for the study, but shall only be presenting data from the professionals for this paper. We constructed a snowball sample of professionals, ensuring a spread of research participants across the four dispersal areas mentioned above and across a variety of organizations and roles. We made contact with research participants via the project steering group for the commissioned research. This steering group's membership was drawn from a wide range of voluntary and statutory sector agencies. Research participants came from social services (11), the health service (17), housing providers (8), education (4), the police service (2) and the voluntary sector (12). Additionally, representatives (8) of organizations with an all-Wales brief were involved. This all-Wales category included the Welsh Assembly Government, the Welsh Refugee Council and a consortium of local authorities. In total, 62 professionals participated in the study. Data were gathered via semi-structured interviews (both face-to-face and over the telephone) and focus groups during the period June–September 2004. Data analysis proceeded according to a code-and-retrieve model and coding was facilitated by the NVivo software.

Research Findings

The complexity of policy

The constant legislative changes posed significant challenges to those working in this field. Some of the professionals we spoke to were often called upon to update colleagues and staff in other services. For example, one social worker told us that she often had to provide relevant information when approaching other services for support.

> *"The government doesn't help much. Immigration law changes so much that even people who are in the business of this, they cannot catch up with everything, never mind people who only see asylum-seekers once in a while. We are very proactive and then we tell them what the legislation is and not to educate them, but to help our asylum-seekers."* (Social worker)

The difficulties of dealing with the complexity of policy were noted by several respondents. For example, we were told of differences in the support systems for accompanied as opposed to unaccompanied children, unaccompanied children living semi-independently and those living in foster placements. The further differences between mainstream regulations and NASS regulations gave rise to yet more complications and apparent inconsistencies. As one team leader from a local authority education department observed:

> *"You know you just learn one system and then they change it. For instance, destitute asylum-seekers, asylum-seekers either who didn't claim asylum in the beginning or whose claim has failed and should be going back, errmmm, and we are still unclear as to Welsh Assembly Government policy."* (Education team leader)

The complications of dispersal

Many of our respondents spoke of the profound problems for both unaccompanied children and families seeking asylum in the NASS system. These are, of course, primarily problems for asylum-seekers rather than for professionals. However, the dispersal system, for example, not only creates problems for the families being dispersed but also generates professional dilemmas for those having to work with such families. Children are seen to be particularly vulnerable in a system that can move them from one part of the country to another.

"It is hard because, you know, the children were happy and they had friends here. They had so many friends and they were going to playgroups and things like that and now that is all gone now they have been sent to England. The other side of that, of course, as a professional is that I am sure that other professionals will care for these children but you always worry that somebody will not have the same (it sounds awful to say that you are the only dedicated person) but you worry that people will miss something and that what they miss is going to be essential to the child's well-being . . . These children are in limbo and have been in limbo all along anyway. The move on, of course, isn't you know, it is not just about moving a house, it is about child school places, it is about GPs, it is about dentists, it is about solicitors, it is about all of the other services that they might currently be using, being informed of the change of address. And it is about those children and them thinking, 'Oh my gosh, have I got to move schools again?'" (Senior project manager in local authority housing department)

Doctors frequently see the consequences of dispersal because of both children and adults having to start their wait for appointments afresh when they are moved. A paediatrician made this point. She had a specific family in mind, but saw their situation as typical of a general problem:

"The Bristol family of that child needed an urgent orthopaedic review of a hip problem and had been dispersed to Cardiff and then taken, you know, time to come through the system to me again and then I've had to make all of the referrals all over again for our consultants here. So, you know, they've missed their appointment in Bristol and then they've had to wait again and it's all had to start all over again here. That's you know, just a common example where they've missed out on their medical care because they've been moved." (Paediatrician)

Nurses are on the front line in having to cope with the dispersal system. One of the nurses we interviewed thought that "the asylum system to my knowledge is quite abusive to families and children in particular". Another told us her views that

"People are dispersed inappropriately. We all know the issues for adults concerning dispersal but specifically to children, we are having children being dispersed with special needs. For instance, if you have been living somewhere else for two years you may have already been top of the list on speech therapy. And then when you are dispersed you have to start again at the bottom of the list. We had one woman who was dispersed and she was in the late stages of pregnancy and she was actually due the next week. And they told her if she didn't get on the train, she'd miss the house here. She thought her other children needed to be in a house rather than a bed and breakfast hotel in London. So this woman she had a miscarriage. You can imagine you know getting on a train, you know lots and lots of people about." (Nurse)

Similarly, a worker from a local authority accommodation support service also saw the consequences of dispersal at first hand. He thought there was a marked lack of knowledge of where families were being dispersed to and that some would clearly have been better served by staying in the place they had come from.

> *"The main thing that we find is that sometimes people haven't been given much information prior to coming. And they don't know where Wales is you know, they really haven't got a clue of the geography of the country and don't even know that it is a separate country, they are just put on a coach, sometimes I think with fairly little information so it is a big change for them. There have been some people dispersed and we really felt it wasn't appropriate for them to get dispersed, you know they were getting the support they needed in the area they had come from and it is just the whole thing of getting used to a new place and settling in and kind of acclimatizing."* (Local authority accommodation support worker)

Problems of coordination

Some professionals also felt that they were not able to do the job for which they had been trained and, indeed, are being paid to do. This project manager in a voluntary sector drop-in centre thought his service was going beyond its remit in order to make up for other services' failure to provide what they should:

> *"I think the frustration I find is not being able to get on with the job that I'm actually contracted for in a lot of instances. Because you have to wear so many hats. There are so many other failings in other areas that you feel that you have to fill that void . . . The people you're helping are very grateful for the work you do but it's not actually the work that you should be doing. But they don't see that because they still see all the help that you're giving. But it's not, there should be other providers providing that, not you."* (Manager of voluntary sector drop-in centre)

Administrative errors also add to professionals' frustration. A manager of one local authority refugee team described an example of an administrative error that had affected her planning:

> *"We had been expecting an Afghan-speaking Muslim and when they have arrived they are Punjabi-speaking Sikh. We have had children thinking a male gender is arriving and they are females. We have had dates of birth that have been out by 10 years. All this impacts upon service delivery because the accommodation size, a two-bedroomed property against a three-bedroomed property for example, there are good guidelines, best practice guidelines about the age a child should share and about mixed gender sharing so you know, you book accommodation based on that information and when they arrive they are not the family that we thought they were going to be."* (Deputy manager of a local authority refugee team)

Ethical dilemmas

Many of the respondents were of the view that interpretations of recent legislation, together with new procedures and processes arising from this legislation, actually compromised some of the basic principles of their professional practice. A project worker in a local authority asylum team expressed considerable anxiety about having to evict families who had been refused the right to remain. There was evidence here of a potential challenge to NASS. This worker at least was not passively (and certainly not happily) just implementing immigration policy.

> *"We do have families that have been refused and they become overstayers. We have to report them to NASS. They will say they have to leave and we say we are not going to evict them because they will be on the street and then they will go down the homeless route and then there will be no access to services . . . . NASS do put pressure on us."* (Project worker in local authority asylum team)

This worker told us, however, that her team does take part in evictions. She spoke of building up attachment to families but nonetheless having to evict them. There was clearly an ethical difficulty for her here but, in the last analysis, there seemed little room for sustaining a challenge to NASS.

> *"With singles in particular, they will evict, I know that they do and it is actually in our contract that if need be we can change the locks on our doors although we would never do that but it has been done and can be done legally. That is the thing, it is about you get to know the families and you get attached to them to a certain extent."* (Project worker, as above)

This project worker felt she was coping with the situation but had misgivings about others in her team. She mentioned "therapy" and "counselling" for her staff to help them deal with distressing situations.

> *"It has been a problem for the support workers. I have just arranged some staff training with occupational therapy for them now because they do hear some quite desperate situations and they see that and it is really hard, yes I can supervise them and offer them counselling during supervision as much as possible on a daily basis if need be but it is hard for them to detach. But at the end of the day you have to be able to go in and say this is my job, I will help you. Your values are still the same, your attitudes are the same, you don't judge people but there comes a point where you cannot be everything for that family you know and that is really, really hard."* (Project worker, as above)

Note the project worker's view that, although there are limits to what you can do for people, you can nevertheless maintain liberal values, such as the importance of being non-judgemental. There are certainly echoes here of one of Humphries's (2004) arguments about social workers and the asylum system. She sees individualized notions about anti-oppression as being rather meaningless in the face of policies that are so overtly racist, that social workers themselves help to implement. The same tension could be noted with regard to the above project worker: we might wonder what is the value of being non-judgemental when one is evicting people because of their nationality (and arguably their "race").

One of the paediatricians felt she was torn between the ways that different laws could be interpreted. Indeed, several of the research participants mentioned the tension between the conception of child welfare in the Children Act 1989 and asylum law, as also the tension between human rights law and asylum law.

"I mean according to the Children Act, all of these children are children in need and they should be treated just as a child and also according to the Human Rights Act. You know their rights should be respected but according to Immigration, you know the Immigration and Asylum department, they don't look at that at all. It's all a political decision depending on the country that people come from; they don't appear to look at individuals. I feel a great conflict about that and sometimes you just hope that people will be able to stay and get leave to remain. Sometimes I feel that we have no control on it and it can be a bit demoralizing you know because we don't have control over it. Even if we write letters of support, the Home Office often doesn't take that into account at all. It's all a political decision." (Paediatrician)

This paediatrician was very unhappy about asylum law. She saw herself as making minor challenges in the form of letters of support, yet felt quite powerless to countermand political decisions.

Likewise, one of the social workers interviewed saw her professional standards being compromised. Her role of ensuring the welfare of young children (themselves fairly powerless in the asylum process, since they "don't have any choices") was being undermined by decisions taken elsewhere:

"Because we do say don't we that children don't have any choices, and they are here and that we should look after them. That is our job. But you see the asylum process is so long. How can you turn around to someone who's been here for four years and, you know the child may come here at four and you ask them to leave at eight years. That's the worst thing of all. The fact is that everything that society does to pass this legislation impacts seriously on our work." (Social worker)

The significance of discretion

Although the scope for resisting asylum law from within the system is very limited indeed, it does seem possible to use discretion so as to undermine the system. The proportion of failed asylum-seekers who are removed from the country is (arguably) relatively low at 21 per cent in 2002 and 2003 (Home Office 2004b: 22). Although some of the 79 per cent who remain will be supported informally via their own social networks, there are also probably large numbers of welfare professionals continuing to support families whose asylum applications have failed. Both the following workers in the housing field spoke of deliberately not evicting tenants, when they "ought" to be doing so.

"There have been problems where people, you know for one reason or other, don't fit into policy and then they become difficult, you know it is difficult for us to make sure they are getting what they need. The big example of that is destitution and some families, although at the moment it is supposed to be only single asylum-seekers who have the final refusal but end up with no support, it has actually happened to a few families now because we have got women who are pregnant when they got their termination support when they subsequently went on to have a baby. Their asylum claim is all finished so they have got no means of support whatsoever and it has been

really, really difficult because they have actually been still in our properties when technically we are supposed to evict them." (Local authority housing officer)

"Lots of people, OK they might have failed their asylum claim but they're still quite terrified of returning home so they have stayed in our properties and we have had to refer them to Children's Services for money to keep them going. We have got a system with the Welsh Refugee Council providing food parcels as well and we have tried to make sure that the children are OK. We have also got a family where a woman with an 18-year-old daughter had come to the end of their asylum claim, got the NASS termination but then another daughter joined them who had travelled to the country separately and she was 14. She is in the property now because she is not counted on the NASS scheme. NASS wouldn't reinstate their support so again you have got a family with a child in it who is not on the NASS scheme who has got no other means of support. We are supposed to be evicting them . . . we have been holding off doing that because we know the consequences would be so severe because there is a very high chance that the child could be taken into the care of the local authority because mum wouldn't have any means to support and the mother would be destitute." (Local authority accommodation support worker)

There is also some evidence of welfare staff taking on a minor campaigning role in advocating for the rights of children. While one would not necessarily expect statutory agencies to be openly critical of policies they are obliged to implement, there is some room for them to exert pressure via the voluntary sector. For instance, although Save the Children makes displaced children an important focus of its campaigning on a UK (as well as an international) level in any case, staff at Save the Children's Wales office were approached by frontline practitioners from statutory agencies concerned at the plight of asylum-seeking children, and were asked to raise some of these children's problems in their campaigning. The steering group members of our own research project (see above) gave us very useful information on details of policy and practice. They also showed by their membership of this group a willingness to support a campaign to improve the welfare of children and challenge asylum law.

Discussion

There is evidence of problems for professionals with the asylum system: coping with complex and ever-changing specialist knowledge and experiencing several different kinds of problems with the dispersal system. There is certainly evidence of staff questioning policy and speaking of ethical conflict about their own roles. We have limited evidence of actions to undermine policy, but some does exist. Certainly, the numbers of failed asylum-seekers who are not removed is suggestive of much more undermining by welfare professionals as well as social networks. We found there to be support from some committed practitioners in Wales for campaigning via the voluntary sector on the welfare of asylum-seeking children.[1]

There is little evidence of profound reflexivity from frontline staff—fundamentally questioning their roles in relation to asylum-seeking children. Yet they clearly find it frustrating to work within legislation which is complex and which challenges their professional ethics. Our findings could be seen as more encouraging than the most pessimistic accounts of frontline staff in the asylum system. These workers are not accepting the system, but doing what they can to tinker around the edges of policy. On the face of it, the comprehensive NASS regulations allow little room for discretion on the part of practitioners, and yet, as indicated above, the large majority of failed asylum-seekers are not removed from the country. In part, this must arise from professionals "turning a blind eye" or by not actively pursuing such individuals according to the letter of the law. The research reported here provides at least some indication of such practices. As Evans and Harris (2004) have recently argued in relation to social workers, Lipsky's (1980) work on "street level bureaucrats" (whereby he saw "policy" not so much in the decisions of governments as in the actions of frontline staff such as social workers, teachers and housing officers) can still be relevant 25 years on. Even in an area such as asylum, where the government is under considerable scrutiny and the law is rapidly shifting in order to tighten up procedures, welfare professionals can still manage to exercise some discretion, invoking their personal interpretation of policy, in this case to the advantage of the client.

We should note that our sample is not representative of all welfare staff who encounter asylum-seekers. We did not survey the experiences of staff in mainstream services who may encounter asylum-seekers without having any specialist role in that regard. It could be that such mainstream staff have more judgemental attitudes to asylum-seekers than do specialists who are committed to working with this particular group. In other words, our own research may have been biased towards "committed" practitioners. Nevertheless, since the number of welfare staff in Wales who are in a specialist role in relation to asylum-seekers is not high, we are confident we interviewed the *majority* of key staff in these specialist roles, not merely those seen as especially sympathetic to their clients.

Humphries (2004) sees the inherent racism of immigration policies as fatally undermining any attempts to use anti-racist approaches while implementing asylum policy. She seems to suggest that asylum policies are of a different order of repression from other aspects of contemporary social policy. There is an interesting question to be addressed here: is asylum fundamentally different from other policy areas, where frontline professionals have to deal with the victims of profound inequalities and extreme relative poverty? Are the professional dilemmas involved not in some measure familiar territory within the welfare state? Following Bauman (2004), we could see the asylum system as one of managing the human waste that modernity creates. But so much of social welfare work targeted on the most vulnerable groups in society is also about managing the human waste created by profound inequalities. Although our respondents suggested areas of particular concern over the provision of services in Wales, it is likely that parallel concerns could be articulated by professionals in other areas of service provision. It is familiar territory for welfare staff, for example, to have to ration eligibility for services, denying help even to those they regard as being in need.

However, we might consider that scenarios such as children potentially being deported—or going hungry through termination of any financial support—are not scenarios familiar to workers with children of British citizens. Citizenship is fundamental to welfare entitlement and it is citizenship that is at stake for asylum-seekers. While mainstream staff concerned with child welfare may be faced with dilemmas such as eligibility for services, removing children from parents and so on, there will always be a baseline level of care and protection that welfare workers can rely upon, because at the end of the day the Children Act 1989 is the primary legislation adhered to. By contrast, children and young people seeking asylum are especially vulnerable and usually relatively impotent, when confronted by the exigencies of the dispersal system. The effects of moving on their school places, on health care and their friendship networks are profound. Equally, the pressures of waiting for decisions, the racism and harassment routinely experienced, the delays in providing school places and the absence of specialist services and staff impinge particularly on children and young people. Against such a backdrop, it is unsurprising to learn of the frustration of professionals having to implement this system and attempting to seek ways of working to improve the lot of their clients, in such a rigid, formalized and codified context.

Conclusion

Our research covered the experiences of a range of professional groups and reveals some interesting indications in the staff responses. Some of these findings could confirm a pessimistic stance about the role of welfare professionals in the asylum system, but some could challenge an overly pessimistic perspective. There are very clear limitations on the freedom of staff to promote what they see as the welfare of children. But many staff are not passively accepting their roles. They are at least questioning them, if not acting to undermine aspects of policy that do not sit comfortably with their professional ethics. It may be argued that some of the dilemmas faced by staff in the asylum system are not of a wholly different order from the routine ethical difficulties of working for the welfare of any other poor and marginalized people in a context of profound inequality. It is also the case, however, that asylum-seekers are uniquely marginalized within the welfare state because they lack citizen status; and that children and young people are especially vulnerable to some of the most damaging effects of this marginalization. The fact is that asylum and immigration is clearly one of the most contentious areas of New Labour's policy and is one likely to continue to dominate the political agenda. So long as political parties continue to use migration to better their election chances, one can expect immigration policy to become increasingly punitive and detrimental to children.

Note

1. We should also note that on a UK-wide basis there is a body called the Refugee Children's Consortium, which is largely made up of child care organizations and established itself in response to the increasingly punitive immigration policies. The Refugee Children's Consortium is made up of Amnesty International, Barnardo's, the British Agencies for Adoption and Fostering, the National Children's Bureau,

the Children's Rights Alliance, the Children's Society, the Medical Foundation for the Care of Victims of Torture, the NSPCC, the Refugee Council, Save the Children and UNICEF UK.

References

Audit Commission (2000), *Another Country: Implementing Dispersal under the Immigration & Asylum Act (1999)*, London: Stationery Office.

Barnardo's (2000), Children first and foremost: recent survey findings from local authorities. Presented at a Barnardo's seminar, London (July).

Bauman, Z. (2004), *Wasted Lives: Modernity and Its Outcasts*, Cambridge: Polity Press.

Bloch, A. and Schuster, L. (2002), Asylum and welfare: contemporary debates, *Critical Social Policy*, 22, 3: 393–414.

Christie, A. (2002), Responses of the social work profession to unaccompanied children seeking asylum in the Republic of Ireland, *European Journal of Social Work*, 5, 2: 187–98.

Christie, A. (2003), Unsettling the "social" in social work: responses to asylum-seeking children in Ireland, *Child and Family Social Work*, 8: 223–31.

Cunningham, S. and Tomlinson, J. (2005), "Starve them out." Does every child really matter? Section 9 of the Asylum and Immigration (Treatment of Claimants, etc.), Act, 2004, *Critical Social Policy*, 25, 2: 253–75.

Dennis, J. (2002), *How Refugee Children in England Are Missing Out: First Findings from the Monitoring Project and the Refugee Children's Consortium*, London: Children's Society, Save the Children and Refugee Council.

Department for Education and Skills (DfES) (2003), *Every Child Matters*, Cm 5860, London: DfES. Available at: http://www.dfes.gov.uk/everychildmatters/pdfs/EveryChildMatters.pdf

Evans, T. and Harris, J. (2004), Street level bureaucracy, social work and the (exaggerated) death of discretion, *British Journal of Social Work*, 34: 871–95.

Hewett, T., Smalley, N., Dunkerley, D. and Scourfield, J. (2005), *Uncertain Futures: Children Seeking Asylum in Wales*, Cardiff: Save the Children. Available at: http://www.savethechildren.org.uk/scuk_cache/scuk/cache/cmsattach/2654_Uncertain%20futures_eng.pdf (accessed June 2005).

Home Office (2004a), *Asylum Statistics: 2nd Quarter 2004*, Office for National Statistics. Available at: http://www.homeoffice.gov.uk/rds/pdfs04/asylumq204.pdf

Home Office (2004b), *Asylum Statistics United Kingdom 2003*, Home Office Statistical Bulletin 11/04. Available at: http://www.homeoffice.gov.uk/rds/pdfs04/hosb1104.pdf

Humphries, B. (2004), An unacceptable role for social work: implementing immigration policy, *British Journal of Social Work*, 34: 93–107.

Kidane, S. (2001), *"I did not choose to come here": Listening to Refugee Children*, London: British Agencies for Adoption and Fostering.

Lipsky, M. (1980), *Street Level Bureaucracy*, New York: Russell Sage Foundation.

Robinson, V. (1999), Research note. Cultures of ignorance, disbelief and denial: refugees in Wales, *Journal of Refugee Studies*, 12: 78–87.

Russell, S. (1999), *Most Vulnerable of All: The Treatment of Unaccompanied Refugee Children in the UK*, London: Amnesty International United Kingdom.

Rutter, J. (2003), *Working with Refugee Children*, London: London Metropolitan University and Joseph Rowntree Foundation.

Urry, J. (2000), Mobile sociology, *British Journal of Sociology*, 51: 185–203.

7

When the Export of Social Problems Is No Longer Possible: Immigration Policies and Unemployment in Switzerland

Alexandre Afonso

Introduction

In many industrialized European countries, immigration became a major political issue in the early 1980s, when the end of sustained economic growth gave rise to major social and economic problems, such as mass unemployment, spatial segregation, urban violence and xenophobia. As a response to these new socio-economic conditions, most Western states tried to stop flows of labour migration after the first oil shock of 1973, and in some countries extreme-right parties, such as the *Front National* in France, used the equation "immigration = unemployment" to take advantage of the growing fears linked to social and economic uncertainty among the public (Bade 2002). In Switzerland, the issue of immigration was politicized by xenophobic movements as early as the 1960s, and this had led the authorities to limit immigration through a system of quotas *before* the recession of the mid-1970s. Paradoxically, the social and economic problems related to migration, such as large-scale unemployment and social marginalization, really became visible only at the beginning of the 1990s, that is, *later* than in other comparable countries.

Until the beginning of the 1990s, the Swiss economy had been able to cope successfully with international economic downturns, and was seen as a model of economic and political stability. Unemployment remained at very low levels during the 1970s and 1980s, whereas wages and living standards remained very high. The good economic performance of Switzerland in this period in comparison with its neighbours—as well as the apparent absence of poverty or social instability—led many observers to consider Switzerland a *Sonderfall*, an exception (Armingeon 2004). Analysts trying to account for this success emphasized a tradition of dialogue between economic and political forces (Katzenstein 1985), weak intervention of the state in economic affairs (Freiburghaus 1988), and a high flexibility of the labour market, due in part to a large proportion of immigrant workers functioning as a cyclical buffer (Flückiger 1998; Bonoli and Mach 2000).

Indeed, over the last 50 years, Switzerland has been one of the countries with the largest share of immigrants[1] in Western Europe, this share now accounting for around 21 per cent of the population and 25 per cent of the workforce (Egger 2003). When the economy was hit by the oil crisis of the mid-1970s, a wide variety of precarious stay permits linked to employment status, as well as the absence of compulsory unemployment insurance, constrained many foreigners who lost their jobs to leave the country, so that the unemployment rate remained under 1 per cent during the 1970s and 1980s. According to some authors, the manipulation of this flexible workforce "[made] it possible to absorb virtually all of the costs of change in the international trade system" (Katzenstein 1985: 59).

In the 1990s, however, Switzerland experienced a significant change as regards its ability to escape economic difficulties. Unemployment increased to levels unseen since the 1930s, which had a strong effect on public deficits and social expenses. Even if the impacts of the economic downturn, particularly in the domain of unemployment, did not reach the extreme levels of some other European countries, Switzerland no longer seemed to be a *Sonderfall* (Bonoli and Mach 2000). Observers and analysts no longer focused on the factors explaining the *success* of the Swiss economy, but rather on the causes of its *failure*. In particular, the fact that economic growth in Switzerland was perceptibly lower than in the EU became a subject of worry (Borner *et al.* 1990).

Among the factors explaining the end of the *Sonderfall*, in particular regarding the labour market, immigration and immigration policy were considered central (Flückiger 2001). Existing policies in this field were challenged in many respects. As a majority of foreigners had access to more stable stay permits (owing to pressures from their countries of origin), it was no longer possible to send them back to their countries of origin, as had been done in the past. This new configuration made the side effects of past patterns of recruitment of foreign labour more visible: the majority of foreigners in Switzerland have much lower qualifications than nationals, and are thus over-represented among the unemployed. Besides, the rise of the national-populist *Swiss People's Party* (SVP-UDC) has put growing pressure on public policies in this field. Taking advantage of the xenophobic fears linked to a more uncertain social and economic situation, this rightist party has constantly used arguments about the *burden* of immigrants and asylum-seekers on welfare services.

In this new context, the responses adopted by the Swiss government in the domain of immigration and integration policy have been conditioned by specific institutional factors. Although some important adjustments have been made in admission policy (the most important of which is the introduction of the free movement of persons within the EU in 2002), they have been quite slow and limited in scope regarding the admission of third-country nationals, as well as in the domain of integration policy. The purpose of this article is to analyse the developments in these two domains affecting the labour market, and especially to highlight the institutional factors that account for their patterns.

Institutions and Immigration Control

The central idea is that developments implemented in the fields of immigration and integration policy to respond to the socio-economic problems of the 1990s have been determined by existing *institutions*, defined in a very generic way as stabilized rules constraining actors' preferences, interests, representations and strategies.

In a historical institutionalist perspective, institutions are defined as legal or administrative structures (laws, state structures . . .) and rules (formal or informal) which stabilize a distribution of rights, power, costs and benefits (Hall and Taylor 1996; Immergut 1997). A central notion in this perspective is the concept of *path-dependence*. It is asserted that a historically constructed set of institutional constraints and policy feedbacks structures the behaviour of political actors and groups, so that opportunities for policy change are limited by choices made in the past. Once the path has been established, the costs of changing direction become too great. Actors thus adapt to a specific institutional arrangement, construct their interests within it and oppose changes which threaten these vested interests, reinforcing existing institutions through "feedback mechanisms" (Pierson 2000).

The major factors inhibiting the possibilities for change in immigration policy in Switzerland in the 1990s were four: the constraints of direct democracy; a defensive migration regime; state structures and their effects; and the overall improvement of the legal status of immigrants mainly due to bilateral agreements with some sending countries.

Direct democracy

Direct democracy is often presented as the major originality of the Swiss political system and certainly constitutes the most decisive institutional factor in the development of all policy domains. Every legal change proposed by the government is dependent on the approval of all potential veto players who could launch a referendum, which makes the state only weakly autonomous *vis-à-vis* societal interests (Kriesi 1998). If in most receiving countries opinion polls have shown widespread latent hostility towards immigration, in Switzerland this hostility has found decisive institutional channels of expression through direct democracy.

Apart from the compulsory referendum on constitutional revisions (introduced in 1848), the most important direct democracy procedures are *optional referendum* on federal laws, and *popular initiative*. Virtually all federal laws, as well as international treaties, are subject to optional referendum. In this case, a popular ballot is held if 50,000 citizens request it by way of a petition; this makes legislators very careful about satisfying potential veto players who could use this tool—or threaten to do so—as a way of opposing decisions they do not like. Popular initiative allows 100,000 citizens to call for a ballot proposing an amendment to the constitution. This procedure is typically used by opposition parties with no direct access to the political agenda to raise new policy issues *from below*, and has had a remarkably great influence on Switzerland's immigration policy. Seven popular initiatives proposing to limit or reduce the number of foreigners were launched between 1960 and 2000. All of them were voted down, but the possibility that one might succeed has constantly acted as a sword of Damocles hanging over governmental policies in this field. Given these xenophobic pressures being expressed through direct democracy, the government was constrained to establish a system of overall quotas in 1970.

The impact of direct democracy procedures on immigration policy has been considerable, but more because of their latent implications (the authorities taking into account xenophobic sentiments among the population and instituting a system to limit immigration) than their actual results (all xenophobic initiatives having been voted down at the polls). In essence, every legal change in the domain of immigration or integration policy is subject to the approval of all significant political groups, which tends to limit the scope of changes and slow every reform.

Defensive migration regime

Although *immigration* policy in Switzerland in the postwar period has been quite liberal, owing to a structural labour shortage and sustained economic expansion, the policy on *immigrants* has, by contrast, been rather restrictive (Piguet 2004). As Ireland (1994: 148) puts it, "since World War II, Swiss governments and institutions have worked . . . earnestly . . . to keep foreigners out of host-society politics and divided among ethnic lines". Indeed, whereas virtually every foreign worker was granted a work permit in Switzerland until the mid-1960s, legal and administrative procedures inherited from the interwar period explicitly prevented their social and political integration into Swiss society. The Aliens Law (still in force) was established in 1931 and is strongly marked by the uncertainty and xenophobia of that period. Its explicit aim is to fight against "over-foreignization" (*Überfremdung*), a concept which has recurred in public debates up to the present day (Arlettaz and Arlettaz 2004). This institutional framework has been preserved in the postwar period because of its high level of flexibility. It permits a response to the needs of the labour market, which does not have to assume the costs of economic downturns. Foreign workers were thus seen as a rather flexible aid to production: easy to send back to their countries of origin in case of recession. As in other countries with established guest worker programmes, such as Germany or Austria, immigrants were intended to work and stay for a while, but not to settle.

The acquisition of Swiss citizenship is difficult, and procedures vary greatly between cantons. Besides the *jus sanguinis* principle, according to which children of foreigners born in Switzerland have no automatic right to Swiss citizenship, at least 12 years of stay are required to apply for a naturalization procedure. Applications are subject to administrative controls at three levels of government (communal, cantonal, federal), which discourages many foreigners from applying. Together with Germany and Italy, Switzerland evinces an ideal-type *ethnic-assimilationist* approach to citizenship, whereby immigrants face "both an exclusionary national community and a demanding environment in terms of the extent to which they have to adapt to the rules and cultural codes of the host country" (Giugni and Passy 2004: 58).

These dispositions, coupled with the sustained economic expansion of the postwar period, have notably contributed to the creation of a large population of "denizens": people who are granted most social and economic rights, but no *political* rights (Hammar 1985). Nevertheless, contrary to the expectations of the postwar period, immigrants settled and brought their families, as will be shown in the next section.

This defensive and exclusionary conception of national identity and citizenship could be considered quite striking in a multicultural country like Switzerland, with three languages and two religions. But while Switzerland is pluralist "towards the cultures traditionally recognized within the context of federalism . . . it is much less pluralist toward ethnic minorities of migrant origin, especially those who arrived most recently" (Giugni and Passy 2004). Cantonal identities are thus "legitimate" normative frames for public policies mostly implemented by the cantons, whereas particularistic policies aimed at immigrant populations are only weakly legitimate. For many major political groups such as the Swiss People's Party, Switzerland is still "no immigration country". Although the idea that immigration is a mere temporary phenomenon has been progressively eroded, very few active measures to integrate the foreign population have been implemented until the last decade.

Until 2002, three main types of stay permits for foreigners existed in Switzerland. The seasonal worker statute was an example of the Swiss exclusionary conception of immigration, allowing workers to stay in Switzerland for nine months in the year (to work in agriculture, construction, the hotel trade) without right of family reunification or unemployment insurance. Renewable *annual permits* allowed working for the whole year; while *residence permits* were permanent and granted most economic and social rights, but not political rights. The two first categories conferred very limited socio-economic rights on foreigners: they could not change profession nor move to another canton without authorization, and had to leave the country if they lost their jobs. The existence of this wide variety of precarious permits, together with the fact that unemployment insurance was not compulsory until 1977 (which implied that most foreigners who lost their jobs had no right to benefits and had to leave the country) and the difficulties of attaining Swiss citizenship, made possible what has been called the "export of unemployment" in the 1970s.

When the Swiss economy was hit by the recession of 1974–6, around 180,000 foreign workers—a significant proportion of the workforce—were forced to leave the country because their work permits were not renewed (Flückiger 1998). So, although the Swiss economy lost around 258,000 jobs in this period, unemployment only increased by 21,000 people (Weber 2001). The reduction in foreign worker employment was around six times larger than for Swiss workers during this period, and the costs of economic change were thus externalized to a large extent on foreigners holding precarious stay permits (Bonoli and Mach 2000).

Immigrant rights

Despite this restrictive migration regime, some expansion of immigrant rights has nevertheless been possible, which explains to a certain extent the

97

loss of flexibility of the Swiss labour market in the 1990s. Indeed, the development of immigrant rights accounts for the impossibility of sending large numbers of foreigners back to their countries during the economic crisis of the 1990s, as had been done in the 1970s.

Whereas the proportion of foreigners holding residence permits (having the right to stay in Switzerland and being entitled to social assistance) was only 21 per cent in 1970, it was around 60 per cent by 1990. The overall social and legal conditions of foreigners had improved over this period, mainly owing to pressures from the sending countries.

In Switzerland, a majority of immigrants are from Western European countries which, being part of the European Union, have been able to exert great pressure on the Swiss government to improve these immigrants' social and legal conditions. Whereas active courts and judges using judicial liberal principles have been a major factor in the expansion of immigrant rights in liberal democracies such as Germany, Britain or the United States (Joppke 2001), courts have not played such an important role in Switzerland, owing to the Swiss Supreme Court's very restricted powers of constitutional review, as regards federal laws and international treaties (Rothmayr 2001).

The bilateral agreement the Swiss government concluded with Italy in 1964 notably improved the situation of Italian workers in Switzerland (representing 70 per cent of all foreigners at that time), by reducing the period required to obtain residence permits and the right to family reunification. At the time, Italy enjoyed considerable blackmail power since, at a time of strong labour shortage, the Swiss government was nevertheless reluctant to recruit workers from more distant countries such as Turkey or Yugoslavia, these being considered too "culturally distant" and their nationals "inassimilable" (Cerutti 2000). After this bilateral agreement, the proportion of foreigners holding residence permits steadily increased, as a result of permit transformations, births and family reunifications. In 1976, during another negotiation, seasonal workers from all southern European countries obtained the right to have their permits transformed into annual permits after 36 months of work in Switzerland (Niederberger 2000). During the 1980s, strong economic expansion in the traditional sending countries of southern Europe reduced the labour flows from these countries, thus placing them in a strong position to improve the living conditions of all their nationals in Switzerland. The Swiss government duly signed agreements with Italy, Spain and Portugal which reduced the time required to obtain permanent stay permits (from 10 to 5 years of stay) (Piguet 2004). Besides specific immigrant-related rights, the reinforcement of the welfare state after the recession of the 1970s, and notably the introduction of compulsory unemployment insurance in 1977, has also strengthened the position of foreigners on the Swiss labour market.

The development of immigrant rights can now be considered from a path-dependent perspective, since the effects of the agreements with sending countries have reinforced themselves over the years. Foreigners gained access to more stable stay permits, with which they could not be expelled, and were allowed to bring their families. This was a major mechanism limiting the room for manoeuvre of the Swiss authorities in this domain. By 1989, only

20 per cent of immigrant flows could legally be limited (Cosandey 1989); by the same token, 80 per cent could not be limited by the Swiss authorities—particularly regarding their social characteristics. The great majority of new immigrants entering the country were unskilled (Sheldon 2001).

Fragmented state structures

If institutional factors account for the "loss of control" of the Swiss authorities over the entry of immigrants, one should not consider that the preferences of the state regarding "wanted" and "unwanted" immigrants have been unambiguous. In fact, the question of *which* immigrants are needed has been controversial until now. On the one hand, the Federal authorities, multinational companies and economic experts wish to admit exclusively skilled immigrants, less liable to become unemployed; on the other, some cantons and economic sectors such as agriculture, catering or the hotel trade are highly dependent on unskilled foreign labour to do low-paid jobs for which the workforce is hard to find on the Swiss labour market.

The relatively weak autonomy of the Swiss Federal state *vis-à-vis* economic and regional interests would seem a decisive factor, especially with regard to the structural reliance of many regions and economic sectors on unskilled foreign labour. Until now, Switzerland has entertained a tradition of weak statutory intervention in economic affairs (Armingeon 2004). Hence, private arrangements between economic actors (firms) and social partners (unions and employers) have played a central role in the functioning of the economy and labour markets (Bonoli and Mach 2000). The weakness of the Federal state in relation to economic (corporatist) and regional (cantonal) interests, in addition to the existence of direct democracy procedures granting great power to potential veto players, helps account for this pattern (Kriesi 1998).

This has had important implications for immigration policy. Unlike in France or even in Germany—where expansion strategies, via the import of foreign labour in the postwar period, were characterized by strong state intervention (Martin and Miller 1980; Hollifield 1992)—the Swiss Federal government adopted a hands-off policy, at least until the mid-1960s, when xenophobic pressures led to the establishment of a system of quotas. In the 1950s, Swiss employers were permitted to contract directly with foreign workers, there being no state agency responsible for such recruitment. Up to 1960, furthermore, practically all foreigners with valid contracts were given residency authorization—a practice which gave no cause for concern since, as already mentioned, most economic actors believed immigration to be a temporary phenomenon.

This hands-off policy had significant effects: weak or declining industries had abundant, unskilled and cheap labour at their disposal. Hence they had no incentive to modernize their production systems and, instead, expanded the labour force. This kept wages in these sectors at a relatively low level by Swiss standards and reinforced the segmentation of the labour market. Indeed, one of the major characteristics of the labour market in Switzerland has been the disjuncture between well-paid, export-oriented sectors and low-paid domestic sectors (Flückiger 1998; Bonoli and Mach 2000).

When the Federal government established its system of immigration quotas, this trend was actually reinforced. Since the demand for labour was superior to the supply, the Federal government opted for a system of administrative allocation of work permits. However, since it did not have the administrative resources to proceed to the centralized allocation of work permits, the *cantons*—already in charge of a majority of public tasks—became responsible for attributing most of the work permits (Lavenex 2004).

Empirical research has shown that the implementation of public policies in Switzerland can vary considerably from one canton to another (Kissling-Näf and Wälti 2004). Logically enough, rural cantons tended to favour regional, labour-intensive, low-productive sectors (hotel trade, catering, construction) with which they had close ties. Significant protectionist measures (such as the impossibility of changing canton or sector for a few years) were aimed at keeping foreign workers in these sectors or regions, yet they proved inefficient. A significant proportion of immigrants, who came to work in peripheral regions, then moved to bigger cities where wages were higher, but where they faced major difficulties on the labour market owing to their lack of skills (Dhima 1991). The automatic transformation of seasonal permits into permanent permits after four years, a result of the 1964 negotiation with Italy, contributed to the settlement of a large unskilled foreign population. At the same time, as Swiss workers gained better-paid jobs and improved their own qualification profile, the labour-intensive sectors became more and more dependent on unskilled foreign labour.

Thus the weak autonomy of the central government *vis-à-vis* economic and regional interests accounts to a large extent for the "path-dependent" reliance of some economic sectors on an unskilled foreign workforce which itself is more liable to become unemployed. These economic sectors and cantons were strongly opposed to reforms aimed at stopping the flow of unskilled labour. Furthermore, the strength of the cantons and organized interests relative to the central state made it more difficult to achieve coordinated policies in the domain of integration.

Unemployment, Immigration and Policy Responses

The institutional logics highlighted above can be considered key intermediary variables, in respect of responses adopted in the fields of immigration and immigrant policy in the context of economic stagnation in the 1990s. To a certain extent, they even account for the rise of unemployment among immigrants in Switzerland in the 1990s. Indeed, it can be argued that improvements in the legal status of foreigners, together with patterns of immigration policy advantaging low-skilled migration, coupled again with the non-existence of an integration policy, are factors which go far to explain why the labour market was no longer able to cope so successfully with economic downturn in the 1990s. Whereas the weak development of immigrant rights had partially hidden the "economic dysfunctions" of this policy in the 1970s, this was no longer the case by the end of the century.

Indeed, the 1990s have witnessed a kind of normalization of the Swiss economy by European standards. Whereas simultaneous increases in unemployment and inflation had led many European countries to undertake radical changes in their economic and social policies in the 1980s (Jobert 1994), there was no such radical change in Switzerland during this period. To a certain extent, significant reforms were not needed. Many of the policy reforms being undertaken by other countries were already in force in Switzerland: a flexible labour market (no minimum wage legislation and decentralized wage bargaining), an independent central bank, low taxes and a lean welfare state (Bonoli and Mach 2000).

In the 1990s, however, Switzerland had to face problems similar to those of its neighbours and witnessed a strong increase in unemployment—up from 0.5 per cent in 1990 to 5 per cent in 1997—and in public deficits, owing to an even greater increase in social expenditure. For many observers, one cause of the increase in unemployment (by comparison with the 1970s) was that the foreign population was no longer so "flexible". It became apparent that a majority of the foreign workers that had been hired on a temporary basis and then stayed on permanently were low-skilled and hence more liable to face difficulties in a more competitive labour market.

Unemployment and poverty among immigrants

In 2003, people of foreign origin represented around 20 per cent of the total resident population, 25 per cent of the workforce (including frontier commuters) and 41 per cent of the unemployed (Egger 2003). During the 1990s, the unemployment rate for foreigners was consistently at least twice as high as that for Swiss citizens.[2] Immigrants, particularly non-Europeans, are also over-represented among the "working poor". Apart from the discrimination problems affecting some categories of immigrants—such as Turks and Yugoslavs (Fibbi *et al.* 2003)—this state of affairs is principally due to the lack of qualifications of migrant workers, often recruited to work in labour-intensive domestic sectors on a temporary basis.

The overall lack of qualifications is particularly visible among "older" immigrants from southern Europe: half of them have not gone beyond elementary school, and less than 10 per cent have a tertiary degree (Egger 2003: 15). (The trajectories of non-European immigrants—from African asylum-seekers to American executives—are even more diversified.) An important proportion of southern Europeans (from Italy, Spain, Portugal, Yugoslavia, Turkey) originally came as seasonal workers, on a *temporary* basis. They then benefited from a permit transformation and brought their families, on a *permanent* basis. But the hotel and construction sectors, in which these foreigners are strongly over-represented, have the highest unemployment rates. Jobs in these sectors are often unstable and subject to strong seasonal variations.

Whereas qualification profiles were not so significant in the expanding economy of the 1950s and 1960s, and their weaknesses have been "hidden" by the departure of a significant part of the foreign population in the 1970s, they became highly visible in the 1990s context of economic stagnation and unemployment. Existing immigration policies have increasingly been criticized by economists and big business, on the grounds that those who entered Switzerland in the past are not "adapted" (or adaptable) to the new "post-Fordist", knowledge-based economy (Wimmer 2001). The immigrant-related social problems of the 1990s, many experts claimed, were a legacy of the period of strong economic growth, when immigration had been considered merely a temporary phenomenon. No active integration policy had been implemented and unstable legal status had even explicitly prevented integration.

However, if the problems facing Switzerland in the 1990s could be considered a legacy of the past, the responses adopted in the context of economic stagnation and unemployment had also been institutionally "pre-determined".

Reforms in immigration policy

The first measures considered by the Swiss government were similar to those which had been tried by neighbouring countries in the mid-1970s: stopping the flow of unskilled migration from outside Europe. These faced considerable opposition from the economic sectors and regions which had become highly dependent on an unskilled foreign workforce, as well as from unions and social democrats opposed to the exclusion of migrants on humanitarian grounds. The weak autonomy of the state *vis-à-vis* political forces, and economic and cantonal interests, made any significant change very difficult to effect.

The room for manoeuvre of the Swiss government was further limited owing to the proportion of inflows which could not be reduced, because they derived either from family reunifications (partly regulated by bilateral treaties) or asylum requests (granted by international conventions). In 2003, for instance, family reunifications represented 40 per cent of the annual inflow (Piguet 2004). Moreover, even within the scope of legal limitations, the restriction of extra-European immigration to skilled immigrants has had to face much opposition from regions and economic sectors which had benefited from the import of unskilled labour.

Major changes in immigration policy were at last triggered by the acceleration of the process of European integration. The negotiation of the EEA (European Economic Area) agreement notably prompted the Swiss authorities to make significant adjustments to their admission policy: liberalization of the labour market at the European level stood to be of great benefit to Swiss export industries in need of skilled personnel. In return, Switzerland would have had to abolish the seasonal workers statute, which benefited domestic sectors.[3]

For the Swiss government, mindful of xenophobic pressures from the ever-stronger SVP-UDC, opening the borders to western European workers meant reducing the inflow from outside Europe, to prevent an overall increase in the foreign population. In 1991, a model instituting three "circles", corresponding to regions of immigration, was established. The first circle comprised the "traditional" sending countries of the European Union, who enjoyed priority in anticipation of the establishment of the free movement of persons with the EC. The second comprised other "culturally near" industrialized countries such as the USA, Canada, Australia and New Zealand. The third included all other countries, from which only "indispensable" workers (IT specialists, executives) were to be admitted. The guiding principle of the three-circles policy was "cultural distance" (immigrants from the third world were supposedly more difficult to integrate), which faced major criticisms not only from human rights groups and the left, but also from some employers opposed to the ban on Yugoslav workers—here classified in the third circle although Yugoslavia had been a "traditional" sending country for many years.

In the end, the EEA agreement was voted down by a popular referendum led by the Swiss People's Party in December 1992, and the seasonal workers statute was retained. Only after a long and painful negotiation process did Switzerland and the EU finally conclude an agreement on the free movement of persons (enforced in 2002) which finally put an end to the seasonal workers statute. Several concessions were made in order to get around the opposition of unions (who feared social dumping) and xenophobic parties (who feared an "invasion" of foreigners) (Fischer *et al.* 2002). The agreement introduced many innovations regarding the working conditions of European nationals in the domains of residential and employment mobility, social security, pensions and recognition of foreign diplomas. As a central feature, it introduced more competition in the labour market, the consequences of which—regarding wage levels and qualification requirements—remain as yet uncertain.

If the European question is now partially solved, thanks to strong international pressure, the question of extra-European immigration remains deadlocked, owing especially to vested interests which are themselves the product of former policies. On the one hand, businesses and cantons reliant on seasonal workers look for substitutes outside Europe, and strongly oppose every reform proposed by the Federal government, which is geared to stopping the flow of unskilled immigration. On the other hand, federal bureaucrats—as well as the largest multinationals, economic experts and right-wing parties— have advocated the strict limitation of extra-European migration to executives, wealthy taxpayers, IT workers and other high-skilled, "less costly" immigrants (Afonso 2004).

This latter vision of "useful immigration" seems to have become dominant in the context of economic difficulties and growing competitive pressures on the Swiss economy; nevertheless, future developments regarding immigration policy remain uncertain. Recent debates on the revision of the Aliens Law (in force since 1934) have seen the watering down of many initiatives promoted by the Federal Council to impose restrictive criteria for the issuing of work permits. In all likelihood, the preservation of cantonal competences in this domain will ensure there is no radical change to existing practices (Sheldon 2001; Piguet 2004).

Developments in integration policy

In Switzerland, "integration problems" have been rendered more visible by many factors over the last 15 years. First, deteriorating economic conditions have meant a far less favourable context for the arrival of immigrants than in the past. Second, the motives of new immigrants from more distant countries (Africa, South America or elsewhere) are also "less favourable"—since they are often fleeing conflicts and poverty in their home countries by applying for asylum or entering illegally, and this makes them obviously more vulnerable to "precariousness".[4] Third, family reunifications and births within migrant communities increased, contributing to the decoupling of migration flows from labour market conditions. All of these factors have made many political actors aware of the need for an integration policy, not least to improve the employability and qualifications of both first- and second-generation foreigners. However, the development of active integration measures has had to face many difficulties.

There was no explicit legal framework pertinent to the integration of foreigners—at least at the national level—until 2000, when a Federal ordinance on integration was adopted. This was the first legal reference to integration as a public task, since the Aliens Law of 1931 made no mention of the topic. The principal federal public entity active in the domain of integration—the Federal Commission for Foreigners, created in 1970—has only a limited capacity for action. Since 2000, it has been in charge of grant-aiding integration projects (out of a relatively small budget) besides consultative and expertise tasks; but it has no pro-active competencies. Naturally, any policies aimed specifically at immigrants are liable to face major opposition from right-wing parties, notably the Swiss People's Party.

The limited scope of developments at the Federal level in the domain of integration can also be explained by specific state structures (the major role of the cantons and the social partners) that have to a large extent determined the strategies adopted on integration. Indeed, there is no substantive "state capacity" to implement active integration policies. After all, many of the public tasks related to integration are either in the charge of the cantons (education) or (in the case of wages, working conditions) are settled through negotiations between the social partners. A wide variety of programmes aimed at first- and second-generation immigrants does exist at the cantonal level to promote the integration of foreigners in the labour market, but these are characterized by extreme diversity and unequal development (Egger 2003). While some cantons have created administrative positions in charge of integration programmes in the domain of education, language teaching or the re-qualification of the unemployed, others have hardly done anything. Hence, if federalism allows scope for experimentation and innovation, it can also slow reforms and pose problems of (in)equality of treatment across the Swiss territory (Kissling-Näf and Wälti 2004).

To be sure, coordination policies and national initiatives are now starting to materialize at the Federal level, under the auspices of the Federal Commission for Foreigners, even if these are still only weakly developed. Projected measures focus on the transition from education/training to work, the integration of foreigners in the workplace, and the reintegration of the unemployed in the labour market. Language courses and training measures are also being provided by unemployment programmes (Egger 2003). All of these policies need a high level of coordination—yet the Federal state is not able to implement them directly, being reliant, rather, on the cantons and social partners. The financial participation of subnational units (cantons, communes) is required for the attribution of federal subventions for integration projects. Cooperation and coordination is also required from unions and firms, the latter of which are often reluctant to assume the costs of integration measures. As a new policy domain which has to draw upon existing institutional arrangements, integration policy is developing a pattern of "governance" whereby the state uses *encouragement, cooperation* and *persuasion* rather than *coercion* (Pierre and Peters 2000). This may be a convenient pattern to adopt in such a complex institutional setting, and in a context of such low legitimacy and financial difficulty, but the concrete results have yet to be demonstrated.

At the legal level there has been major opposition, on the part of the Swiss People's Party and other right-wing movements, to the inclusion of integration objectives in the Aliens Law. As they see it, integration should not be a task for the receiving society but exclusively one for the immigrants themselves. Above all, the best way of achieving integration is by reducing the proportion of foreigners. Bearing in mind the tools of direct democracy and the xenophobic sentiments latent among the population (as demonstrated by recent popular votes), such views have to be taken into account by public actors and limit the possibility of their undertaking active integration policies. In addition, financial problems and public deficits can be considered major obstacles in themselves to the establishment of a coherent integration policy across the Swiss territory. Indeed, new policies aimed at diffuse and weakly organized groups are often the first victims of budgetary restrictions.

Conclusion

The central aim of this article has been to show how existing institutional arrangements and representations shape opportunities and limit the possibilities for change in respect of migration-related policy in Switzerland. Direct democracy (as a tool of expression for hostile sentiments towards immigrants), a rather defensive conception of national identity, the development of immigrant rights and specific state structures conferring low autonomy on the central state act as important intermediate variables in accounting for the responses adopted after the increase in unemployment among foreigners from the early 1990s. Developments in immigration and integration policy have been slow and rather limited in scope because of the opposition of actors whose ideas and interests have been shaped by existing formal structures and collective understandings.

However, one should not consider institutions immovable and innovation impossible. Many improvements have indeed taken place regarding the ways in which immigrants have been considered and incorporated into Swiss society since the Second World War. For instance, recent research has shown that second-generation Italian and Spanish immigrants, who belong to older immigration flows, have performed very well as regards education and labour market integration (Bolzman *et al.* 2003). Policy change can also happen through learning processes on the part of the actors involved. In the domain of integration, it can be argued that developments should be possible once hostile and indifferent actors begin to think that the better integration of foreigners might be in their interest. Recent events have actually shown such processes to be at work. Recently, the largest employers' associations have advocated integration measures, such as the facilitation of naturalization procedures, because they have started to think that a more "open" posture might be a good way of attracting high-skilled immigrants needed by the economy. Thus, for these actors, a legal framework favourable to integration could be construed as a comparative advantage in the international competition for skilled labour. Nevertheless, even if a growing number of political and economic actors now support the very general statement that "integration matters", more concrete propositions—such as the financing of pro-active integration measures—remain the subject of disagreement.

Acknowledgements

The author would like to thank the editor and Yannis Papadopoulos for helpful comments and stylistic improvements.

Notes

1. I use the expressions "foreigner" or "immigrant" as generic expressions to designate people who do not have Swiss citizenship. The expression "foreign-born" is not suitable for Switzerland since children of immigrant parents are not automatically entitled to Swiss citizenship.
2. In 2003, the unemployment rate of foreigners was 6.5 per cent, as compared with 2.7 per cent for Swiss citizens (Egger 2003). Great variations exist between nationalities: the unemployed represent 12.6 per cent among Yugoslavs and almost 15 per cent among Turks (Piguet 2004: 110).
3. Southern European countries that were part of the European Community (namely Italy, Spain and Portugal) were willing to improve the working conditions of their nationals living in Switzerland, and strongly criticized the precarious seasonal workers statute (under which family reunification was not permitted) on ethical grounds.
4. Moreover, unlike southern Europeans (Italians, Spaniards, Portuguese), their states of origin enjoy much less blackmail power to improve the living conditions of their nationals since they are not in the European Union, on which the Swiss economy is very dependent.

References

Afonso, A. (2004), *Internationalisation, économie et politique migratoire dans la Suisse des années 1990*, Lausanne: Institute for International and Political Studies.
Arlettaz, G. and Arlettaz, S. (2004), *La Suisse et les étrangers: immigration et formation nationale 1848–1933*, Lausanne: Antipodes.
Armingeon, K. (2004), Economic and financial policy. In U. Klöti, P. Knoepfel, Y. Papadopoulos, H. Kriesi and W. Linder (eds), *Handbook of Swiss Politics*, Zurich: NZZ Verlag, pp. 633–73.
Bade, K. J. (2002), *L'Europe en mouvement: la migration de la fin du XVIIIe siècle à nos jours*, Paris: Seuil.
Bolzman, C., Fibbi, R. and Vial, M. (2003), Que sont-ils devenus? Le processus d'insertion des adultes issus de la migration. In H.-R. Wicker, R. Fibbi and W. Haug (eds), *Les migrations et la Suisse*, Zurich: Seismo.
Bonoli, G. and Mach, A. (2000), Switzerland: adjustment politics within institutional constraints. In F. W. Scharpf and V. Schmidt (eds), *Welfare and Work in the Open Economy*, Oxford: Oxford University Press, pp. 131–73.

Borner, S., Brunetti, A. and Straubhaar, T. (1990), *Schweiz AG: vom Sonderfall zum Sanierungsfall?* Zürich: Verlag Neue Zürcher Zeitung.

Cerutti, M. (2000), La politique migratoire de la Suisse 1945–1970. In H. Mahnig (ed.), *Histoire de la politique de migration, d'asile et d'intégration en Suisse depuis 1948. Research Report for the Swiss National Fund for Scientific Research*, Neuchâtel and Geneva: Swiss Forum for the Study of Migrations and Population, pp. 82–122.

Cosandey, J.-D. (1989), Les travailleurs étrangers en Suisse: réglementation actuelle, *La Vie Économique*, 5: 21–4.

Dhima, G. (1991), *Politische Ökonomie des schweizerischen Ausländerregelung*, Chur/Zurich: Rüegger.

Egger, T. (2003), *Intégration et travail*, Bern: Federal Commission for Foreigners.

Fibbi, R., Kaya, B. and Piguet, E. (2003), *Le passeport ou le diplôme? Etude des discriminations à l'embauche des jeunes issus de la migration. Research Report no. 31*, Neuchâtel: Swiss Forum for Migration Studies.

Fischer, A., Nicolet, S. and Sciarini, P. (2002), Europeanisation of non-EU countries: the case of Swiss immigration policy towards the EU, *West European Politics*, 25, 4: 143–70.

Flückiger, Y. (1998), The labour market in Switzerland: the end of a special case? *International Journal of Manpower*, 19, 6: 369–95.

Flückiger, Y. (2001), Le changement du contexte économique international et les transformations du marché du travail. In H. Mahnig (ed.), *Histoire de la politique de migration, d'asile et d'intégration en Suisse depuis 1948*, Neuchâtel/Genève: Swiss National Fund for Scientific Research, pp. 432–54.

Freiburghaus, D. (1988), *La relation entre la stabilité politique et la prospérité économique*, Lausanne: IDHEAP.

Giugni, M. and Passy, F. (2004), Migrant mobilization between political institutions and citizenship regimes: a comparison of France and Switzerland, *European Journal of Political Research*, 43: 51–82.

Hall, P. A. and Taylor, R. C. (1996), Political science and the three new institutionalisms, *Political Studies*, 44, 5: 936–57.

Hammar, T. (ed.) (1985), *European Immigration Policy: A Comparative Study*, Cambridge: Cambridge University Press.

Hollifield, J. F. (1992), *Immigrants, Markets and States: The Political Economy of Postwar Europe*, Cambridge, MA: Harvard University Press.

Immergut, E. (1997), The normative roots of the new institutionalism: historical institutionalism and comparative policy studies. In A. Benz and W. Seibel (eds), *Theorieentwicklung in der Politikwissenschaft: eine Zwischenbilanz*, Baden-Baden: Nomos.

Ireland, P. R. (1994), *The Policy Challenge of Ethnic Diversity: Immigrant Politics in France and Switzerland*, Cambridge, MA: Harvard University Press.

Jobert, B. (1994), Introduction: le retour du politique. In B. Jobert (ed.), *Le tournant néo-libéral en Europe*, Paris: L'Harmattan, pp. 9–20.

Joppke, C. (2001), The legal-domestic sources of immigrant rights: the United States, Germany and the European Union, *Comparative Political Studies*, 34, 4: 339–66.

Katzenstein, P. (1985), *Small States in World Markets: Industrial Policy in Europe*, Ithaca, NY: Cornell University Press.

Kissling-Näf, I. and Wälti, S. (2004), The implementation of public policies. In U. Klöti, P. Knoepfel, H. Kriesi, W. Linder and Y. Papadopoulos (eds), *Handbook of Swiss Politics*, Zurich: NZZ, pp. 563–600.

Kriesi, H. (1998), *Le système politique suisse*, Paris: Economica.

Lavenex, S. (2004), Whither the liberal democratic model? Immigration politics in Switzerland and Japan, *Swiss Political Science Review*, 10, 3: 179–210.

Martin, P. L. and Miller, M. J. (1980), Guestworkers: lessons from Europe, *Industrial and Labor Relations Review*, 33, 3: 315–30.

Niederberger, M. (2000), Die Entwicklung einer Integrationspolitik. In H. Mahnig (ed.), *Histoire de la politique d'immigration, d'intégration en Suisse 1948–2000*, Zurich: Seismo.

OFS (2003), *La population étrangère en Suisse*, Neuchâtel: Office Fédéral de la Statistique.

Pierre, J. and Peters, B. G. (2000), *Governance, Politics and the State*, London: Macmillan.

Pierson, P. (2000), Increasing returns, path dependence, and the study of politics, *American Political Science Review*, 94, 2: 251–66.

Piguet, E. (2004), *L'immigration en Suisse: 50 ans d'entrouverture*, Lausanne: PPUR.

Rothmayr, C. (2001), Towards the judicialisation of Swiss politics? *West European Politics*, 24, 2: 77–94.

Sheldon, G. (2001), Foreign labour employment in Switzerland: less is not more, *Swiss Political Science Review*, 7, 1: 104–12.

Weber, B. A. (2001), Le chômage en Suisse dans les années nonante, *La Vie Economique*, 6/2001: 4–9.

Wimmer, A. (2001), Ein helvetischer Kompromiss: Kommentar zum Entwurf eines neuen Ausländergesetzes, *Swiss Political Science Review*, 7, 1: 97–104.

8
Why It Is Bad to Be Kind. Educating Refugees to Life in the Welfare State: A Case Study from Norway

Anniken Hagelund

Introduction

Everyone is talking about integration and how important it is that immigrants are integrated in the societies they have moved to. Most agree that integration is good. But what does integration actually mean? Or more precisely, what kind of policies and practices does it entail? What must governments actually do in order to promote integration?

A number of studies have addressed the debates and philosophies underpinning the integration policies of European countries (Favell 1998; Hvenegård-Lassen 2002; Silvermann 1992). In my own work on Norway (Hagelund 2003) I have seen how the meaning of integration and the purposes of integration policy have changed imperceptibly over time, from being a project concerned with how to avoid enforced assimilation, to one more concerned with how to produce actively participating citizens out of immigrants. However, such analyses often fail to address the institutionalization and implementation of integration policy. Integration is no doubt a slippery notion, incorporating an appealing, but diffuse, functionalist image of the harmonious coexistence of social inclusion and cultural diversity within nation-state boundaries. Nevertheless, it is also more than a catchy word in political debates. In a well-developed welfare state, such as the Norwegian one, institutions are set up to produce integration; integration is something people are employed to do. From the Home Office and the Directorate of Immigration to hundreds of local municipalities, integration is a practical task entailing a whole range of institutions, practices and occupations. It is towards this apparatus that I have directed my focus in this paper.

One of the most concrete measures Norwegian authorities have ever taken to produce integration is the recent establishment of a compulsory two-year introduction programme for newly arrived refugees, effected nationally from 2004. In the first part of this paper I will locate the establishment of this policy within a broader context of integration crisis, before I move on to look more specifically at the background for the programme and the problems it is set up to address. The introduction programme is an activation-style pro-gramme involving both a financial and an educational component, where out-payments depend on participation in a full-time training programme aimed at enabling participants to become self-sufficient members of Norwe-gian society. In the latter part I present the introduction programme as it is being implemented in one medium-sized Norwegian city. The local discourse here is one of before and after, where the failings of previous policies have been overcome and new and productive practices have been established. One of the themes of progress concerns the past tendency to be *kind*, which is now about to be overcome. Why is it so bad to be kind? And what does this tell us about changes in integration policies as well as about social perceptions of immigration, immigrants and the welfare state?

Integration Crisis

There is a grave sense of crisis with respect to integration in Norwegian politics and in the public debate. Why is this so?

Immigration to Norway started later than in many other Western European countries, but has otherwise developed along lines that are quite comparable to those of better-known countries of immigration. The first significant number of labour migrants from poorer countries arrived in the late 1960s. Following the introduction of immigration restrictions in other European countries, Norway established an "immigration stop" in 1975 that effectively put an end to third-world labour immigration. As elsewhere, immigrants continued to arrive as specialists (mostly westerners), via family reunification schemes, and later as refugees and asylum-seekers. Today, the immigrant population, comprising first-generation immigrants and their children, constitutes 7.6 per cent of the population (as of 1 January 2004; Statistics Norway: http://www.ssb.no). About a third of these have a refugee background.

Why crisis? Research on immigrants' living conditions repeatedly comes up with the same depressing pattern. Non-Western immigrants fare worse on most indicators—unemployment figures are higher and living standards lower (Djuve and Hagen 1995; Blom 1998). Considering that the Nordic welfare state model relies on high employment in order to secure universal access to relatively generous services, the low employment rates are particu-larly disconcerting. Only 48 per cent of the refugees settled after 1986 are employed, compared to 70 per cent of the total population (Olsen 2004: 73), which again means that income levels are lower and dependence on social security higher (Kirkeberg and Kleven 2004). The discrepancies between immigrants and natives get narrower with longer times of residence, but do not disappear. And as Grete Brochmann has pointed out, good welfare states do not have the time to wait for equality to occur after two, three or four generations (2004: 352). To wait is simply not a legitimate response to current problems in ambitious welfare states. They have social problems on their hands now and need to find remedies.

Immigration and integration have been big and heated issues in the public debate since the mid-1980s, stirring strong feelings and often provoking highly polarized positions. Furthermore, no issue has contributed to the cross-political sense of integration crisis in the way that gender issues have done in Norway, since the turn of the century (Hagelund 2002, 2005). Television documentaries about issues such as enforced marriages (Bredal 2004) and female genital mutilation have provoked massive outrage, as did the "honour killing" of Swedish-Kurdish Fadime Sahindal, killed by her father and brothers because she had had a Swedish boyfriend. Such stories have spurred not only big headlines but also parliamentary debates and a sense that a "rethink" on integration was necessary.

Young women are both the heroes and victims in these stories, that all revolve around dichotomies of tradition vs. modernity, force vs. freedom, family vs. individual, and foreign ways—particularly Islamic—vs. core Norwegian values. It was impossible not to be affected by the stories, both because they *were* upsetting and because a public climate developed wherein everyone was required to take a stance. Gradually the horror stories of abuse and violence were also incorporated into a more general narrative about integration failure, pivoting on a parental generation which gives priority to maintaining transnational relations with their own ethnic community, rather than focusing their efforts on gaining the knowledge necessary to succeed in Norwegian society. At the heart of this kind of discourse is a problem representation which is focused on a mixture of ignorance and unfit values within immigrant communities. And, as always, when lack of knowledge and understanding appear as the problem, education and work on people's attitudes easily come up as the solutions.

However, Islam, traditional values and ignorance are not the only villains in the tales that have emerged to explain the integration crisis. Equally to blame has been the state: the state that has failed to intervene when women's rights have been violated, the state that has failed in making demands on immigrants, the state that has failed in making integration happen. Norwegian politicians of all political persuasions have admitted shortcomings with respect to integration, and a willingness to take more drastic steps than have been taken previously.

One of the common explanations that keeps coming up for how and why things had failed is the untranslatable word *snillisme*. It is constructed by combining the adjective "kind" with the suffix "-ism"—*kind-ism*. The claim, or diagnosis, was that Norwegian politicians, policy-makers and academics had been *kindist*; that this was why integration had failed and grave injustices had been allowed to continue. *Kindism* is devising new benefit schemes, rather than telling people what they have to do for themselves. The concept has been used by right-wing liberalists, and by social democratic reformers of the welfare state. The argument is a nostalgic one. It speaks of a past where the ideal was to "do your duty and demand your right" and a present where the focus on rights has outgrown the doing of duties. Integration policy provides the "anti-kindists" with a potent example: instead of stressing what immigrants have to do— like learning Norwegian—Norwegian authorities and opinion leaders have been more concerned with securing their rights to this or that benefit.

A scholarly version of the same argument has been formulated by the social anthropologist Unni Wikan. In the poignantly titled *Generous Betrayal* she writes about the "well-meaning Scandinavian, whose cherished identity is that of world champion of all that is kind and good" (2002: 25). Through the state's efforts to be good, in the sense of respecting immigrants' culture, Wikan argues that it has ignored the situation within immigrant families where daughters have been married off by force, and where mothers, who have not been allowed to learn Norwegian and participate in society, are incapable of helping their children to succeed in Norway. According to her analysis of welfare colonialism, the Norwegian welfare state works to undermine the idea that Wikan has found so vital in the Muslim communities where she has done fieldwork: God helps the one who helps himself. That is not true in Norway, says Wikan, where he who does not help himself receives social benefits. The result is a situation where minorities systematically obtain less education, do not learn the language and are more often unemployed than the majority population—in other words, an "ethnic underclass".

The kindism argument incorporates the diverse concerns of integration—culture, gender, welfare, social equality, language skills and employment—into one explanatory narrative. However, the location of responsibility is ambiguous in many of these accounts. At one level it is placed within migrant communities as a partly cultural problem. But at another level, the responsibility for the integration crisis is located in the welfare state itself, more specifically, in its generosity and good intentions.

The Introduction Programme

Everyone blames the state; yet, it is the very same state that is called upon to sort out the mess. In this context of crisis, one of the most concrete and ambitious things the authorities have done is to introduce a compulsory introduction programme for refugees, successful asylum-applicants and their families.[1] In what we shall here be referring to as *Midtown* (along with a dozen other municipalities), such programmes have been running as pilot projects since 2000. In 2004 they became national law.

The introduction programme is to provide newcomers both with the qualifications they need to integrate successfully and with a source of income. Basically, the new law gives refugees the right, and in practice also a duty, to participate in a two-year full-time education and training programme. It has a financial and an educational component—and arguably also a third, less acknowledged, mental component.

Participants receive a monthly introduction benefit. The amount is fixed, not means-tested, meaning that work on the side is both possible and encouraged, without affecting payments. Benefits are, however, subject to attendance in the full-time introduction programme, and each class missed without legitimate reason results in reduced benefits.

Each participant has a contact person—a *primary contact*—who, in collaboration with the participant, develops an individual career plan consisting of an aim—normally a type of job—and various classes and training schemes deemed relevant to achieve this. This element of individual *tailoring* is emphasized by policy-makers and practitioners alike, but in practice, all municipalities will have a more or less limited set of classes and courses to offer, which will suit some better than others. The programme will always consist of a huge dose of language classes, and in many cases also of so-called language apprenticeships, where students spend two days a week in a specific work-place in order to pick up work-related vocabulary and get to know the Norwegian labour market. In Midtown, they also have computer courses, a women's group, a traffic course, sewing courses, job-seeking courses, courses directed specifically towards work in the health sector or in catering, as well as schemes for introducing participants to the city and civil society activities.

The programme also has a mental component in the sense that it aims to foster a certain kind of attitude to work and welfare. The economic incentive structure is designed to encourage participation, and illustrates clearly that immigrants have both rights *and* obligations. Also, in the actual teaching there is a marked emphasis on creating the motivation to work and to become financially independent.

Carol Bacchi has suggested that when we look at policies, we should ask, "What's the problem?" What are the problems that make integration policies necessary? Within every policy proposal there is an explicit or implicit diagnosis of the "problem", which we may call its *problem representation* (Bacchi 1999: 1). By asking this kind of question we can also critically address the broader understandings of society and social problems that underpin policy—the explanations and simplifications that make political action possible. So what is the problem the introduction programme is set up to remedy?

A closer reading of the reports and analyses that preceded the law reveals a problem representation founded in the idea of welfare dependency. Social assistance dependency is relatively high for refugees, even after many years of residence. This is partly caused by lower employment figures, but also by the fact that few alternative income support schemes are available to new foreign residents. They have simply not lived or worked long enough to earn the rights that would qualify them for rights-based income support, such as unemployment benefits or incapacity pensions. Instead, they rely—often for many years—on means-tested social assistance, which in theory is meant to be only short-term. However, the problem is not merely poor skills and subsequent employment problems, but the detrimental effects of being on welfare. Social assistance, particularly over time, is seen as a form of support that creates *passive* recipients. This is aptly formulated in this quote from the "introduction bill":

> The socialization of newcomers does to a too large extent consist of arguing on the basis of needs with respect to social assistance. Over time, this may result in permanent dependency on public assistance and a subsequent passive way of life for the individual. This will work to stigmatize the group in society and prevent an active participation in social life from their side.

> The Government is of the opinion that the natural starting point is that it is primarily the newly arrived immigrants themselves who are responsible for participating actively in society. The society must arrange conditions in an appropriate manner so that this may actually be possible. (Ot prp nr 28 2002–3: 7)

The introduction programme is precisely an attempt to provide such enabling conditions and, not least, to construct incentives that may make this kind of active participation come true.

Midtown: Before and After

Midtown is a medium-sized city with a well above average size immigrant population. In recent years, awareness of multicultural issues has grown in the municipality, and a number of projects have been established in order to create a positive vision of and for a *Multicultural Midtown*. One such establishment is the Introduction Centre for Foreigners, where the new introduction programme is located.

The Introduction Centre is a recent institutional creation in the city, the result of a merger between the Norwegian Language Training Centre and the former refugee section of the Social Assistance Centre. Now, this new institution is in charge of the whole reception and introduction process. Once the municipality has agreed to receive a new refugee, the centre will apply to the housing office to find accommodation for the newcomer and furnish the flat. The assigned *primary contact* will help the newcomer settle in and soon take him or her to the introduction centre to be enrolled in the introduction programme. The programme largely consists of courses offered by teachers at the Introduction Centre and supervised work placements. After two years the participant should be ready for work or further education. In practice, quite a few are instead transferred to other types of income support or training schemes, while others continue to take classes at the centre.[2]

The establishment of the Introduction Centre and of Midtown's pilot version of the introduction programme have been two sides of the same process. Some very resourceful and dedicated individuals have been involved in engineering the merger, and this is no doubt a crucial factor in its success. There is a great sense of enthusiasm at the centre. People feel they have brought about some good changes and that things are moving in the right direction. What has happened in Midtown is also, it seems to me, generally regarded as a success story in the Norwegian world of integration work— members of staff are often invited to speak at conferences, and they have been quite successful in attracting state funding for their projects. Most probably, the intentions of the introduction programme have been followed up more thoroughly here than in most other municipalities. In this sense, it may be more of a showpiece version of the introduction programme than a representative one, which makes it ideal for studying the philosophies and ideals of the programme, if not its general workings.

In 2003 and 2004, I spent time at the introduction centre, taking part in meetings and classes, interviewing, observing and chatting informally with dozens of staff and management. From the stories they told me, I got the impression of a young and confident institution, which had already developed an identity based in a narrative of "before and after", where the before chapter had a definite touch of "bad, old days".

One reason given for the restructuring of Midtown's integration work was pedagogical. They had wanted a new approach to language training that was focused more directly on the purposes of the training, namely to enable participants not only to speak the language, but also to find work and be financially self-sufficient. This implied taking a more practice-orientated approach, translated into out-of-school language apprenticeships, but also to a more practical orientation in classroom teaching with more focus on life in Norway and how to find employment, and less on grammar.

Another reason given for the merger was to remove integration work away from the sphere of social work. Primary contacts are not social workers, but make up a new type of occupational category. When recruiting new staff, management actively tries to avoid too many social workers, instead recruiting people from more diverse backgrounds. People with business experience, for example, are considered highly desirable, which is in line with the focus on employment. The merger also increased the status of the refugee workers. What used to be an understaffed subsection at the Social Assistance Centre is now part of an attractive and independent institution solely dedicated to work with refugees and immigrants.

The problem with the Social Assistance Centre was that refugees had to go there in the first place. For most newly settled refugees, it had been their only option for subsistence. The problem, according to the stories my informants told me and each other, was the sort of socialization into Norwegian life they had been offered (and here they echoed the official discourse I referred to earlier). There had been few resources to supervise and inform people on how to organize themselves. Instead, all manpower was busy paying out benefits and sorting out people's bills. One ex-social worker told me:

> *"It worked like this then that everyone is given a certain sum of money each month for what the social assistance centre calls subsistence, meant for all kinds of expenses. But with for example rent and electricity they simply give the bill to the social office, which then pays it automatically. I had a real aha-experience with a specific family who had been with us for three years and after three years he got a disability pension and she got a small job, so they no longer qualified for social benefits because their income was too high. Then came their shock when they realized that they had to pay rent. They hadn't noticed previously that there was something called rent that they had to pay. It was really bad. So this is much better now. It was very much like this, you took away their courage and motivation by saying that here is a system that looks after you and they learn it really quickly, that there is not much point, we just hand in the electricity bill so whether we switch the lights off or not or no matter how much heat we put on, it doesn't matter."*

The before-and-after narratives also include an analysis of changed attitudes among staff. The past was associated with the idea that refugees would not be able to sort out things themselves, that staff had to do it for them. In the new era, refugees were seen as capable of solving their own issues—with a little assistance. The refugees are no longer *clients* in the social system, but *participants* in the introduction programme.

One pair of concepts that staff often use to explain this change of mind is *helper* versus *supervisor*. A helper is doing things for the other and thus incapacitating him. The supervisor is teaching the other how to do things himself. A primary contact with long experience from refugee work talks about her past as a helper—with a hint of embarrassment:

Primary contact: *"It has perhaps been easy to consider the refugees as if they have started here, as if their lives began on the Norwegian border and now we need to help, and perhaps not thought so much about what resources they have taken with them from before that they can use here. They are grown-up capable people like everyone else who can manage as long as they get a little supervision, then they are OK. We don't need to run around with a screwdriver and light bulb and drive them everywhere."*

Anniken: *"Is that what happened before? Did you put in light bulbs for people?"*

Primary contact: *"Yes, I did carry a hammer and a screwdriver in my bag, I must admit I did. And a floor cloth."*

This dichotomy—helper vs. supervisor—is not one the primary contacts have come up with themselves. They have read about it in training manuals developed by the Directorate of Immigration, and it has been the focus of internal seminars at the Introduction Centre. Every week all the primary contacts meet to put forward and discuss cases that are troubling, and many of these cases revolve precisely around this balancing act, of knowing when it is acceptable to do something for the participants and when they should be left to their own devices. One of the noteworthy aspects of these meetings was how the introduction workers' desires to intervene were constantly scrutinized and problematized by themselves and others. When someone, feeling sorry for an exhausted mother, had spent time finding her a reasonable baby buggy, was that right or should the participant have done her shopping alone? It is not that helping in itself is always wrong, but when kindness motivates the action there is reason to be wary.

Controlling Kindness

The helper/supervisor dichotomy is a key discursive resource when trying to work out solutions to these dilemmas. The aim is to guide without eliminating responsibility. Introduction workers speak about the lure of helping; the temptation is always to be the helper—it is easier to help people than to supervise them. Being a helper is the default position. To become a supervisor, training, work on attitudes, and discipline are necessary. It is convenient to take on the role of the helper because it is easy to feel compassionate when encountering other human beings who have suffered and feel helpless and lost. To be a good primary contact one needs to curb this natural inclination to be a helper. In a sense, the introduction workers are busy fighting their own *kindist* instincts. A range of strategies, discursive as well as more practical, are employed to achieve the right balance.

One strategy is to explicitly emphasize the element of participants' choice and responsibility by saying "this is your choice", or "this is your responsibility". Let us look at one example: primary contact John has organized a meeting with Ahmed and Ahmed's teacher to discuss his progress. Ahmed's family has just arrived in Norway after many years of separation. Tomorrow the primary contact will meet him at the house to drive him, his wife and their eldest daughter to the girl's new school. The parents can spend the day with her there and help her to settle into her new school life. Ahmed asks: "What about our younger children?" "Well, you need to get someone to look after them", says John. Then he bites his tongue. "I mean, I should rather ask, what do you intend to do to sort out childcare?" Ahmed replies that he will call his brother and ask him to babysit. John nods approvingly: "I know that you can sort these things out yourself. You don't need me to explain to you how to do it." However, while encouraging Ahmed to find his own solutions, there are also things that John is more than happy to tell Ahmed how to do. When Ahmed expresses reluctance about doing a language apprenticeship, for example, John is very persuasive when telling him that he is ready for this challenge and that he should follow the steps set up in his individual career plan. While individual choice is encouraged, the alternatives need to be commensurate with the framework of the introduction programme.

Another method of controlling the inclination to help is to speak about the introduction programme as work and to use work as the basis for comparison in difficult cases. When discussing such cases the winning argument will often be the one that can claim similarity to how things are in the workplace. This is not surprising, given that the introduction programme can in many ways be described as an attempt to simulate working life. It aims to generate the kind of mental state that is associated with waged work as opposed to welfare dependency. Participants receive a flat-rate "wage"; there is no means-testing; rules for holiday and sick leave resemble those of working life, and work placements are a treasured part of the teaching methodology.

Another parallel to working life goes through the attendance register, also a favourite topic at staff meetings. The introduction programme is like a job, so participants are obliged to attend classes just like one is obliged to show up at work every day. The teachers are instructed to register attendance at the beginning of each lesson, and illegitimate absences should result in deduction of benefits. The teachers, however, are sometimes reluctant collaborators in this effort. Rigid attendance registering takes time, but also fits badly with teachers' ideals about adult students who should take responsibility for their own learning. Furthermore, the elaborate rules regarding legitimate and illegitimate reasons for absence do not cover all the stories teachers face in the classroom. There are so many things going on in their lives, says one teacher: children are sick, wives must be taken to the dentist because they are scared of taking buses alone, there are meetings with the immigration police, calls at the Social Security Office and appointments with the primary contacts. It is tempting to connive at their absences—tempting to be kind.

The attendance register works to discipline the participants, they must be present in order not to suffer financial sanctions, or even lose their place in the programme. But in a sense, these rules also work to discipline the teachers. They are obliged to be strict, to perform their control duties.

Teacher 1: *"There were fewer demands previously. We really feel it as teachers, that a much stronger control is imposed with respect to attendance registry, the absences should be documented and that they have consequences. For some, not all of course, it means that they lose their places. What do we think about it?"*

Anniken: *"Yes."*

Teacher 1: *"In a way it can be a double-edged sword. In a way I think it is right, it is important and it should have consequences and that is something every one must understand sooner or later. It is something we in a way are responsible for communicating also. But at the same time I see that it is not always easy for me as a teacher to keep to it that strictly for the participants I know. It is . . ."*

Teacher 2: *"It is something about us seeing the human being."*

Teacher 1: *"Yes, we see the human being."*

Teacher 2: *"We know a little about the background and we know why it happens. So then we are a little kind anyway, aren't we . . . I was much kinder before. In tutorials and meetings and such things, if they didn't come I made new appointments again and again and again, but I am much better now at saying no, you have lost that chance."*

Teacher 1: *"And I think that is good."*

Teacher 2: *"Yes, but I do feel a little bad."*

Teacher 1: *"Yes, I must admit I do too. It's something about our [students[3]]. Have they understood it? What have they understood? We do not have interpreters available normally, and we've had lessons now about how to apply for leave and the rules for attendance and what are they actually left with in their heads? We do not actually know. But at the same time, it can be a way of learning in practice which can be quite brutal."*

Teacher 2: *"But this is where they are supposed to learn it. For it is like this out there in society, so if they do not learn it here, they won't learn it."* (Emphasis added)

This quote well illustrates the double quality of kindness. It is something the introduction workers try to contain. They should not be too kind—and progress in introduction work has partly been achieved by moving away from kindness. On the other hand, the act of not being kind leaves them with a disconcerting feeling of having been "bad". This can partly be interpreted as a paternalist reaction, grounded in uncertainties about whether the refugees really understand what is best for them. But it is also an expression of compassion, based on a closeness to the actual lives and experiences of programme participants, and a sense of discrepancy between these and the formalized bureaucratic system and ideals embodied by the introduction programme. So while kindness may be bad, not being kind is not an entirely desirable option either.

While work skills and employment are crucial parts of the introduction programme, I think it is equally apt to describe it as an introduction to Norwegian welfare bureaucracies. One day, a primary contact and I took a refugee to a meeting at the social assistance centre, and afterwards the primary contact decided to take him on a little sightseeing tour in the car. It was a sightseeing tour of the welfare state. We showed him the social security office (where he should go to apply for child benefits), then to the tax office (where he should go to get his tax forms), and to the job centre (where he should go to try and find work). When the primary contacts and teachers talk about what they see as the aim of their work, they do not only talk about work and further education, in the way the official discourse does; they talk about "finding one's way around society", about "understanding how things work". For the refugees this means being able to fill in forms, to deal with the social security office, to attend parents' meetings at school, apply for a place in the kindergarten for their toddlers and book appointments with the health centre.

For the refugee workers, however, the bureaucratic character of their own institution is also a way of avoiding *kindism*. Sticking to the rules means less space for individual considerations and fewer temptations to feel sorry for people and to help more than one should. When refugees try to negotiate for more support, a better flat, a bigger fridge or more leave, the introduction workers are quite happy to be able to say, "sorry, this is the rule, there is nothing I can do". It also relieves the refugee workers of the responsibility for controlling their personal sympathies, as expressed by this primary contact:

> *"It is better then to be able to show some empathy in the situation one is in, but then to say that this is life and this is how the system is. Yes, it is actually limited, the extent to which the system will adapt to you later in life too."*

This also points to a factor which makes kindness problematic in any kind of bureaucracy: If emotions and personal sympathies are given too much space, unequal treatment and unfairness may result. More importantly, perhaps, the strict insistence on following the rules is presented as an imperative "reality check". There is a tough world out there, which the participants on the introduction programme will sooner or later have to face. In other words, the introduction programme should not be a cushioned protection against the demands of the "real world", but a simulation of it.

Why Is Being Kind So Bad? Concluding Remarks

It is noteworthy that while immigration and integration are highly contentious issues in public and political debate, the introduction programme has been introduced with hardly any debate and to universal applause. Lydia Morris (2002) reminds us that welfare rights can also be means of control. For example, many rights operate through premises of conditionality—you have the right to A (introduction benefits), but only if you fulfil condition B (participation). Within this double quality lies a considerable potential for appealing to opposite forces of claims-making. For those who are welcoming to refugees, the introduction programme represents a vigorous pull to improve refugees' lives and future chances of success in Norway. For the more sceptical crowd, it means that the authorities "finally" are doing something to "make demands" on immigrants; there is an element of force which is welcomed. Furthermore, with its strong emphasis on learning the Norwegian language and the skills deemed necessary to succeed "here", it is a far cry from multicultural celebrations of diversity or complex attempts at forging increased levels of tolerance towards foreign practices. At the same time, it is hard to argue against the value of such skills. For all parties, it is a chance of saying that they are *doing something* to tackle the problems of integration. The programme promises long-term reductions in social welfare expenditure, and it represents some of the hottest trends in improving the welfare state's efficiency (individual plans, activation). For those more concerned with refugees' welfare than state finances, the right to introduction benefits is considered preferable to means-tested social assistance. The counter-arguments that one might imagine being pertinent—such as the paternalism inherent in a programme that instructs people on what is good for them—have, so far as I have been able to register, hardly been uttered.

We have seen how the street-level introduction bureaucrats of Midtown feel that they are part of a project that is moving refugee and integration work forward. The introduction programme and the methodologies it entails are in their view an improvement on how things were done in the past, although they sometimes feel that the programme is structured on an unrealistic conception of the individual refugee's capacity. In general, though, they accept that too much kindness, as epitomized in the role of the "helper", is counterproductive and a threat to efficient introduction work. Kindness has become an embarrassment.

The changes in Norwegian integration policy and the attacks on *kindism* in the public debate can all be understood in light of what the British anthropologist Ralph Grillo has called a "backlash against diversity" (2005). This is a complex, multivocal phenomenon played out in many different ideological versions and forms on different levels. At its heart lies disenchantment with multiculturalism, concerns about social cohesion and, not least, about Islam. The question being asked with increasing strength is whether diversity threatens the unity of European societies. These concerns are raised also in Norway in multiple forms and guises by actors ranging from feminists on the left to the populist anti-immigration right, and government policies are responding to them in various ways. The introduction programme certainly appeals to those who desire more clearly defined responsibilities for newcomers, and it does respond to some of the issues presented in the kind of anti-*kindist* discourse that has quite successfully been propagated in the Norwegian public.

It could be argued that the programme deals more explicitly with welfare state concerns about inactivity and exclusion than with cultural diversity. This is true, but at the same time, the non-inclusion of immigrants in the labour market appears as a particularly troubling scenario because it generates patterns of exclusion along ethnic, cultural or religious lines, which again are seen to threaten social cohesion in a way that, say, the large number of people on incapacity benefits do not. Thus, welfare exclusion and cultural diversity can be understood as mutually reinforcing issues rather than distinct ones.

How do we understand the street-level bureaucrats' struggle to contain their own drives for kindness within this context? They are in the middle of it, to a large extent managing the results of it, but at the same time peculiarly untainted by it. According to the anti-*kindist* narrative of integration failure the welfare bureaucracies must take a large part of the blame for the crisis. The risk of being accused of racism has made welfare officials shy away from "making demands on immigrants", it is argued; they have been more concerned with being good people than with doing good work (see, for example, the anthology edited by Brox *et al.* 2003). None of my informants spoke of the risk of being labelled as racist. Their discourse was rather about encounters with genuine distress and complicated lives, where the default reaction was one of helping and being kind—reasonable enough but unproductive in the long run. Their story of change was not one of reassessing diversity, but rather of reassessing past practices. They too blame the state, as produced by their own work, but also call on it and their own renewed and professionalized efforts to save the situation.

The backlash diagnosis is not sufficient to capture the endeavour to rationalize, institutionalize and professionalize integration that the introduction programme represents, but they are related. The programme and the way it is implemented at the Introduction Centre provide the people who work there with a comprehensive professional discourse for integration work, which they seem to appreciate. There is a problem analysis of welfare dependency, aid-induced incompetence and misconceived helping, substantiated by tales of colleagues' experiences from the old Social Assistance Centre. There is a methodology based on individual plans, a language of goals, subgoals and means, and a syllabus aimed at enabling refugees to cope in a complex welfare state. The primary contacts obtain a professional role and identity as supervisors. The teachers feel part of something larger than language courses. There is an economic incentive system designed to encourage participation and self-sufficiency, which also comes with the ideological baggage and offerings of new public management. There is a legal framework in the introduction law, and a national network of support with conferences and inter-municipality meetings. This process of professionalization has equipped the introduction workers with a shared language and a shared understanding which makes it easier for them to talk about and make sense of the work they are doing. And as is so often the case, meaning is produced through contrasts, and ideas become much clearer when explained in opposition to something else. At the Introduction Centre, this opposite is the bad old days of kind helping.

Acknowledgements

An earlier version of the paper was presented at the Migration Research Seminar at Sussex University, 26 January 2005, and at the SPA conference in Bath, June 2005. Thanks to the participants for their comments. I am also grateful to the Norwegian Research Council for funding my research with grant no. 156983/540. Finally, I'd like to thank the many introduction workers who gave generously of their time during my fieldwork.

Notes

1. Family members' right to participation has since been restricted, so that those who are reunited with asylum-claimants granted residence on humanitarian grounds are no longer included in the programme.
2. One evaluation report found that of the 176 former participants who were interviewed 16.5 per cent had found work and 5.7 per cent had entered the ordinary education system (Lund 2003). This evaluation was done at an early stage and many participants had a relatively short career in the introduction programme, which may partly explain the low figures.
3. These teachers teach classes aimed at some of the weaker students.

References

Bacchi, C. (1999), *Women, Policy and Politics: The Construction of Policy Problems*, London: Sage Publications.

Blom, S. (1998), *Levekår blant ikke-vestlige innvandrere i Norge*, Reports 98/16, Oslo: Statistics Norway.

Bredal, A. (2004), "Vi er jo en familie". Arrangerte ekteskap, autonomi og fellesskap blant unge norsk-asiater. Dr. polit. thesis, University of Oslo.

Brochmann, G. (2004), Velferdsstatens utålmodighet i det flerkulturelle Norge, *Nytt norsk tidsskrift*, 3–4: 348–60.

Brox, O., Lindbekk, T. and Skirbekk, S. (eds) (2003), *Gode Formål—Gale Følger. Kritisk Lys på Norsk Innvandringspolitikk*, Oslo: Cappelen.

Djuve, A. B. and Hagen, K. (1995), *Skaff meg en jobb! Levekår blant flyktninger i Oslo*, Fafo-report no. 234, Oslo: Fafo.

Favell, A. (1998), *Philosophies of Integration: Immigration and the Idea of Citizenship in France and Britain*, Basingstoke: Macmillan/Palgrave.

Grillo, R. D. (2005), *Backlash against Diversity: Identity and Cultural Politics in European Cities*, Working paper 14, Oxford: Centre on Migration, Policy and Society. Available at: www.compas.ox.ac.uk/publications/papers/Ralph%20Grillo%20WP0514.pdf

Hagelund, A. (2002), Problematising culture: discourses on integration in Norway, *Journal of International Migration and Integration*, 3, 3–4: 401–16.

Hagelund, A. (2003), *The Importance of Being Decent: Political Discourse on Immigration in Norway 1970–2002*, Oslo: Unipax.

Hagelund, A. (2005), The Progress Party and the problem of culture: immigration politics and right wing populism in Norway. In J. Rydgren (ed.), *Movements of Exclusion: Radical Right-wing Populism in the Western World*, New York: Nova Science.

Hvenegård-Lassen, K. (2002), På lige fod. Samfundet, ligheden og Folketingets debatter om udlændingepolitik 1973–2000. PhD thesis, University of Copenhagen.

Kirkeberg, M. I. and Kleven, L. (2004), 5. Inntekt. In K. R. Tronstad (ed.), *Innvandring og innvandrere 2004*, Statistical Analyses, Oslo: Statistics Norway.

Lund, M. (2003), *Kvalifisering for alle. Utfordringer ved obligatorisk introduksjonsordning for nyankomne flyktninger*, Fafo-report no. 414, Oslo: Fafo.

Morris, L. (2002), *Managing Migration: Civic Stratification and Migrants' Rights*, London/New York: Routledge.

Olsen, B. (2004), 4. Arbeid. In K. R. Tronstad (ed.), *Innvandring og innvandrere 2004*, Statistical Analyses, Oslo: Statistics Norway.

Ot prp nr 28 (2002–3), *Om lov om introduksjonsordning for nyankomne innvandrere (introduksjonsloven)*, Oslo: Ministry of Local Government and Regional Development.

Silverman, M. (1992), *Deconstructing the Nation: Immigration, Racism and Citizenship in Modern France*, London/New York: Routledge.

Wikan, U. (2002), *Generous Betrayal: Politics of Culture in the New Europe*, Chicago/London: University of Chicago Press.

9

How Studies of the Educational Progression of Minority Children Are Affecting Education Policy in Denmark

Bjørg Colding, Hans Hummelgaard and Leif Husted

Introduction

Denmark is not a traditional country of immigration. Until the mid-1980s, immigrants accounted for less than 3 per cent of the total population (second-generation immigrants accounting for only about 0.4 per cent). However, as in many other European countries, there has been a large increase in the percentage of immigrants and their children since then. By 2004, 8.2 per cent of the total population was minority (6.3 per cent immigrants, 1.9 per cent second-generation immigrants, i.e. children of immigrants born in Denmark). Most of this increase was due to immigration from less developed countries, particularly from Turkey and Pakistan.

The increase in the presence of immigrants is a matter of social concern, because it is well documented that the unemployment rate among immigrants from less developed countries is much higher and the educational attainment of their children much lower than among native Danes. As educational qualifications are increasingly a prerequisite for employment in Denmark, the low attainment of minority youth is likely to perpetuate the weak integration of their parents into economic and social life. Hence, since minorities are projected to account for an increasing share of the population of working age, the Danish welfare state may come under pressure over and above its demographic ageing problem. Furthermore, the socio-economic differences between minorities and native Danes are likely to result in increased geographic segregation and eventually, possibly, in social unrest.

There are only a few existing European studies focusing on education and ethnic minorities (Gang and Zimmerman 2000; Riphahn 2003; Ours and Veenman 2003; Nielsen *et al.* 2003), all of which analyse educational attainment rather than educational progression. However, to formulate effective policies geared to increasing the educational attainment of minority youth, it is necessary to have a thorough understanding of where in the educational system minority youth are facing barriers to educational progression, and what factors may be affecting their educational choices at different stages.

In 2000, the Danish government appointed the Think Tank on Integration in Denmark. Its assignment was to analyse future development in the number of minorities and the social consequences of this development. This paper presents results from a number of studies prepared for the Think Tank, regarding the educational choices of minority children from less developed countries. The studies identify the main barriers to educational progression and investigate the effect of socio-economic status and other factors on educational choices.

The Danish Educational System

The Danish educational system is predominantly publicly funded and is among the most expensive in the world. Tuition is free at all levels of the system, including all universities. As depicted in figure 1, the system consists of nine years of compulsory grade school, followed by an optional tenth year of grade school, upper secondary school, and finally tertiary education. The upper secondary level is divided into one vocational and one academic track. Academic upper secondary schools qualify the student for entry into advanced education at the tertiary level, but do not qualify him/her for any particular job category. Education to provide students with formal qualifications of direct use in the labour market involves vocational upper secondary education and tertiary education. Hence vocational education is both an upper secondary education comparable to academic upper secondary education *and* a qualifying form of education comparable to a tertiary education. Tertiary-level education is usually divided into three groups according to its duration.

There are approximately 85 different vocational upper secondary educational programmes, ranging from clerical education to training in such skills as carpentry, plumbing and car mechanics. These programmes consist partly of time spent at vocational schools and partly of an apprenticeship with an employer and take between two and four years.

The state has to a large extent taken over the financial responsibility for students above the legal age of 18. The fundamental principle is that everyone 18 years of age and older is entitled to economic support from the government if they attend an eligible educational programme and are personally eligible.[1] The support is provided by the State Educational Grants and Loans Scheme. The grant is sufficient to cover living expenses and study-related expenses, including books. The grants and loans scheme is the only source of economic support of any significance for students in Denmark, since universities and other education institutions play no direct role in the financial support of students, and parental support is limited.

In 2001, some 298,100 students received student grants; of these 116,500 attended upper secondary education while 181,600 were enrolled in advanced education. The total amount disbursed was DKK 10.5 billion (equivalent to about 1.4 billion US$, or about US$ 4,700 per student recipient) which accounted for 0.77 per cent of Denmark's GDP.

Figure 1

The Danish educational system

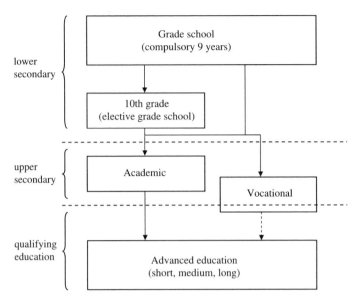

Data and Sample Characteristics

The quantitative analyses presented in this paper use two large data sets, originating from administrative registers provided by Statistics Denmark. One data set includes information about all immigrants and their children (about 396,000 individuals in 2001) for each of the years 1984–2001. The other set includes a 10 per cent random sample of the entire Danish population (about 500,000 individuals) also covering the period 1984–2001. Information is available on a wide variety of topics, including demography, labour market attachment, and educational enrolment and attainment. The analytical unit in both data sets is the individual and not the household, but for ethnic minorities, household information can be readily computed from the census.[2] For native Danes, parental information is available in a separate data set for selected cohorts of children.

Unlike survey data, administrative data from statistical registers are not susceptible to errors in reporting due to memory issues, self-presentation concerns or comprehension. Another advantage is that attrition only occurs at death or emigration. On the downside, however, administrative data do not provide the kinds of information available from clarifying behavioural questions in surveys such as reasons for dropping out of school, Danish language proficiency, religious affiliation, and expectations and ambitions.

The two samples used include native Danes and minority children, respectively, from the age of 15 and for as long as they are present in the data. The sample of minority children includes individuals born in Denmark to immigrant parents, so-called second-generation immigrants, and children who immigrated before the age of 13. The importance of age at immigration is explored by differentiating between children who immigrated at preschool age, i.e. before the age of 6, and children who immigrated at age 6 or older. Furthermore, the analyses of minority children only cover individuals from so-called less developed countries, because it is the educational attainment of children from these countries of origin which most differs from that of native Danes. These and a few additional sample selection rules (see Colding *et al.* 2004, for details of the restrictions) produce a data set containing 101,787 native Danish children, 8,065 second-generation immigrants, 5,223 immigrants who arrived in Denmark at preschool age, and 7,641 immigrants who arrived at age 6–12 years.

Empirical Evidence

Because of the longitudinal data available, it is possible to analyse the educational trajectories of individuals from when they leave grade school (typically at age 16 or 17) and thus to identify the stages of the educational system at which minority youth face barriers to progression, as well as to separate out the quantitative effects of background characteristics—such as socio-economic status—on the educational choices made. In addition, final exam grades for children leaving grade school in 2002 and 2003 have been analysed to compare the educational preparedness of native Danes and minority children. Finally, a qualitative study of children who drop out of vocational schools has been undertaken.

Educational progression

Table 1 shows that about 88 per cent of native Danes start an upper secondary education, but that age at arrival in Denmark matters for the transition rates of minority children. About 85 per cent of second-generation immigrants continue in the educational system, compared to only about 69 per cent of the immigrant children who arrived in Denmark at ages 6–12 years. Interestingly, children who arrive in Denmark during school age are more likely to choose the vocational over the academic branch, whereas over 55 per cent of the children in the other three ethnic groups (i.e. second-generation immigrants and those who arrived aged 0–5 years, as well as native Danes) choose the academic branch.

About the same share of women and men start an upper secondary education in all four ethnic groups. However, women in all ethnic groups are more likely than men to choose the academic over the vocational branch. This is particularly so among native Danes and immigrants who arrived during school age, due to the fact that a large share of men in these two groups chooses a vocational education.

The analysis also shows (figures not presented here) that substantial differences exist among children from different countries of origin. For example, the transition rates to an upper secondary education for children from Iran and Vietnam are very similar to those of native Danes, though the minority

Table 1

Transition rates from grade school to upper secondary schools by ethnic group and branch of upper secondary education

	Total	of which		N
		Academic (%)	Vocational (%)	
Native Danes				
Women	88.8	64.6	35.4	49,670
Men	87.6	46.7	53.3	52,117
All	88.2	55.6	44.4	101,787
Second-generation immigrants				
Women	86.1	59.7	40.3	3,938
Men	83.1	51.0	49.0	4,127
All	84.6	55.3	44.7	8,065
Immigrants 0–5				
Women	81.0	59.6	40.4	2,480
Men	80.6	52.1	47.9	2,743
All	80.8	55.7	44.3	5,223
Immigrants 6–12				
Women	69.1	51.7	48.5	3,518
Men	68.1	40.5	59.5	4,123
All	68.6	45.6	54.4	7,641

Source: Colding *et al.* (2004).

children are much more likely to choose the academic branch. In contrast, children from Lebanon and particularly from Turkey are less likely to start an upper secondary education at all, and are more likely then native Danes to choose the vocational branch when they do so.

As is evident from table 2, the dropout rates from both branches of upper secondary education are about twice as high for minority youth as for native Danes. However, it is the level of the dropout rates from vocational upper secondary education that is most striking. About 60 per cent of minority youth who start a vocational education drop out. The rate is similar for all three minority groups though, interestingly, the dropout rates from both branches of upper secondary education are lower for minority women than men (whereas the opposite is true for native Danes). The gender gap in dropout rates is particularly large among minority youth at vocational schools.

Socio-economic status

It is well documented that children from relatively disadvantaged families tend to have lower educational attainment (see Haveman and Wolfe 1995 for a review of the US literature). One possible explanation for the observed ethnic

Table 2

Dropout rates from upper secondary schools by ethnic group and branch of
upper secondary education

	Dropout rates	
	Academic	Vocational
Native Danes		
Women	9.1	36.4
Men	8.4	29.1
All	8.8	32.2
Second-generation immigrants		
Women	11.1	49.0
Men	16.0	65.9
All	13.4	58.0
Immigrants 0–5		
Women	14.8	50.6
Men	16.6	63.8
All	15.7	57.8
Immigrants 6–12		
Women	18.4	53.8
Men	20.3	67.1
All	19.3	61.4

Source: Colding *et al.* (2004).

differences in educational choices in Denmark could be that minority youth
come from families with lower socio-economic status, as is evident in table 3.

The table shows that the average educational attainments of minority
mothers and fathers are about 7.5 and 9.5 years, respectively, compared to
11–12 years for native Danish parents. Furthermore, the real gap in parental
educational attainment is likely to be substantially greater than this, because
the averages are only computed for individuals for whom relevant information is available. As the table shows, educational information is missing for
three-quarters of minority mothers and for between 58 and 65 per cent of
minority fathers; the reason for this is that information about education
completed abroad is not available in the administrative registers of Statistics
Denmark. So this information had to be collected by Statistics Denmark by
means of a questionnaire.[3] The response rate was only about 50 per cent—
and was particularly low among immigrants from less developed countries,
of whom many were likely to be illiterate or to have very low educational
attainment. (In the case of native Danes, educational information is missing
for about 3 and 7 per cent of fathers and mothers, respectively.)

Ethnic differences in work experience, especially of mothers, are much more
obvious. For example, the mothers and fathers of immigrants who arrived
during school age have on average worked 1 and 3.7 years respectively in

Table 3

Socio-economic background by ethnic group

	Second-generation immigrants		Immigrants (0–5)		Immigrants (6–12)		Native Danes	
	Mean	Std	Mean	Std	Mean	Std	Mean	Std
Parental background								
Educational attainment (years)								
Mother	7.7	4.8	7.7	5.4	7.4	5.3	11.2	3.1
Father	9.6	3.9	9.6	4.1	9.4	4.3	12.0	3.3
Missing educational data (%)								
Mother	65.1	—	66.9	—	67.7	—	2.8	—
Father	58.4	—	59.6	—	65.4	—	7.5	—
Work experience (years)								
Mother	4.9	4.6	2.8	3.6	1.0	2.3	11.1	7.0
Father	10.9	6.3	6.8	5.9	3.7	5.7	16.0	8.5
Duration of stay in Denmark (years)								
Mother	17.8	4.6	11.6	3.7	5.4	3.2	n/a	n/a
Father	20.0	4.8	13.7	6.1	8.3	6.6	n/a	n/a
Neighbourhood characteristics								
Disadvantaged neighbourhood (%)								
	14.2	—	22.7	—	25.9	—	1.2	—

Denmark, compared to 4.9 and 10.9 years for the parents of second-generation immigrants and 11.1 and 16 years for native Danish parents. However, the table also shows that the duration of stay in Denmark varies substantially among the minority groups.

Finally, an important feature of the socio-economic background of the ethnic groups is the proportion living in a disadvantaged neighbourhood; about one-quarter of the immigrant children live in a disadvantaged neighbourhood compared to only 1 per cent of the native Danes.

Minority youth thus come from more disadvantaged backgrounds than their native Danish peers. Nevertheless, surprisingly, Colding *et al.* (2004) conclude that although the socio-economic status of minority youth may significantly affect their transition rates from grade school to upper secondary education, it has very little effect on their dropout rates thereafter.

Educational preparedness

The level of educational preparedness acquired in grade school is undoubtedly very important for the subsequent educational achievement of a student. One measure of educational preparedness is the exam grades a student gets at the end of grade school. Unfortunately, information on individual-level exam grades is only available from 2002 on, and could thus not be included in the statistical analysis presented above.

However, a recent study (Colding 2005) shows that the grades obtained by minority youth from less developed countries in the five core subjects (written maths, oral maths, written Danish, oral Danish, Danish spelling) are much lower than among native Danes. In particular, immigrant children who arrived in Denmark during school age have substantially lower grades than the two other minority groups—and immigrants who arrived in Denmark at age 0–5 years actually do slightly better than second-generation immigrants. In all the ethnic groups, women do better than men in the three Danish topics, while men do slightly better than women in the two maths topics.

In fact, the ethnic differences in grades are likely to be substantially larger than reported in the study, because—as the study itself points out—a larger share of minority children leave grade school without taking the final exams. It seems reasonable to assume that it is the academically weaker students who (with the consent of their parents) opt out of the exams. (It is possible to leave grade school without taking the exams in Denmark because, though students have nine years of compulsory education, final exams are elective.)

The lower grades being achieved by minority youth—particularly by those immigrants who arrived in Denmark during school age—suggest that their educational preparedness is much lower than that of their native Danish peers, which may, at least in part, explain the difference in dropout rates at the upper secondary level. Results from the Danish PISA[4] 2003 study (Mejding 2004) corroborate this conclusion. The study concluded that about 50 per cent of minority youth did not have sufficient reading and writing proficiency to complete an upper secondary education successfully. The figure for native Danes was about 20 per cent.

Mechanisms underlying dropout

To further investigate the very high dropout rates from vocational schools, a qualitative study (Højmark Jensen and Tovby Jørgensen 2005) was undertaken. Interviews were conducted with guidance counsellors at vocational schools and municipalities as well as with minority dropouts, minority youth who had completed a vocational education, minority parents, native Danish youth, and representatives from private companies which hire apprentices.

Inadequate Danish language proficiency was identified as a very important direct and indirect reason for the high dropout rates among minorities. For many minority youth, Danish is their second language; it is not spoken at home because their parents are not proficient in Danish. Minority students thus enter grade school with low Danish proficiency, and this negatively affects learning and consequently the students' educational achievement. The combination of low language proficiency and low educational achievement implies, in turn, that many minority students form social networks exclusively with other minority students, with whom they communicate in the language of their parents' country of origin. Consequently, minority students may leave grade school functionally illiterate in the Danish language.

The inadequate Danish language proficiency of minority parents also implies that they are unable to help their children with homework or provide the necessary guidance with regard to educational choices and opportunities, because the parents are unable to acquire sufficient knowledge for themselves about the institutional structure of the Danish educational system. These adverse effects of minority parents' language skills on minority children's educational performance are further reinforced by the low educational attainment and the low labour market integration of the parents. Female respondents also mention that noise at home, from younger siblings and family conflicts, negatively affects their homework and thus contributes to any decision to drop out of vocational school.

To counter this "negative intergenerational transmission" from disadvantaged parents to their children (minority as well as native Danish), guidance counsellors are available in grade schools and at the municipal level. However, the study shows that minority children are less likely to use the services of the guidance counsellors. Another possible source of support and guidance for minority youth could be from their Danish peers and their parents—but, as already mentioned, social networks tend to be ethnically divided.

Then again, it seems that minority youth do not merely start vocational education at a disadvantage, but that some of this disadvantage carries over into vocational schools. For example, the curriculum includes academic subjects such as English, Danish and maths. This comes as a surprise to many minority students, who have chosen a vocational over an academic upper secondary education precisely because they did not do well in academic studies at grade school.

In addition, group work and project-based learning are important educational instruments at vocational schools. Low educational preparedness from grade school and inadequate language proficiency imply that minority students tend to form groups, both in and out of class, with other minority students. This division widens the gap between themselves and the native Danes, who generally do better academically and have more resources. Furthermore, because Denmark is not a traditional immigration country, knowledge of and experience with bilingual education is limited. Consequently, teachers and guidance counsellors generally do not have adequate training in the cultural and linguistic aspects of teaching and interacting with minority youth.

Finally, another important barrier to the successful completion of a vocational education—as identified by the study—relates to the apprenticeship market. Overall, the supply of apprenticeships is smaller than the demand. According to the respondents interviewed from private companies, there is a perception that it is more costly for the firm to hire a minority apprentice; this is due to possible social problems with the other native Danish employees or to loss of business if clients are unwilling to deal with a minority employee. In any case, a minimum requirement for hiring a minority apprentice is that s/he speaks Danish fluently. Consequently, minority students are at a disadvantage, since firms are more likely to reject their application. Lastly, many apprenticeship positions are filled with students who have a recommendation from someone in their family network. Since the unemployment rate is very high among immigrants, this again puts the minority student at a disadvantage.

Policy Changes

Based on the studies reviewed above, the government has already implemented a number of new policy instruments to reduce the dropout rate of minority youth at vocational schools. Minority youth will in the future be offered lessons in Danish as a second language at the vocational schools; incoming minority students will be offered a mentor who is an older minority student at the school; and vocational schools with large numbers of minority students will target their efforts to ensure these students obtain an apprenticeship with a private company. In addition, a task force has been appointed to investigate the possibility of restructuring the curriculum in vocational schools, to emphasize the vocational aspects of the study more in the early stages, so as to avoid putting off less academically inclined students.

To improve the Danish language proficiency of minority children, the language stimulation of both preschool and school-age children with inadequate Danish skills is now mandatory in kindergartens and grade schools. In addition, a bill has recently been presented in parliament to strengthen the teaching of Danish as a second language in grade schools. Finally, the system of educational guidance has been reformed to improve the quality and to put more emphasis on disadvantaged youth, including minority youth.

Still, the studies reviewed have pointed to a number of additional policy changes that could play an important role in reducing dropout rates from vocational schools among minority youth in Denmark.

Policy recommendations

The government has implemented a number of initiatives to strengthen minority students' Danish language skills. However, far from all teachers have the necessary training in and knowledge of the special pedagogy involved in teaching Danish as a second language and in bilingual education in general. In consideration of the fact that the number of bilingual students in grade schools will increase rapidly over the coming years, there is a need for teaching in Danish as a second language and bilingual education to form an obligatory part of teacher training.

Research from Canada and the USA (referenced in Egelund 2003) shows that mother-tongue teaching has a positive effect on knowledge acquired at school in general. Mother-tongue teaching can reinforce and build on what children already know. Regrettably, the present government has cut back the financial support for mother-tongue education carried out by the municipalities.

Two other important policy instruments to improve educational achievement of minority children and other disadvantaged children are help with homework at school and supplementary classes after school hours. In the education literature, "parenting practices"—or, more narrowly, parental involvement in children's learning and schooling—are identified as important determinants of educational achievement (Esther and Willms 1996). Minority parents with poor Danish skills and low integration in economic and social life are poorly equipped to help their children with their schoolwork. Help with homework at school and supplementary classes would therefore be an obvious mode of compensation, as is proposed in the government's most recent integration plan.

In this context, there could also be a need for strengthening educational and vocational guidance in the schools, aimed especially at students whose parents have inadequate knowledge of Danish society and the Danish educational system. The counselling reform implemented by the government in 2004 aims at this, but it remains to be seen how effective the reform will be at reaching minority students.

The lack of apprenticeships for minority youth in particular at vocational upper secondary education is one of the most serious barriers to completing vocational education. Because many enterprises expect it to be more costly to offer an apprenticeship to a minority than a native Danish young person, it may be beneficial to provide enterprises which hire a minority apprentice with an economic subsidy.

Better counselling of students who are about to apply for an apprenticeship is needed to motivate minority students to write applications and to search actively. For example, counsellors should help students formulate applications that more effectively stress the qualities that the enterprises value highly and that are written in a satisfactory Danish, to avoid falling through the employers' round of first elimination. Counsellors should also encourage students to attach a personal recommendation from a teacher, to improve their chances of getting an interview.

Some enterprises have found that the minority apprentice finds it difficult to adapt to the unwritten rules of the workplace and the colloquial language used among craftsmen, particularly at construction sites. It would, therefore, also be an advantage if classes in "general conventions at the workplace" were set up at vocational schools. It would probably also be advantageous to introduce a mentor scheme at the workplace so that one of the staff at the enterprise becomes responsible for introducing the apprentice to the work culture there.

At the vocational schools, there would, in addition, seem to be a need for the teachers to be actively involved in forming the social networks between students by, for example, putting together project groups cutting across ethnic group lines and academic qualifications. Working together with native Danish students might be expected to have a positive effect on both the minority student's educational achievement and their social lives, and in this way improve their integration at the study programme. Research shows (Rangvid 2003) that academically weak pupils generally do better if they are in the same class with academically strong pupils, without any resulting impairment of the proficiency of the strongest.

It appears, moreover, that some teachers in the vocational study programmes lack the necessary pedagogical competencies and knowledge of foreign cultures to teach minority youth. This points to a need for the supplementary training of teachers, focusing on how to communicate with minority youth, how to handle culture-specific problems, and how to strengthen the student's self-esteem by focusing and building on his/her resources in the classroom. In this context, it would be an advantage to appoint more teachers with a foreign background who know the special needs of the young foreigners and can function as role models for them.

Concluding Remarks

Ensuring that more minority youth secure educational qualifications is high on the political agenda in Denmark. This was expressed most recently in a new plan for integration presented by the government in the spring of 2005. The empirical studies reviewed in this paper suggest a number of policy instruments at different stages of the educational system to improve the educational achievement of minority youth. Some have already been implemented by the government.

The focus of the instruments discussed is to counter the negative effects of minority children's socio-economic background, i.e. to interrupt the intergenerational transmission from parent to child, and thus target the children rather than the family. However, it is also important to focus attention on how well the parents are integrated, because efforts to improve the social and economic well-being of the parents will also benefit their children.

Notes

1. For the 18- and 19-year-olds who are attending an upper secondary school, the support depends on parental income; for all others the support is independent of parental income.
2. However, information about family members who have not resided in Denmark from 1984 to 2001 is not available.
3. The questionnaire was sent to all immigrants who were 18–59 years old on 1 January 1999, who were 16 years old or above when they first came to Denmark and had not completed a qualifying education in Denmark at the time of the survey.
4. The OECD's Programme for International Student Assessment (PISA) is an internationally standardized assessment that was jointly developed by participating countries and administered to 15–16-year-olds in schools. Most recently, tests were administered to 4,200 students in Denmark in 2003.

References

Colding, B. (2005), En sammenligning af udlændinges og danskeres karakterer fra folkeskolens afgangsprøver og på de gymnasiale uddannelser. In *Tænketanken om udfordringer for integrationsindsatsen i Danmark, Udlændinge på ungdomsuddannelserne—frafald og faglige kundskaber*, Copenhagen: Ministry for Refugee, Immigration and Integration Affairs.

Colding, B., Hummelgaard, H. and Husted, L. (2004), Indvandreres og efterkommeres uddannelse. In *Tænketanken om udfordringer for integrationsindsatsen i Danmark, Udlændinges vej gennem uddannelsessystemet*, Copenhagen: Ministry for Refugee, Immigration and Integration Affairs.

Egelund, N. (2003), *Bilinguals and Danish Speakers—Differences between Academic and Social Skills for 15–16 Year-Olds*, Copenhagen: Danish University of Education Press. (In Danish)

Esther Ho Sui-Chu and Willms, J. D. (1996), Effects of parental involvement on eighth-grade achievement, *Sociology of Education*, 69, 2: 126–41.

Gang, I. N. and Zimmermann, K. L. (2000), Is child like parent? Educational attainment and ethnic origin, *Journal of Human Resources*, 35: 550–69.

Haveman, R. and Wolfe, B. (1995), The determinants of children's attainments: a review of methods and findings, *Journals of Economic Literature*, 33: 1829–78.

Højmark Jensen, U. and Tovby Jørgensen, B. (2005), Det vigtigste i livet er at få en uddannelse—undersøgelse af etniske minoritetsunges frafald fra erhvervsuddannelserne. In *Tænketanken om udfordringer for integrationsindsatsen i Danmark, Udlændinge på ungdomsuddannelserne—frafald og faglige kundskaber*, København: Ministeriet for flygtninge, indvandrere og integration.

Mejding, J. (ed.) (2004), *PISA 2003—Danske unge i en international sammenligning*, akf, Danmarks Pædagogiske Universitet og Socialforskningsinstituttet.

Ministry for Refugee, Immigration and Integration Affairs (2005), *Foreigners in Youth Education Programmes: Dropout and Academic Skills*, Copenhagen. (In Danish, English summary.)

Nielsen, H. S., Rosholm, M., Smith, N. and Husted, L. (2003), The school-to-work transition of the 2nd generation immigrants in Denmark, *Population Economics*, 16: 755–86.

Ours, J. C. van and Veenman, J. (2003), The educational attainment of second-generation immigrants in the Netherlands, *Journal of Population Economics*, 16: 739–53.

Rangvid, B. S. (2003), Do schools matter? The influence of school inputs on student performance and outcomes. PhD dissertation no. 2003:9, Aarhus School of Business.

Riphahn, R. T. (2003), Cohort effects in the educational attainment of second-generation immigrants in Germany: an analysis of census data. *Population Economics*, 16: 711–37.

10

New Destinations? Assessing the Post-migration Social Mobility of Minority Ethnic Groups in England and Wales

Lucinda Platt

Introduction

According to the 2001 Census, minority ethnic groups made up just under 9 per cent of the population of England and Wales. These minority groups show diversity in terms of whether they were born in Britain or migrated here (in childhood or adulthood), in their origins and migration histories, and in their current demographic, social class, educational, geographical and economic profiles. For some researchers, the unexplained differences between minorities and the majority are regarded as direct evidence of discrimination (e.g. Blackaby *et al.* 2002); for others, the differences are regarded as an ethnic penalty (or, perhaps more properly, as ethnic penalties) of which at least a part can be put down to discrimination, but where other, unobserved differences—including in migration histories—may also be playing a part (Heath and McMahon 1997). It remains to be seen, however, what are the relative contributions of within-Britain experiences (including discrimination), separately from the contribution of diverse origins and histories and the different combinations of those origins and histories to particular occupational and educational patterns.

This paper addresses that topic in two parts. The first examines the current state of knowledge and theory in relation to the diversity in social class outcomes between Britain's ethnic groups, thus setting up points of reference and potential explanatory frameworks for the empirical analysis which follows. It summarizes the legal and social context of the migrant generation, in order to clarify the context experienced by migrants in this period (which includes the parents of those minority group members in the empirical study that follows), as well as providing a broad picture of patterns of migration. This enables some sense to be made of the differences in origins explored and discussed in the empirical analyses. This first part then examines diversity within the "second generation", from whom the minority group members in the study are drawn. It draws on a range of sources to illustrate the experiences of different minority groups in relation to education and employment in the 1990s, and the ways these differences have been accounted for. Commentators have not, though, been able to support explanations with empirical evidence that directly relates parents' backgrounds to the second generation's outcomes. This is the unique contribution that the empirical analysis in the second part of the paper has to offer.

The second section presents analyses of representative survey data for England and Wales, following individuals from 1971 to 2001. It examines the backgrounds of children born between 1956 and 1967 and growing up in England and Wales in 1971, and relates this background information to study members' outcomes measured at 1991 and again in 2001, capturing their progress into adulthood and through the labour markets of the 1980s and 1990s. The analyses attempt to separate out the effect of the migration histories of the children's parents from the study members' own experience of growing up in Britain. The analysis presents results for four different "ethnic groups".

The determination of an ethnic group is much discussed and contested in the ethnicity literature (see e.g. Weber 1978; Barth 1969; Cornell and Hartman 1998; Rex and Mason 1986; Ratcliffe 1994; Platt forthcoming). It is, however, constrained in the secondary analysis of survey data by the classification schemes used by those surveys. In England and Wales these have followed the Census categories: using or adapting first the 1991 Census question from the beginning of the 1990s and subsequently the 2001 Census question from 2001. The 1991 question has been subject to extensive criticism (e.g. Ballard 1997; see also Salt 1996; Ratcliffe 1996), including the claim that "what is clear about the census ethnic group question is that the one thing it does not measure is ethnicity" (Ratcliffe 1996: 5; see also Karn et al., 1997). Similar criticisms could be made about the 2001 Census. However, in practice, despite some modifications in surveys (e.g. the introduction of an East African Asian category into the 1993 PSI survey; Modood et al. 1997) and some refining of the definitions and categories in smaller-scale qualitative studies, the Census categories largely determine what we know and can investigate in relation to Britain's ethnic groups.

Accounting for Diversity: An Overview

Background: migration to Britain up to 1971

Migrants who arrived in Britain before 1971—and who therefore correspond to the parents' generation of the study sample analysed in the second section, below—had experienced to a greater or lesser extent the shift from the inclusive tenor of the 1948 Nationality Act to increasing controls on entry and settlement (and a high degree of politicization of these issues) up to the 1971 Act which, together with the British Nationality Act of 1981 (and despite some modifications since), forms the main source of law in relation to immigration (Supperstone and O'Dempsey 1994).

During the period of postwar reconstruction, migrant labour was eagerly sought from within Europe; at the same time, anxiety about immigration from non-white colonies and former Commonwealth countries preceded any substantial immigration from them (Solomos 1989). Nevertheless, the freedom of British subjects freely to enter and settle in Britain was enshrined in the 1948 Nationality Act, and in the following years some industries actively sought labour from the Caribbean and India. However, the growth of Britain's established minority ethnic groups, where it has occurred at all, has been, since the 1970s, predominantly through reproduction rather than primary immigration. Nowadays, the majority of British Caribbeans and British Indians originating in India rather than East Africa are British-born.

The first restrictions on immigration of British nationals came with the Commonwealth Immigrants Act 1962, which introduced a voucher system to limit entry for those wishing to exercise their Commonwealth right to settle in the UK. In the late 1950s immigration had been taking place at a low annual rate, which appeared to be declining (Evans 1983), but the introduction of the Act resulted in a rush to beat the bill by those wishing to exercise their citizenship rights before they disappeared. Thereafter, immigration from the Caribbean was practically at an end, while immigration from the Indian subcontinent largely took the form of chain migration and later, following further restrictions, was mainly family reunification.

Despite the limitations imposed by the 1962 Act, access to Britain remained possible for those UK passport-holders who had no alternative citizenship when their countries of residence gained independence. The majority of those in this position were East African Asians. On Kenyan independence in 1963, some of the Asian population gained Kenyan citizenship automatically, some registered for it, and some retained their CUKC (Citizen of the United Kingdom and Colonies) status. The Kenyan government began to impose restrictions on those without Kenyan citizenship, culminating in the legislation of 1967 which effectively removed their right to be in Kenya, and during 1965–7 roughly 6,000 Kenyans a year took up their right to live in Britain. The 1968 Commonwealth Immigrants Act, introduced in direct response to the arrival of such nationals, required ancestral links to the UK for settlement, despite the fact that by doing so it removed the right of abode from those who did not have that right elsewhere. Later East African expulsions (i.e. from Uganda in 1972) were accepted only in terms of international obligations to the stateless rather than rights of residence for holders of passports that were nominally British (but this was after 1971, the cut-off for the sample in this study).

The period up to 1971 also saw the first Race Relations acts. The first was in 1965, when the Labour government developed a formulation to explain its change of heart over reversing the 1962 Commonwealth Immigrants Act: strict immigration control was presented as part of "good race relations". Covering only access to public amenities such as hotels and swimming baths, it was followed by the 1968 Race Relations Act, which made discrimination in housing or employment unlawful. According to Hepple (1992), the second Act was an attempt to compensate for the 1968 Commonwealth Immigrants Act and served again to link "good race relations" to tight immigration policy. A third Race Relations Act was passed in 1976, modelled on the sex discrimination legislation of the previous year. This remained the basis of race relations legislation till it was strengthened by the 2000 Race Relations Amendment Act.

Diversity among minority ethnic groups in the 1990s

The diversity of outcomes for minority ethnic groups is now well known (e.g. Modood *et al.* 1997; Parekh 2000; Platt 2002). This section highlights some of the crucial differences that are pertinent to understanding the analysis. It focuses on Indians and Caribbeans, two of the three minority groups who are central to the analysis in the next section and for whom (unlike the white migrant group) information is typically available, with comparisons to the white majority.

In terms of occupational success, attainment of professional jobs by Indians (and Chinese) has been noted. Almost one in five Indians was employed in professional occupations in 2001, with one in 20 Indian men being a doctor (National Statistics 2004). This compared with just over one in ten white British men in professional occupations. Caribbeans had rates of professionals that were even lower than the white British; and the patterns across groups were similar for managers. While the high unemployment rates of Pakistanis and Bangladeshis have been a particular source of concern, Caribbeans, too, typically have well above average rates of unemployment: in 2002/3 these were, for men, around 13 per cent in Great Britain, around three times those of white British men (5 per cent). Indian men's unemployment rates were substantially lower than their Caribbean counterparts, but still higher than the average at around 7 per cent (National Statistics 2004). Indian women's unemployment was comparable to Indian men's while white women's was around 4 per cent, one percentage point lower than white men's. However, Caribbean women's unemployment levels were substantially lower than Caribbean men's, though still higher than white women's. Caribbean women tend to show a distinctive profile in the labour market as well as in educational terms compared to other groups (Modood *et al.* 1997; Platt 2002).

Ethnic minorities' labour market disadvantage has been linked to a range of factors: demographic profiles, in that young people have the highest rates of unemployment (e.g. Berthoud 1999; National Statistics 2004); geographical distributions, and thus impacts of local labour markets; concentrations in particular sectors of employment (Platt 2002); and educational achievement. When these have been accounted for, a gap still remains, however, and "ethnic minorities have to be not just as good as but better than their white competitors to get the job" (Modood 1997: 145). Similarly, Blackaby *et al.* (2002) concluded that once other relevant factors had been taken account of, there was evidence of persistent discrimination in both pay and unemployment, which was as significant in the 1990s as in the 1970s and was affecting the British-born generation as much as the migrant generation.

When it comes to exploring differences between minority groups rather than between minority and majority, extensive attention has been paid to educational outcomes. Table 1 shows the distribution in the mid-1990s. The high proportions of Indian men with higher qualifications and of unqualified Caribbean men are apparent. These patterns partly reflect different demographic profiles.

Table 1

Proportions of working-age people at different qualifications levels by ethnic group,
average for 1996–8

	Higher qualification (%)	Other qualification (%)	No qualification (%)
All			
White	22	61	16
Caribbean	19	62	19
Indian	25	57	18
Men			
White	22	62	14
Caribbean	15	62	23
Indian	29	57	15
Women			
White	21	60	19
Caribbean	22	62	16
Indian	20	58	22

Source: Adapted from B. Twomey, Labour market participation of ethnic groups, *Labour Market Trends*, January 2001, table 2, p. 31.

Turning to contemporary outcomes, after Chinese children, Indian girls were most likely to achieve five or more GCSEs at C grade or above, with 70 per cent of them doing so and 58 per cent of Indian boys (National Statistics 2004). At the other end of the spectrum, 38 per cent of Caribbean girls and only 23 per cent of Caribbean boys achieved such levels of qualifications in 2002. Education is often seen as the key to occupational success. The puzzle then comes in understanding why educational achievement should vary so widely between minority groups, with explanations varying from those highlighting different expectations and aspirations within the groups to those focusing on school systems which act on (and thus perpetuate) stereotypes regarding potential achievement. It has also been argued that some groups may have more resources to support their children's education, through their own levels of human capital, through mobilizing their networks, or through prioritizing the success of the second generation over current well-being.

The analysis in the next section attempts to explore whether we can locate ethnic groups' differential potential for success within education and considers how that relates to other resources. Moreover, the pattern of GCSE results at 16 is not the full story. There is substantial evidence that some minority group members remain in education for longer periods, not just gaining higher qualifications, but also "catching up" to compensate for underachievement during school years. Another possible reason for staying on is awareness of the difficult conditions ahead: "an expectation of discrimination in the labour market may encourage some ethnic minority young people to stay longer in education than they would otherwise do with the aim of increasing their competitiveness in the labour market" (Pathak 2000: 8). It is therefore important to examine whether there is evidence of occupational catch-up.

Arguments to explain diversity between minority groups

Several explanations have been put forward to account for both differences between generations of the same ethnic group in a particular country and the long-term outcomes of different ethnic groups. It is argued that the migrant generation can be expected to differ from the succeeding generation, born and brought up in the country of immigration, in a number of ways, within which the migrant's migration history and own characteristics are given different degrees of attention.

Initially, lack of networks and familiarity with the "host" community can be expected to depress the occupational achievement of the migrants, relative to their skills and education. This may be exacerbated if the migration was forced rather than voluntary. In this model, assimilation leads to the second generation being much closer to their peers from the host community in educational and occupational terms. This assimilation model is particularly associated with the USA, and with Park in particular (Park 1950; see also Alba and Nee 1997; Gordon 1964). While, at the institutional and analytical level, assimilation has been less fully endorsed in British accounts, there has been a related argument for the "recovery" of the underlying or latent class position of the first generation in the second generation (e.g. Modood 1997; see also Heath and McMahon 1999 for a consideration of the international salience of higher class origins). This has been used in particular to explain the high levels of achievement of Indians and African Asians in successive generations.

On the other hand, migrants are acknowledged to be a selected sample. They may have particular motivation that caused them to migrate in the first place, but not pass this directly on to their children. Thus, the second generation might fare worse than their parents in occupational terms, particularly if the children find that being born and bred in a country does not exempt them from racism and discrimination. The poor health status of certain minority groups in Britain has, on occasion, been discussed in these terms (e.g. Marmot *et al.* 1984; Nazroo 1997).

A perspective which amalgamates elements of the two discussed is one which suggests that the crucial differentiating factor between groups is the aspiration and determination to succeed, despite a sometimes hostile environment, that certain migrant parents bring with them and transmit to their children (e.g. Modood 2004; Archer and Francis forthcoming). This view, without endorsing a beneficent assimilation process, nevertheless locates potential for relative success within the second generation, but links it to particular, selected characteristics of the parents. In particular, parental commitment to education and to achieving upward mobility through education is regarded as critical.

Finally, there has been some attention paid to geographical factors in mediating the possibilities and therefore outcomes of the second generation.

It has been argued that, in so far as location of initial settlement varies by migrant group, it is likely to result in systematic differences in the experiences of different ethnic minorities in the longer term (Galster *et al.* 1999; see also Dorsett 1998).

In the British context the complexity of the issue and practical constraints of measurement and investigation have limited the possibilities for adjudicating between these explanations. Which account best describes relative positions in the course of the transition from "immigrant groups to new ethnic minorities" (Castles 2000) can shift with the way the first and second generations are defined, and according to which ethnic group is the principal focus of interest.

There are few British sources which can directly relate minority group parents' and children's outcomes. Therefore, for the purpose of understanding change across time and between groups and developing inferences, "first" and "second" generations are usually constructed from cross-sections of minority groups at particular time points (e.g. Modood 1997; Robinson 1990). Obviously, in such cases the "first generation" are not, strictly speaking, the parents of the "second generation", and the probability that the two even approximate migrant parents and their British-born children will vary with ethnic group (and migration histories). If ethnic groups are still forming and expanding, then the later time point will capture new migrants as well as the "second generation". If the group is subject to substantial return or onward migration, many of the potential second generation from the first time point will have been lost. Moreover, the point in their career at which they are measured will contribute to whether upward mobility is observed or not, with those who are younger overall being less likely to have reached their final class destination. In addition, the stage at which "success" is achieved may vary by ethnic group: substantial investment in education may produce later returns. While it is of inherent interest to observe the changing profile of a group over time by examining succeeding cross-sections, it is more difficult to make confident claims about the processes involved in shaping those profiles.

There have been two attempts to explore ethnic group differences in mobility between parents and children directly (Heath and Ridge 1983; Heath and McMahon 1999). However, the former considered the migrant's parents' class in the country of origin and their children's occupational situation in Britain, and in the latter it was not possible to distinguish processes of migration (and factors outside Britain) from those operating within Britain.

There is therefore a gap in our understanding of the precise relationship between parental origins and diversity in minority groups outcomes when considering those for whom other circumstances are held in common, i.e. parental class is observed within Britain and the children have experienced common educational structures and entered similar labour markets. It is this gap which the ensuing analysis aims to fill.

Intergenerational Social Class and Social Class Background among Four Ethnic Groups 1971–1991/2001

This study is novel in its empirical examination of the relative impact of migration history and relationship to wider British society for a set of minority

Figure 1

Tracking individuals from different ethnic groups over time and linking them
to parents' backgrounds

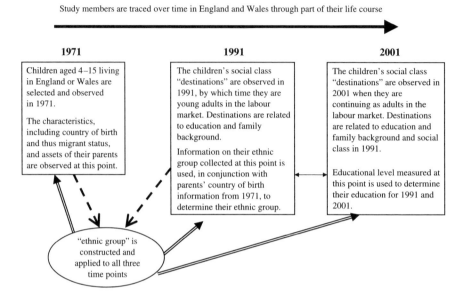

Study members are traced over time in England and Wales through part of their life course

1971

Children aged 4–15 living in England or Wales are selected and observed in 1971.

The characteristics, including country of birth and thus migrant status, and assets of their parents are observed at this point.

1991

The children's social class "destinations" are observed in 1991, by which time they are young adults in the labour market. Destinations are related to education and family background.

Information on their ethnic group collected at this point is used, in conjunction with parents' country of birth information from 1971, to determine their ethnic group.

2001

The children's social class "destinations" are observed in 2001 when they are continuing as adults in the labour market. Destinations are related to education and family background and social class in 1991.

Educational level measured at this point is used to determine their education for 1991 and 2001.

"ethnic group" is constructed and applied to all three time points

groups of the same age and growing up in the same temporal and geographical context—England and Wales in the 1960s and 1970s. The ONS Longitudinal Study data used in this study are the only ones that enable the
systematic tracking of individuals from different ethnic groups over time and
therefore of relating their childhood context to their occupational and social
class outcomes in adulthood (by contrast with the large-scale cross-sectional
surveys on Britain's ethnic groups used by Daniel 1968; Smith 1977; Brown
1984; Modood *et al.* 1997). This tracking over time and linking to migration
background is illustrated in figure 1.

The longitudinal approach provides a unique handle on the extent to
which there is diversity within members of minority groups once we both
hold their backgrounds constant and constrain the time-point at which, and
the country in which, those origins are measured. It allows a way of determining which aspects of the diversity of Britain's ethnic minorities can be
explained through an examination of the backgrounds of the "second generation", and how these backgrounds intersect with the study members' own
life courses, including educational achievement and marriage, and with the
economic and social circumstances within which they find themselves (e.g.
periods of high versus periods of low unemployment). It therefore indicates
which speculative explanatory frameworks and theories are supported by
empirical evidence, and which questions remain unanswered and invite
further investigation and analysis.

The groups selected—and constructed—for the purpose of this analysis have been based on the study members' self-identification in relation to the 1991 Census question. Of the nine main minority groups that were classified and measured by that question, this study focuses on the two largest and those which experienced the majority of their migration before 1971 (the point at which the study sample is selected): Indians and Caribbeans. It should be emphasized that it is the study members' own identification as Indian or Caribbean[1] in 1991 that is used, rather than that of their parents. It is therefore assumed that they retain this identification throughout the period observed (i.e. from 1971 to 1991 and on to 2001). Although ethnicity is not a fixed characteristic, and identification with a category can change over time (Platt *et al.* 2005), the only way we can talk about outcomes over time for groups is to make the assumption of stability for individuals.

The Indian and Caribbean groups constructed for this study are further restricted by the condition that at least one of the parents of the Indian or Caribbean child was born outside the UK. This ensures that they came from a migrant background, with the implications of original motivation to migrate, adjustment to a new society and potential downward mobility on migration that that implies. A reference group was created from those who identified as white at the 1991 Census and for whom neither of their co-resident parents was born outside the UK (called "white non-migrant" in this study). A fourth, composite group was constructed from those who identified as white in 1991 but where both co-resident parents were born outside the UK. Although comprising a range of white ethnicities, this group was constructed to identify whether migrant effects could be observed and separated from processes experienced uniquely by "non-white" minorities (cf. Heath and Ridge 1983).

Approach

The initial analysis is designed to explore whether we can observe a migration effect for the parents of the cohort under study. The analysis ascertains whether the experience of the white migrants is distinct from that of the white non-migrants, the Indians and the Caribbeans, in terms of their social class origins. It considers whether, in exploring apparent downward mobility following migration to Britain, there is an additional, colour-related discrimination effect, or whether ethnic-group-specific effects cannot be understood in such terms.

Drawing on standard social mobility analyses of the relationship between parents' class (the child's origins) and the grown-up children's achieved class (the child's destinations), subsequent analyses attempt to unpick what patterns a "non-discrimination" scenario would show in terms of the relationship between the group members' origins and their own outcomes. The analysis explores different probabilities of "success", measured as attainment of a professional or managerial class position in 1991, across groups; and it examines the role of education in mediating—or explaining—such success. It questions how far the results, in terms of comparison with the "non-discrimination" scenario, indicate the persistence of group-specific "ethnic penalties".

The final section of the analysis explores whether there is evidence that the level and nature of "ethnic penalties" are changing over time, by comparing outcomes at 1991 with those at 2001. The results from all these analyses are linked to the discussion in the first section.

Data source and variables used

As explained above, the data used for this paper are from the ONS Longitudinal Study (LS), which is a 1 per cent sample of the population of England and Wales that is followed over time. The LS was initially obtained by taking a sample of the 1971 Census, based on those born on one of four birth dates (day and month). Information from samples taken at each subsequent Census has been added to the study. Members are also added to the study by linking information on births and immigrations using the same selection criteria. No more information is linked where study members have records indicating that they have died or left England and Wales, though linking recommences for returning emigrants.

My focus is on a cohort of LS members who were aged from 4 to 15 years in 1971. Four ethnic groups (see earlier) were defined by linking information from 1991 back to 1971 and combining that with information on country of birth of the children's parents. The LS members were grouped into three age groups: 4–7 years old; 8–11 years old, and 12–15 years old at the date of the 1971 Census. These age groups were intended to indicate both the *minimum* period of schooling that the children had experienced in Britain (given that some were born abroad), and also how far they had proceeded towards their final class destinations by the time these were measured in 1991 and 2001.

Information on parents' occupation and economic status in 1971 was used to construct parental social class or the children's social class of origin. CASMIN scale values were aggregated into four categories: service (the highest social class), intermediate, working and "other" (where respondents did not fit one of the former classes). Variables describing parents' education in 1971 and economic status indicators for the household of origin (car ownership and tenure) were also created. In addition, a five-level measure of ethnic minority concentration in the area of residence was constructed to capture geographical factors.

Study members' own class (based on their and their (cohabiting) partner's occupation and economic status) was constructed for both 1991 and 2001. This destination social class was based on the NS-SeC social class classification, with the main distinction being between the highest aggregate social class (professional or managerial) or any other social class position. Variables summarizing study members' education, partnership status, car ownership, and housing tenure were also constructed for 1991 and 2001.[2]

The social class composition of the individuals observed in 1991 and 2001 is illustrated in figure 2. The figure also gives the composition of origin social class, showing the shift from predominantly working class origins in 1971 to predominantly professional and managerial destinations in 2001, with 1991 forming an intermediate point, but closer to the pattern for 2001.

Figure 2

Class composition of the study members' origins and of their destinations at 1991 and 2001

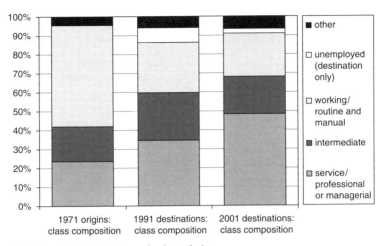

Source: ONS Longitudinal Study, author's analysis.

The analysis that follows focuses on relationships at the three time-points: when the individual was living with their parent(s) and growing up and going to school in England or Wales; the study members' own class outcomes in 1991 and how these relate to their educational achievement and parental backgrounds; the study members' class outcomes in 2001 and how these relate to their educational achievement, parental backgrounds and class position in 1991. The sample sizes at the three time-points, broken down by ethnic group, are given in table 2.

The probability of service class origins in 1971

A series of logistic regressions of the probability of parental (origin) class being service class were run, broken down by ethnic group (see table 3). According to model 1, compared to their white non-migrant counterparts, study members from the three minority groups were all less likely, in 1971, to have service class backgrounds (controlling just for basic characteristics of age, sex and birth abroad (of the child)). That is, parents from all three groups showed a greater concentration in lower classes than white non-migrant parents. Model 2 adds in the ethnic minority group concentration in the ward where parents were living. This reduces the ethnic group effects a little, as the characteristics of the area of settlement on migration can both enhance and inhibit possibilities for occupying particular occupational niches (Smith 1977). Such niches could either correspond to a reduction in class status, thus corresponding to downward mobility on migration, or, conversely, enable the retention of class position.

147

Table 2

Size and ethnic group composition of study members

	For analysis of origins (1971) (by ethnicity)	For analysis of origins (1971) and 1991 destinations	For analysis of origins (1971) and 2001 destinations
White non-migrant	72,972	68,188	63,751
Caribbean	1,054	896	719
Indian	653	590	552
White migrant	2,568	2,324	2,084
Total (including other ethnic groups)	80,879	75,164	70,186

Note: Sample sizes vary as some study members will no longer be observed at later time-points.
Source: ONS Longitudinal Study, author's analysis.

When parental educational and economic status variables as well as ethnic minority concentration in the ward of origin were added (model 3), the Caribbeans had probabilities of service class origin that were insignificantly different from those of their white non-migrant counterparts, whereas the Indians and the white migrants had probabilities that were significantly lower. Moreover, the probabilities for each of the three migrant groups were significantly different from each other, with the probability of service class origins for the Indians, once other background factors were controlled, being substantially lower than those for the white migrants as well as those for the Caribbeans.

The results have two implications. First, they illustrate that for migrants, educational and financial assets may not help the migrant generation to find a relatively privileged occupational situation: the benefits from such assets may only appear in future generations. Moreover, some areas of settlement may provide greater opportunities than others and greater scope for utilizing characteristics, including class origins that are brought with the group. Overall, the results highlight downward mobility for those who migrate from relatively privileged positions (as also illustrated by Heath and Ridge 1983, and Daniel 1968).

Second, the results illustrate that mobility processes are not homogeneous. The Caribbean lack of disadvantage in relation to service class origins suggests that the migrants (parents) found their way into occupations for which their education and assets (as far as we can measure them here) fitted them. However, we cannot reject the possibility that those with greater levels of assets were already subject to high rates of return migration, a feature of the subsequent period. Model 1 showed that Caribbeans were over-represented in lower social classes; but model 2 indicated that, *like for like,* they were not more disadvantaged than their white counterparts. On the other hand, the experiences of Indians seem to illustrate not only a migration penalty but one that is ethnically specific. It is over and above that experienced by the white

Table 3

Logistic regression showing the effect on the probability of having service class origins by ethnic group and other selected characteristics

Variable	Coefficient (standard error)		
	Model 1	Model 2	Model 3
Ethnic group (base = white non-migrant)[a]			
Caribbean	−.717	−.386	.026
	(.091)***	(.094)***	(.105)
Indian	−1.457	−1.063	−1.244
	(.149)***	(.151)***	(.175)***
White migrant	−.588	−.467	−.578
	(.056)***	(.058)***	(.071)***
Sex (= male)	.027	.026	.012
	(.017)	(.017)	(.020)
Age group (base = oldest (12–15 in 1971))			
4–7	.003	.002	−.254
	(.021)	(.021)	(.025)***
8–11	.046	.045	−.105
	(.021)*	(.021)*	(.025)***
Born abroad	.309	.295	−.026
	(.055)***	(.056)***	(.070)
Minority ethnic group concentration in ward of origin (base = 0% minorities)			
0–1%		.462	.473
		(.025)***	(.031)***
1–5%		.378	.511
		(.031)***	(.038)***
5–10%		.037	.329
		(.048)	(.057)***
10%+		−.191	.232
		(.049)***	(.058)***
Mother absent			−.444
			(.112)***
Qualified mother (base = no higher qualifications)			1.338
			(.033)***
Father absent			−.606
			(.062)***
Qualified father (base = no higher qualifications)			2.192
			(.028)***
Tenure at origin (base = owner occupation)			
Local authority			−1.205
			(.027)***
Private rented			−.628
			(.034)***

Table 3

(*Continued*)

Variable	Coefficient (standard error)		
	Model 1	Model 2	Model 3
Car ownership at origin (base = no cars)			
1 car			.900
			(.028)***
2 or more cars			1.423
			(.036)***
Constant	−1.189	−1.527	−2.302
	(.017)***	(.027)***	(.043)***
LR chi² (df)	500.5	1,090.3	26,642
	(12)***	(16)***	(27)***
Wald test that Caribbean = white migrant (df = 1)	*1.5*	*.62*	24.5***
Wald test that Indian = white migrant (df = 1)	30.9***	14.3***	13.2***
Wald test that Caribbean = Indian (df = 1)	18.7***	15.7***	42.0***
N			80,879

Notes: *: P ≤ 0.05; **: P ≤ 0.01; ***: P ≤ 0.001; coefficients in *italics* are not significant.
[a]Other ethnic groups were included in the model but the results are not given here for simplicity.
Dummies have been used for missing values on variables but the results have not been reported here for simplicity.
Source: ONS Longitudinal Study, author's analysis.

migrants, who also seem to experience some degree of suppressed social class, given their characteristics, in the migrant generation.

The chances of occupational success for the "second generation"

These different patterns of origins might lead us to certain expectations about what happens to the second generation when they grow up. If there were absence of discrimination or ethnic penalty, we might expect to see that the Caribbeans, given their apparent lack of a "migration penalty", would experience similar patterns of outcomes to their white counterparts. Their overall profile would still have a higher concentration at lower levels of the class hierarchy, as a result of greater concentration in working class origins and the on-going and well-attested salience of class origins to destinations, but their chances of occupational success should not be disproportionately disadvantageous relative to their white non-migrant counterparts. For the white migrants and even more for the Indians, we might, by contrast, expect to see higher relative chances of occupational success among the second generation, controlling for class origins. Given the evidence from table 3, that their class origins were suppressed relative to the white non-migrants, we might expect to see some reassertion of "underlying" class position in the second generation as the next generation becomes the route to success denied to the first generation. However, we would also expect that this effect would be hard to discern if those same factors which gave evidence of their suppressed class position on migration (parental education and financial status indicators) were also controlled for.

Table 4 shows the relative chances of a study member's social class success in 1991, both excluding (model 1) and including (model 2) the factors that illustrated the downward mobility of the Indians and the white migrants and the relative parity of the Caribbeans (parental occupation and economic status variables). If we look at probability of professional or managerial class outcomes in 1991, then, consistent with the hypothesis advanced above, there is some indication of greater relative occupational success for the Indians and the white migrants, and that this does indeed become non-significant for the Indians once parental education and economic status indicators are controlled (though it still remains positive). However, for the white migrants, the upwardly mobile effect remains even after such controls are included, suggesting that for this group (or groups) there are some migration selection effects that improve the chances for the second generation relative to the white non-migrants. A Wald test of the hypothesis that the effects for the Indians and the white migrants are the same cannot be rejected. This suggests that the Indians also achieve greater levels of occupational success than either their class origins or their apparent class suppression can account for. Instead of revealing patterns of ethnic discrimination in the second generation, the Indians would appear, as far as their class outcomes are concerned, to be comparable to the white migrants, who also succeed over and above what might be predicted for them.

By contrast, Caribbeans have lower probabilities of achieving professional or managerial positions in 1991 than their white non-migrant counterparts from comparable social class backgrounds, and this effect persists when parental education and economic status variables are controlled for. The effect for Caribbeans can be statistically differentiated from the white migrants and from the Indians in both models, emphasizing the group-specific nature of this effect. The distinctive structure of Caribbean families, with higher rates of female-headed households, and with women relatively highly educated compared to men, which is sometimes employed to help explain the distinctive outcomes of this group (Berthoud 2005; Platt 2002), cannot offer much help in elucidating this pattern as absent fathers and parental education are both controlled for here. Thus, Caribbeans are doing worse than we would anticipate, just as Indians and white migrants are doing better, and this cannot be explained through different migration histories and different patterns of class origins and parental assets.

If, instead, we turn to theories of discrimination, we would have to understand discrimination operating in such a way that it can be observed to impact on Caribbeans in relation to class without impacting on Indians and those of white migrant background. While it is obvious that Caribbeans

Table 4

Logistic regression showing the effect on the probability of ending up in the professional or managerial classes in 1991 of ethnic group and other selected characteristics

Variable	Coefficient (standard error)		
	Model 1	Model 2	Model 3
Ethnic group (base = white non-migrant)[a]			
Caribbean	−.231	−.179	−.336
	(.089)**	(.090)*	(.095)***
Indian	.273	.151	−.006
	(.100)**	(.102)	(.109)
White migrant	.227	.172	.061
	(.048)***	(.049)***	(.053)
Sex (= male)	−.005	−.009	.046
	(.016)	(.049)	(.018)**
Social class of origin (base = working)			
Service	1.201	.534	.326
	(.019)***	(.023)***	(.025)***
Intermediate	.285	.060	.015
	(.022)***	(.023)**	(.025)
Other	−.281	−.230	−.108
	(.044)***	(.053)***	(.057)
Age group (base = oldest (12–15 in 1971))			
4–7	−.154	−.232	−.301
	(.020)***	(.021)***	(.022)***
8–11	−.099	−.145	−.208
	(.020)***	(.020)***	(.022)***
Partnered	.760	.817	.945
	(.019)***	(.019)***	(.021)***
Born abroad	.136	.023	−.016
	(.055)*	(.056)	(.060)
Minority ethnic group concentration in ward of origin (base = 0% minorities)			
0–1%	.158	.160	.158
	(.023)***	(.024)***	(.026)***
1–5%	.166	.194	.247
	(.029)***	(.030)**	(.032)***
5–10%	.108	.168	.251
	(.043)*	(.044)***	(.047)***
10%+	.045	.120	.226
	(.042)	(.043)**	(.046)***
Mother absent		−.391	−.293
		(.081)***	(.087)**
Qualified mother (base = no higher qualifications)		.479	.218
		(.030)***	(.033)***
Father absent		.190	.118
		(.044)***	(.048)*
Qualified father (base = no higher qualifications)		.546	.280
		(.027)***	(.029)***

Table 4

(*Continued*)

Variable	Coefficient (standard error)		
	Model 1	Model 2	Model 3
Tenure at origin (base = owner occupation)			
Local authority		−.627 (.020)***	−.354 (.022)***
Private rented		−.304 (.027)***	−.160 (.029)***
Car ownership at origin (base = no cars)			
1 car		.317 (.020)***	.221 (.022)***
2 or more cars		.458 (.031)***	.345 (.033)***
Educational qualifications (base = none)			
Lower (level 1 NVQ or 1+ GCSEs or equivalent)			.942 (.037)***
Middle (level 2 NVQ or 5 GCSEs A–C or equivalent)			1.379 (.037)***
Further and higher (level 3+ NVQ or A' level+ or equivalent)			2.68 (.037)***
Constant	−1.586 (.031)***	−1.494 (.036)***	−2.895 (.050)***
LR chi^2 (df)	6,341.6 (20)***	9,360.9 (31)***	19,178.9 (35)***
Wald test for Caribbean = white migrant (df = 1)		12.8***	14.4***
Wald test for Indian = white migrant (df = 1)		*0.04*	*0.34*
Wald test for Caribbean = Indian (df = 1)		6.75**	5.9*
N		75,164	

Notes: *: P ≤ 0.05; **: P ≤ 0.01; ***: P ≤ 0.001; coefficients in *italics* are not significant.
[a]Other ethnic groups were included in the model but the results are not given here for simplicity.
Dummies have been used for missing values on variables but the results have not been reported here for simplicity.
Source: ONS Longitudinal Study, author's analysis.

could suffer discrimination where it does not affect those of white migrant origin, it is arguably harder to explain why they should suffer it more than their Indian counterparts.

As discussed in the first section, education is one area that is crucial to occupational success and in which both stereotypes about Caribbeans' "failure" and Indians' "success" abound, as well as clear evidence of differential treatment of Caribbeans, for example in the area of school exclusions (National Statistics 2004; CRE 1985; Gillborn and Gipps 1996). Therefore, it is worth exploring whether we can understand the differential experiences of Indians/white migrants and Caribbeans in terms of the former having higher and the latter having lower chances of occupational success in relation to different levels of educational achievement.

Model 3 in table 4 shows that (unsurprisingly) education has a strong independent effect on the probability of social class achievement. Moreover, the addition of education made the ethnic group effects for occupational success for the white migrants and Indians negligible and insignificantly different from the reference group of the white non-migrants. However, the lower chances of professional and managerial outcomes for the Caribbeans remain, and remain statistically significant. Thus, while Indians and white migrants achieve their greater success *via* education, their Caribbean counterparts are failing to achieve parity *despite* their education. Their success or failure in the classroom and beyond is not sufficient explanation of their relative lack of occupational success. Instead, we have to consider the possibility that they are subject to specific exclusionary or discriminatory processes that inhibit their access to better jobs.

Change between 1991 and 2001

These outcomes were for 1991, when the cohort was aged between 24 and 35 years old. It is possible that achievement of final class position could take longer for some groups than for others. For example, we know that young Caribbean men are particularly disadvantaged in the labour market (Berthoud 1999), but it could be that they recover from that disadvantage over time. Moreover, it is also possible that the particular forms of exclusion that keep Caribbeans from the better jobs have decreased in salience or have been affected by wider changes in the economy, such as the change from high to low unemployment levels between 1991 and 2001. The last part of this discussion will then be concerned with comparing these results for 1991 with occupational outcomes at 2001 and attempting to ascertain whether they tell a different story and whether we can identify "catching up" effects for certain groups.

The models presented in table 5 parallel models 2 and 3 from table 4, but for 2001 class outcomes rather than 1991 ones. The results show that, when origins but not own educational qualifications are taken into account (model 1), all three groups show relatively high levels of movement into the professional and managerial classes. The result is not statistically significant for the Indians, but is highly significant for the Caribbeans as well as the white migrants, indicating that the Caribbean disadvantage was lessened by 2001.

Table 5

Logistic regression showing the effect on the probability of ending up in the professional or managerial classes in 2001 of ethnic group and other selected characteristics, and controlling for being in professional or managerial class in 1991

Variable	Coefficient (standard error)			
	Model 1	Model 2	Model 3	Model 4
Ethnic group (base = white non-migrant)[a]				
Caribbean	.254	.003	.322	.076
	(.085)**	(.092)	(.100)**	(.106)
Indian	.153	−.029	−.010	−.107
	(.102)	(.112)	(.120)	(.128)
White migrant	.201	.033	.151	.022
	(.050)***	(.054)	(.057)**	(.061)
Sex (= male)	−.003	.057	.043	.081
	(.016)	(.018)**	(.018)*	(.020)***
Social class of origin (base = working)				
Service	.514	.276	.366	.206
	(.024)***	(.026)***	(.028)***	(.029)***
Intermediate	.035	−.024	.013	−.031
	(.022)	(.024)	(.025)	(.027)
Other	−.216	−.086	−.175	−.085
	(.049)***	(.054)	(.057)**	(.060)
Age group (base = oldest (12–15 in 1971))				
4–7	−.016	−.124	.161	.044
	(.020)	(.022)***	(.023)***	(.024)
8–11	−.019	−.102	.071	−.017
	(.020)	(.022)***	(.023)**	(.024)
Partnered	1.097	1.179	1.016	1.092
	(.020)***	(.022)***	(.023)***	(.025)***
Born abroad	.011	−.036	−.001	−.030
	(.056)	(.062)	(.066)	(.070)
Minority ethnic group concentration in ward of origin (base = 0% minorities)				
0–1%	.208	.206	.163	.166
	(.023)***	(.025)***	(.026)***	(.027)***
1–5%	.243	.297	.218	.261
	(.029)***	(.031)***	(.033)***	(.035)***
5–10%	.188	.265	.160	.225
	(.043)***	(.047)***	(.049)**	(.052)***
10%+	.197	.291	.185	.255
	(.042)***	(.046)***	(.049)***	(.051)***
Mother absent	−.169	−.056	−.080	−.011
	(.074)*	(.082)	(.085)	(.090)
Qualified mother (base =	.438	.155	.320	.125
no higher qualifications)	(.033)***	(.035)***	(.038)***	(.040)**
Father absent	.208	.114	.146	.089
	(.042)***	(.047)*	(.049)**	(.052)

Table 5

(*Continued*)

Variable	Coefficient (standard error)			
	Model 1	Model 2	Model 3	Model 4
Qualified father (base = no higher qualifications)	.493 (.029)***	.198 (.032)***	.308 (.034)***	.103 (.036)**
Tenure at origin (base = owner occupation)				
Local authority	−.520 (.019)***	−.219 (.021)***	−.334 (.022)***	−.129 (.023)***
Private rented	−.309 (.026)***	−.162 (.029)***	−.215 (.030)***	−.112 (.032)***
Car ownership at origin (base = no cars)				
1 car	.270 (.019)***	.170 (.021)***	.189 (.022)***	.125 (.023)***
2 or more cars	.361 (.031)***	.233 (.034)***	.234 (.036)***	.154 (.037)***
Educational qualifications (base = none)				
Lower (level 1 NVQ or 1+ GCSEs or equivalent)		1.01 (.030)***		.833 (.033)***
Middle (level 2 NVQ or 5 GCSEs A–C or equivalent)		1.45 (.031)***		1.188 (.034)***
Further and higher (level 3+ NVQ or A' level+ or equivalent)		2.81 (.033)***		2.245 (.037)***
Professional managerial class in 1991			2.027 (.021)***	1.657 (.022)***
Constant	−1.292 (.036)***	−2.65 (.046)***	−1.927 (.042)***	−2.902 (.050)***
LR chi^2 (df)	8,971.1 (31)***	18,999.9 (35)***	1,934.5 (32)***	23,715.8 (36)***
Wald test for Caribbean = white migrant (df = 1)	*0.3*	*0.1*	*0.1*	*0.2*
Wald test for Indian = white migrant (df = 1)	*0.2*	*0.3*	*1.6*	*0.9*
Wald test for Caribbean = Indian (df = 1)	*0.7*	*0.1*	5.1*	*1.4*
N	70,186	69,015	64,788	63,718

Notes: *: P ≤ 0.05; **: P ≤ 0.01; ***: P ≤ 0.001; coefficients in *italics* are not significant.
[a]Other ethnic groups were included in the model but the results are not given here for simplicity. Dummies have been used for missing values on variables but the results have not been reported here for simplicity.
Source: ONS Longitudinal Study, author's analysis.

When education is added (model 2), the minority group "advantage" loses size and becomes insignificant, indicating that, for all groups, upward mobility is achieved through education, though success continues to be aided by the social class, qualifications and economic assets of parents as well. The change in the picture for the Caribbeans indicates that they experienced substantial class mobility between 1991 and 2001, catching up to a position that, while not comparable with their peers in absolute terms, does not reflect an additional "ethnically based" disadvantage. In this, they become like the Indians and the white migrants. In so far as Caribbeans remain disadvantaged it is through area of residence, more limited access to parental resources, and an educational system in which they either do less well or achieve comparable levels of qualifications later, during the post-compulsory period.

We can extend this analysis by examining the occupational success at 2001 controlling for occupational position at 1991. This will indicate whether there have been ethnic group-specific patterns of upward mobility between 1991 and 2001. That is, we can specifically examine intra-generational mobility on top of inter-generational mobility. The final two columns of table 4 (models 3 and 4) show the effect of controlling for 1991 class position both with and without educational qualifications. Model 3 shows that there is a relatively high level of movement into the professional and managerial classes (or a disproportionate retention there) among Caribbeans and white migrants, once background factors are taken into account. The age group coefficients show that this upward mobility from one decade to the next is, unsurprisingly, age-related: it is more likely to occur for the younger age groups. This reinforces the impression of a "catch-up" effect for the Caribbeans (and white migrants) where qualifications and relevant experience are either obtained later or take longer to make an impact: they are as if a few years behind. When education is added in, it once again renders the ethnic group effects insignificant and is itself a very strong influence on reaching or staying in the professional or managerial classes between 1991 and 2001, stronger even than presence in the professional or managerial classes at 1991. Age group effects also become insignificant, indicating that age had been representing the ability to realize one's educational qualifications, relative to when they were attained. There is some indication in the Indian coefficient that this group is not, despite its strong representation in the professional classes, as successful as it could be if it could realize all its educational advantage and do so over time; however, the effect remains insignificant here.

The overall message from the multivariate analysis is that education takes longer to have its effect for some groups, and this delay intersects with the strength of the economy, which is likely to impact more heavily on more marginal groups. Like for like, white migrants and Caribbeans improve their class position over the 1991–2001 period, undoing some of the class differences that were revealed for 1991, but this is in line with their educational level.

Conclusions

This paper has produced some suggestive findings about the complex questions related to the effects of particular migration history on the transformation from migrants to ethnic minorities. It indicates that particular migration histories are important, not only in contributing to the class position of the "first generation", but they may also have effects that continue into the second generation with higher than anticipated levels of upward mobility from the depressed initial position. Backgrounds count, and the different aspects of background—class, parental education, economic assets and the fact of migration—all count independently for future generations.

The analysis has shown how minority ethnicity in general is a weak indicator of class and class mobility processes, with the two longest-standing of Britain's main postwar minority groups having little in common in terms of either initial class positions or how life chances are transformed in the second generation. Indeed, in several respects, Caribbeans and Indians shared more with white migrants than with each other. This paper has given some support to the thesis that migrants compensate for their own, often depressed class position following migration through the achievements of the second generation, and that the means to achieving this is education.

Nevertheless, second-generation Caribbeans seemed peculiarly disadvantaged in their class outcomes in 1991, with their disadvantage occurring despite, not as a result of, their levels of educational achievement. By 2001, however, the Caribbeans appeared to have "caught up" with their white non-migrant counterparts and to be achieving in line with their educational success. This is not to say that they are not at risk of more limited success through discrimination within the educational system but, instead, that we cannot observe additional ethnic penalties over and above the processes that may affect their educational attainment, their area of settlement, and so on. This catching up between 1991 and 2001 can be seen as a positive achievement for this group, and is also congruent with discussions elsewhere (see Platt 2002, and the introductory section, above). However, it also reveals how certain minority groups may be peculiarly susceptible to economic down- (and up-)turns. This susceptibility of certain minority groups is itself an issue for concern, along with the fact that the process of delayed achievement of occupational success may also have a negative impact on the group (and may also be partly an artefact of the differential drop-out of those who are not observed who might be guessed to be those faring least well). Moreover, the fact that qualifications (and possibly employment experience) take longer both to be gained and to "tell" for different groups is in itself an issue worthy of further policy attention.

Acknowledgements

The permission of the Office for National Statistics to use the Longitudinal Study is gratefully acknowledged, as is the help provided by staff of the Centre for Longitudinal Study Information and User Support (CeLSIUS), in particular Julian Buxton. The author, however, retains responsibility for the interpretation of the data. I am grateful to David Colclough and Stephen Jenkins for their comments on drafts of this paper.

Notes

1. In addition those who defined themselves as "Black Other" were joined with the Black Caribbean group to make up the Caribbean group measured, given the evidence that many of those who defined themselves as Black Other identified as Black British and were the children of those identifying themselves as Caribbean (Owen 1996). This has also been an approach used elsewhere, for example by Berthoud (1998).
2. As lower levels of education were only comprehensively measured for the first time at 2001, this information is extrapolated back to 1991, when most of the cohort should have completed their education. For information on higher education, for 1991, information available at that date is prioritized over that available in 2001.

References

Alba, R. and Nee, V. (1997), Rethinking assimilation theory for a new era of immigration, *International Migration Review* 31, 4: 826–74.

Archer, L. and Francis, B. (forthcoming), Challenging classes? Exploring the role of social class within the identities and achievement of British Chinese pupils, *Sociology*.

Ballard, R. (1997), The construction of a conceptual vision: "ethnic groups" and the 1991 UK Census, *Ethnic and Racial Studies* 20: 182–94.

Barth, F. (1969), *Ethnic Groups and Boundaries: The Social Organisation of Culture Difference*, London: Allen and Unwin.

Berthoud, R. (1999), *Young Caribbean Men in the Labour Market*, York: Joseph Rowntree Foundation.

Berthoud, R. (2005), Family formation in multicultural Britain: diversity and change. In G. Lowry, T. Modood and S. Teles (eds), *Ethnicity, Social Mobility and Public Policy: Comparing the UK and the US*, Cambridge: Cambridge University Press, pp. 222–53.

Blackaby, D. H., Leslie, D. G., Murphy, P. D. and O'Leary, N. C. (2002), White/ethnic minority earnings and employment differentials in Britain: evidence from the LFS, *Oxford Economic Papers*, 54: 270–97.

Brown, C. (1984), *Black and White Britain: The Third PSI Survey*, London: Heinemann.

Castles, S. (2000), *Ethnicity and Globalization*, London: Sage.

Commission for Racial Equality (CRE) (1985), *Birmingham LEA and Schools: Referral and Suspension of Pupils*, London: CRE.

Cornell, S. and Hartmann, D. (1998), *Ethnicity and Race: Making Identities in a Changing World*, Thousand Oaks, CA: Pine Forge Press.

Daniel, W. W. (1968), *Racial Discrimination in England*, Harmondsworth: Penguin.

Dorsett, R. (1998), *Ethnic Minorities in the Inner City*, Bristol: Policy Press.

Evans, J. M. (1983), *Immigration Law*, London: Sweet and Maxwell.

Galster, G. C., Metzger, K. and Waite, R. (1999), Neighbourhood opportunity structures and immigrants' socioeconomic advancement, *Journal of Housing Research*, 10, 1: 95–127.

Gillborn, D. and Gipps, C. (1996), *Recent Research on the Achievements of Ethnic Minority Pupils*, London: OFSTED/HMSO.

Gordon, M. (1964), *Assimilation in American Life: The Role of Race, Religion and National Origins*, Oxford: Oxford University Press.

Heath, A. and McMahon, D. (1997), Education and occupational attainments: the impact of ethnic origins. In V. Karn (ed.), *Ethnicity in the 1991 Census. Vol. 4: Employment, Education and Housing among the Ethnic Minority Populations of Britain*, London: Stationery Office, pp. 91–113.

Heath, A. and McMahon, D. (1999), *Ethnic Differences in the Labour Market: The Role of Education and Social Class Origins*, CREST Working Paper 69, June.

Heath, A. and Ridge, J. (1983), Social mobility of ethnic minorities, *Journal of Biosocial Science Supplement*, 8: 169–84.

Hepple, B. (1992), Have twenty years of the Race Relations Act in Britain been a failure? In B. Hepple and E. Szyszczak (eds), *Discrimination and the Limits of the Law*, London: Mansell.

Karn, V., Dale, A. and Ratcliffe, P. (1997), Introduction: using the 1991 Census to study ethnicity. In V. Karn (ed.), *Ethnicity in the 1991 Census*. Vol. 4: *Employment, Education and Housing among the Ethnic Minority Populations of Britain*, London: Stationery Office, pp. xi–xxix.

Marmot, M. G., Adelstein, A. M. and Bulusu, L. (1984), *Immigrant Mortality in England and Wales 1970–78: Causes of Death by Country of Birth*, London: HMSO.

Modood, T. (1997), Employment. In T. Modood, *et al.*, *Ethnic Minorities in Britain: Diversity and Disadvantage*, London: PSI, pp. 83–149.

Modood, T. (2004), Capitals, ethnic identity and educational qualifications, *Cultural Trends*, 13, 2: 87–105.

Modood, T. *et al.* (1997), *Ethnic Minorities in Britain: Diversity and Disadvantage*, London: PSI.

National Statistics (2004), *Focus on Ethnicity and Identity*, London: Office for National Statistics/HMSO. Available at: http://www.statistics.gov.uk/downloads/theme_compendia/foe2004/Ethnicity.pdf

Nazroo, J. (1997), Health and health services. In T. Modood *et al.*, *Ethnic Minorities in Britain: Diversity and Disadvantage*, London: PSI, pp. 224–58.

Parekh, B. (2000), *The Future of Multi-ethnic Britain*, London: Profile Books/Runnymede Trust.

Park, R. E. (1950), *Race and Culture*, Glencoe, IL: Free Press.

Pathak, S. (2000), Race research for the future. DfEE Research Topic Paper RTP01, March, London: Stationery Office.

Platt, L. (2002), *Parallel Lives? Poverty among Minority Ethnic Groups in Britain*, London: CPAG.

Platt, L. (forthcoming), Ethnicity. In J. Scott (ed.), *Key Sociological Concepts*, London: Routledge.

Platt, L., Simpson, L. and Akinwale, B. (2005), Stability and change in ethnic groups in England and Wales, *Population Trends*, 121: 2–13.

Ratcliffe, P. (1994), *"Race", Ethnicity and Nation*, London: UCL Press.

Ratcliffe, P. (1996), Social geography and ethnicity: a theoretical, conceptual and substantive overview. In P. Ratcliffe (ed.), *Ethnicity in the 1991 Census*. Vol. 3: *Social Geography and Ethnicity in Britain: Geographical Spread, Spatial Concentration and Internal Migration*, London: HMSO, pp. 1–22.

Rex, J. and Mason, D. (1986), *Theories of Race and Ethnic Relations*, Cambridge: Cambridge University Press.

Robinson, V. (1990), Roots to mobility: the social mobility of Britain's black population, 1971–87, *Ethnic and Racial Studies*, 13, 2: 274–86.

Salt, J. (1996), Immigration and ethnic group. In D. Coleman and J. Salt (eds), *Ethnicity in the 1991 Census*. Vol. 1: *Demographic Characteristics of the Ethnic Minority Populations*, London: HMSO, pp. 124–50.

Smith, D. J. (1977), *Racial Disadvantage in Britain: The PEP Report*, Harmondsworth: Penguin.

Solomos, J. (1989), *Race and Racism in Contemporary Britain*, Basingstoke: Macmillan.

Supperstone, M. and O'Dempsey, D. (1994), *Immigration: The Law and Practice*, London: Longman.

Weber, M. (1978), *Economy and Society*, ed. G. Roth and C. Wittich, Berkeley: University of California Press.

Index

absence: from Norwegian introduction
    programmes   117
absorption capacity, social   9
abuse: of women   111
accession negotiation status, EU   32
accommodation
    administrative errors in providing   86
    in dispersal system   50, 58
    forced migrants   58, 66, 73–4
    overcrowding in   76
    overstayers   76
acronyms, list of   43
administrative errors: in welfare
    planning   86
AENEAS   38, 39
Africans, East: migration to UK   139
age
    intergenerational study   157
    at migration, and educational
        progression   127
agencies for forced migrants
    accommodation   73–4
    informal welfare services   75
aid, humanitarian: EU   35–6
Algeria   39
Aliens Law (Switzerland)   96, 103, 104,
    105
Amsterdam Treaty (1997)   33
annual permits: Switzerland   97, 98
apprenticeships: for ethnic minority
    youth in Denmark   3, 132, 133, 134
aspiration: in minority groups   142
assimilation   142
asylum claims
    EU, processing   65
    forced migrants   67
asylum policies
    common, EU   1, 2, 29–47, 64–8
    national, EU states   15

asylum-seekers
    accommodation in UK   73–4
    child, welfare staff working with   81–
        92
    European states responses to   48–62
    failed   69
        accommodation   76
        destitution   70–2
        eviction   88–9
        non-removal of   89, 90
    principle of *non-refoulement*   19, 34,
        50–1, 55
    protection issues   19–21
    as threat to EU security regime   30–
        2
    welfare rights in UK   69
asylum status: applying for, in UK   66
attendance: Norway introduction
    programmes   117
Australia
    border control   14–15
    formal migration programmes   7
    migration industry   13
    non-white immigration   8
    protection of economic and social
        rights of citizens   10–11
    resettlement places   20–1

Balkans, Western: EU neighbourhood
    policies   38–40
benefits, introduction: Norway   112,
    120
bilateral agreements
    migration control   14–15
    between Switzerland and Italy   98
bilingual education: Denmark   132,
    133
borders *see* control; management
brain drain   13, 18

buffer zones, EU   31, 33, 34, 38
bussing: in UK   57

campaigning role: welfare staff   89
Canada
  formal migration programmes   7
  non-white immigration   8
cantons: Switzerland   100, 104
capitalism, global   13–14
CARDS   38
career plans: Norway   112
Caribbean migrants in UK   139
  educational outcomes   140–2, 157,
    158
  intergenerational study   143–57
  occupations   140, 150–8
  service class origins   148–50
census categories: for ethnic
    groups   138, 145
chain migration: UK   139
charity
  for failed asylum-seekers   71–2
  for forced migrants   67, 76
children
  asylum seekers, welfare staff working
    with   81–92
  detention   56
  ethnic minority, educational
    progression in Denmark   124–
    36
Children Act (1989)   91
  and asylum law   87–8
circles
  EU model of concentric   31–2
  three-circles policy in
    Switzerland   102–3
citizens: protection of rights of
    10–11
citizenship
  Switzerland   96–7
  and welfare entitlement   91
claims, asylum see asylum claims
class, social see social mobility
colonies: migration to   5, 13
Commonwealth countries: migration to
    UK   138–9
Commonwealth Immigrants Acts   139
communities
  support for forced migrants   75–6
  see also social networks

Community Assistance for
    Reconstruction, Development and
    Stabilization in the Western
    Balkans (CARDS)   38
community organizations   58
compliance: problem of   21–2
containment, instruments of: EU   31,
    35–6, 38–40, 42
control, border   5–6, 22
  EU policies   31–2, 34, 49
    internal and external   31
  formal programmes   7, 9
  limits of   12–14
  rationales of   8–12
  Switzerland   95–100
  use of term   14
  welfare rights as   119–20
cooperation: Switzerland   104–5
coordination
  border control   15–16
  Switzerland   104–5
  in welfare, problems of   86
counselling
  for ethnic minority children in
    Denmark   134
  for welfare staff   87
criminalization: of asylum-seeking   65
crisis, asylum: none in Europe   59
cultural distance: Switzerland   102–3
culture
  national, preservation of, in migration
    control   8
  stereotyping   9
cycles of migration: EU   30

democracy
  direct, in Switzerland   95–6, 105
  and EU   29–30
  and migration control   11–12
  in welfare states   2
demographic patterns, European: and
    labour migration   30
denizens: Switzerland   97
Denmark: educational progression of
    ethnic minority children   3, 124–
    36
dependency, welfare   113
deportation   2–3, 59
  children   90–1
  consequences of   52–3

data on 51–2
defined 50
described 50–4
joint 53–4
destitution
children 90–1
failed asylum-seekers 70–2, 88–9
forced migrants 65, 66
see also poverty
detention 2–3, 59
abuses 56
defined 50
described 54–6
psychological damage of 56
determination to succeed: in minority
    groups 142
deterrence policies: EU 31
developed countries
skilled and unskilled migration 18
see also specific countries
developing countries
remittances sent to 13, 17
skilled migration from 18
see also specific countries
development policy: EU 35–6, 42
discretion: of welfare staff 88–9, 90
discretionary leave status 69, 72–3
discrimination 137, 140, 145
intergenerational study 151–4
unlawful in UK 139
dispersal areas: Wales 82
dispersal system
abuse of 57
and children 91
complications of, in UK 84–6
defined 50
described 56–9
negative effects 58–9
dispersed state
and forced migration 68–77
notion of 67
diversion, instruments of: EU 31, 34,
    42
diversity
backlash against 120
in social mobility of UK ethnic
    minority groups 138–57
doctors: and child asylum-seekers 85
dropout rates, Danish education 128,
    129, 133

ethnic minority children 130, 131–
    2, 133
Dublin II regulation 40, 65

economic migration 5–6
see also labour
economy
domestic, effects of migration 10–11
Switzerland 93–4, 97, 99, 100–1
ECRE 33
education
of ethnic minority groups
catching up 141–2, 157, 158
in England and Wales 140–2,
    146, 154, 157, 158
see also schools
educational attainment: parents 129
educational progression study
of ethnic minority groups in
    Denmark 3, 124–36
data and samples 126–7
empirical evidence 127–32
policy changes 133–4
educational system: Denmark 125–6
EEA agreement 102–3
Egypt 39
emigration see migration
EMP 38
employment rates: Norway 110
engagement, European: three degrees of
    32
England: post-migration social mobility
    in 137–60
ENPI 38
ethical dilemmas: of welfare staff 86–
    8, 89–90, 91
ethnic groups, minority
educational progression in
    Denmark 124–36
post-migration social mobility in
    England and Wales 3, 137–
    60
EU see European Union (EU)
Europe
deportation, detention and dispersal
    in 48–62
see also specific countries
European Council on Refugees and
    Exiles (ECRE) 33
European Court of Justice 32

European Economic Area (EEA)
  agreement   102–3
European Mediterranean Partnership
  (EMP)   38
European Neighbourhood and
  Partnership Instrument (ENPI)   38
European Union (EU)
  asylum-seeking in   48–9
  border control   14
    regional cooperation   15–16
  common asylum and immigration
    policy   1, 2, 29–47
  developing   33–40, 64–8
  developing of system   40–1
  directives and regulations   40
  joint deportations   53–4
  model of concentric circles   31–2
  pressure on Switzerland   98
  readmission agreements   34
  welfare rights of forced migrants   3,
    63–80
eviction
  ethical dilemmas of welfare staff
    87
  failed asylum-seekers   88–9
exam grades: Denmark   130–1
exceptional leave to remain (ELR)   69,
    72–3

failed asylum-seekers
  see asylum-seekers, failed
family reunification
  Australia   10–11
  in formal migration programmes   7
  Switzerland   98, 102, 104
  UK   139
Federal Commission for Foreigners
  (Switzerland)   104
force: used at deportation   53
forced migrants   5–6
  self-help   76–7
  welfare rights   3, 63–80
    Leeds   68–77
forced migration
  EU policy on   29–47
  see also asylum-seekers
France
  deportation   51
  detention   54–5
  need for further migration to   59

GAERC   35–6
gender issues
  and integration   110–12
  see also men; women
General Affairs and External Relations
  Council (GAERC)   35–6
geographical factors: and outcomes of
  minority groups   142–3
Germany
  asylum-seekers   48
  deportation   51, 52
  detention   55
  dispersal   57
  need for further migration to   59
Global Commission on International
  Migration   17
global markets: labour   13–14
global migration
  control   16–17
  negotiations   17–19
  problem of compliance   21–2
  protection issues   19–21
goal congruence: in global migration
    18
governance
  and forced migration   63–80
  Switzerland   105
grants, education: Denmark   125
group work: in Danish education   132
guest worker programmes: Switzerland
    96
guidance: for ethnic minority children in
    Denmark   132, 134

Hague Programme   41, 42
health care: child asylum-seekers   85
health requirements for resettlement
    places: Australia   21
health status: ethnic minority groups in
    UK   142
helpers versus supervisors in
    Norway   115–16
High Level Working Group on Asylum
    and Migration (HLWG)
    Action Plans   36–8
homelessness
  forced migrants   76
  hidden   73
homework, help with: for Danish
    minority children   133–4

hostility: towards irregular migrants
9–10
housing *see* accommodation
humanitarian migration
Australia 10–11
in formal migration programmes 7
humanitarian protection: in UK 69,
72–3

illegal migration *see* irregular
illegal work: forced migrants 67
immigration
use of term 1
see also migration
Indian migrants in UK 139
education 140–2, 157
intergenerational study 143–57
occupations 140, 150–8
service class origins 148–50
industry, migration 13
initiative, popular: Switzerland
95–6
initiatives
to address root causes of migration 6
see also aid
instability, social: and irregular migration
10
institutions
integration, in Norway 109
Switzerland 95–100, 105
integration
EU 37
Norway
crisis 110–12
introduction programme 3, 109–
23
of parents of ethnic minority children
135
Switzerland 96–7, 103–5, 105–6
international agreements: migration
management 17–19
international organizations: migration
management 17
introduction programme
Norway 3, 109–23
described 112–14
Midtown 114–16
irregular migration
EU 35
readmission agreements 34

from postcolonial states 13
as threat 9–10
to Western countries 5–6
see also forced; labour
Islam 111, 120
Italy
asylum-seekers 48
bilateral agreement with Switzerland
98
deportation 52
detention 55
need for further migration to 59

justice: welfare 2
Justice and Home Affairs (JHA) 33,
38, 42
EU Asylum and Migration
policy 40–1

Kenya 139
kindism
Norway 3, 111–12, 119–21
control of 116–19
kinship *see* social networks

labour
global markets in 13–14
see also work
labour migration 5–6
Norway 110
Switzerland 93–108
UK 138–9
language classes: Norway 112–13,
114–15
language proficiency
Denmark
ethnic minority children 131–2,
133
parents 131–2
law, rule of: and irregular migrants 10
law enforcement: EU 34
laws
and professional ethics 87–8, 89–90
Switzerland 95, 98, 104, 105, 106
Lebanon 39
Leeds
welfare of forced migrants study 3,
68–77
method and sampling 68–9
sociolegal status 69–73

liberal values
  preservation of, in migration
    control 8–9
  tension with democracy 12
  of welfare staff 87
Libya 34
living conditions
  migrants in Norway 110
  see also accommodation
loans, education: Denmark 125
local authorities: cooperation with
  NASS 67–8
longitudinal study, social mobility of
  ethnic minority groups
  data 143–4, 146–7

management, migration 2, 6
  goal congruence 18
  human waste 81
  responsibility for 14–22
  use of term 14
markets: migration industry 13–14
MARRI 38, 39
MASHREQ countries 39
mass invasion: fears of 11
MEDA 38
men
  Denmark
    educational progression 127
    exam grades 131
  UK
    educational attainment 140–1
    unemployment rates 140
mentors: for Danish minority
  children 133, 134
Midtown, Norway: introduction
  programme 114–16
migrant workers: global agreements on
  17
migration
  explanation for 5–6
  use of term 1
  see also asylum-seekers; control;
    European Union; forced;
    management; root causes;
    specific countries
Migration, Asylum, Refugees Regional
  Initiative (MARRI) 38, 39
migration history: ethnic minority
  groups in UK 143–58

migration schemes: temporary 18–19
minority ethnic groups see ethnic
money see remittances
Morocco 34, 39
mother-tongue teaching 133
multiculturalism: disenchantment with
  120

nation states see states
National Asylum Support Service
  (NASS) 72, 82
  accommodation for forced
    migrants 73–4
  child asylum-seekers 84
  ethical dilemmas of welfare staff 87
  local authority cooperation with 67
  responsibilities of 66
neighbourhood policies: EU 38–40,
  41–2
neighbourhoods, disadvantaged: and
  educational progression 130
neighbouring states: EU 31
Netherlands: dispersal 57
networks, social see social networks
New Zealand
  formal migration programmes 7
  non-white immigration 8
NGOs see non-governmental
  organizations (NGOs)
non-arrival measures of control: EU 31
non-governmental organizations
  (NGOs): support of forced
  migrants 67–8, 75
non-refoulement, principle of 19, 50–1, 55
  and readmission agreements 34
non-white ethnic minorities in UK 145
  see also Caribbean; Indian
non-white immigration 8
normalization: of deportation, detention
  and dispersal 59
Norway: introduction programme 3,
  109–23
nurses: and child asylum-seekers 85

occupations: ethnic minority groups in
  England and Wales 140, 150–8
Office of the United Nations High
  Commissioner for Refugees
  (UNHCR) see UNHCR
over-crowding: forced migrants 76

over-foreignization: Switzerland 96
overstayers
    see asylum-seekers, failed

parents
    of ethnic minority children in
        Denmark
        educational attainment 129
        integration 135
        language proficiency 131–2
        parenting practices 133–4
        work experience 129–30
    in intergenerational ethnic group
        study 143–57
partnership strategy: failure of EU to
    implement 29
paternalism: Norway 120
path-dependence
    concept of 95
    Switzerland 98–9, 100
people-smuggling 13
    global agreements on 17
people-trafficking: global agreements on
    17
permits: Switzerland 94, 97, 98, 100
pluralism: in Switzerland 97
political rights: migrants in
    Switzerland 96–7
poor
    fears of mass invasion by 11
    working 101
    see also destitution; poverty
popular initiative: Switzerland 95–6
populations: superfluous 81
populist pressures: on EU 29–30
poverty
    forced migrants in UK 66
    Switzerland 101–2
    see also destitution; poor
prevention: of migration to EU 36
primary contacts, Norway 112
    control of kindism 116–19
    as supervisors not helpers 115–16
problem representation 113
professional and managerial classes:
    intergenerational study 151–4,
    154–7
professionals
    Norwegian introduction
        programme 109–23

working with child asylum-
        seekers 81–92
project-based learning: for ethnic
    minority children in
    Denmark 132, 134
protection issues
    asylum-seekers 19–21
    refugees 17, 41
    see also non-refoulement
public interest criteria: Australia 21

qualifications, educational
    Denmark 124
    ethnic minority groups in UK 140–
        1, 157
    lack of, for migrants in Switzerland
        101
quotas
    migration to EU 16
    resettlement 20
    Switzerland 93, 96, 99, 100

Race Relations acts (UK) 139–40
racism
    and dispersal 58–9
    of immigration policies 90
    welfare officials' risk of being accused
        of 121
readmission agreements: EU 31, 34,
    37, 42
reception
    of asylum-seekers in EU 64–5
    spread of costs of 50
referendum: Switzerland 95
refoulement see non-refoulement
Refugee Community Organizations
    (RCOs): welfare rights for forced
    migrants 75–6
refugee protection
    EU regional programmes 41
    global agreements on 17
refugee status: welfare rights 72–3
refugee workers: Norway 115, 119
refugees
    research 81–2
    welfare rights in UK 69
    see also asylum-seekers
regions
    border control 15–16
    refugee protection 41

remittances: from emigrant
workers   13, 17
resettlement countries: UNHCR   7
resettlement places   20–1
UNHCR   7
resettlement programmes: EU   15–16
residence permits: Switzerland   97, 98
rights
citizen, protection of   10–11
human, tension with asylum law   87–88
immigrant, in Switzerland   97–9,
105
migrant workers, global agreements
on   17
political, in Switzerland   96–7
welfare, of forced migrants   3, 63–80
women's   110–12
root causes of migration
EU policies   29, 31, 35–6, 41–2
need to address   6

Save the Children   89
Schengen Agreement   32, 33
school exclusions: intergenerational
study   154
schools: black-majority   57
seasonal permits: Switzerland   100
seasonal workers: Switzerland   98
seasonal workers statute:
Switzerland   97, 103
secondary migration: and dispersal   58
security regime, EU: asylum and
immigration as threat to   30–2, 42
self-harm: in detention   56
self-help: forced migrants   76–7
service class origins: of ethnic minority
groups in UK   147–50
skilled migration   12–13
Australia   10–11
in formal migration programmes   7
versus unskilled   18
snillisme see kindism
social assistance: dependency   113, 115
social mobility: of ethic minority groups
in England and Wales   3, 137–60
social networks   13
asylum-seekers   58
for Danish ethnic minority children
134

social order: immigration as threat to, in
EU   30
social policies   1
purposes of   2
social workers
and asylum-seekers   83
ethical dilemmas of   87
and integration in Norway   115
socio-economic status
Danish minority children   135
and educational progression
128–30
socio-legal status: forced migrants
69–73
sponsors: resettlement places in Australia
21
states
formal migration programmes   5, 7
migration policy   1
notion of dispersed   67
welfare of forced migrants   63–80
see also specific countries
stay permits: Switzerland   94, 97
stereotyping: cultural   9
suicide: in detention   56
supervisors: of integration in
Norway   115–16
supplementary classes: for Danish
minority children   133–34
support: for asylum-seekers in UK   58
Swiss People's Party (SVP-UDC)   94,
97, 103, 104, 105
Switzerland
immigration policies   3, 93–108
state structure   99–100, 102, 104–5
Syria   34

TACIS   38
Tampere European Council (1999)   29,
35, 40
teachers: training in teaching ethnic
minority children in Denmark   134
Temporary Protection Directive: EU
40
therapy: for welfare staff   87
three-circles policy: Switzerland   102–3
transborder movement: responsibility for
management of   14–22
Turkey: accession negotiations with EU
32

UK *see* United Kingdom (UK)
underclass, ethnic 112
unemployment
  Norway 110
  Switzerland 100–5
unemployment insurance, compulsory:
    Switzerland 98
unemployment rates
  Denmark 124
  of UK migrants 140
unfounded cases 65
UNHCR 7, 65
  global agreements for migration 16–
    17
  global regime for asylum-seekers 20
  security regime 42
    asylum and immigration as threat
      to 30–2
United Kingdom (UK)
  complexity of immigration policy 84
  deportation 51, 52–3
  detention 55–6
  dispersal 57, 58–9
  migration up to 1971 138–40
  need for further migration to 59
  post-migration social mobility in 3,
    137–60
  welfare of forced migrants 3, 66–8,
    68–77
  welfare rights of forced migrants 66
  welfare staff working with child
    asylum-seekers 81–92
United Nations Commissioner for
    Refugees 65
United States (US)
  border control 14
  democracy 12
  formal migration programmes 7
  liberal values 9
  non-white immigration 8
unskilled migration
  Switzerland 99–100, 102, 103
  versus skilled 18
US *see* United States (US)

Vienna Action Plan (1998) 31–2
violence
  and integration 110–11
  racial, towards irregular migrants 10
  used at deportation 53

vocational education, Denmark 125–
  6, 133, 134
  dropout rates 128
voucher system: UK 139

Wales
  post-migration social mobility
    in 137–60
  welfare professionals working with
    child asylum-seekers study 81–
    92
waste, human 81, 90
welfare
  child asylum-seekers 82
  and forced migration 63–80
  and Norwegian introduction
    programmes 119
welfare dependency 113
welfare professionals
  ethical dilemmas 86–8, 89–90, 91
  risk of accusation of racism 121
  working with child asylum-seekers
    study 3, 81–92
    research design 83–4
    research findings 84–9
  see also social workers
welfare rights
  of forced migrants 3, 63–80
  in Leeds 68–77
welfare services
  informal in Leeds 75–6
  Norway, introduction programme 3,
    109–23
welfare states
  migration policy 1, 2
  see also specific countries
Western countries
  case for migration management 5–
    28
  see also specific countries
White Australia policy 8
white migrants: in intergenerational
    study 143–57
white migration 8
white non-migrants: in intergenerational
    study 143–57
Wikan, Unni 111–12
women
  Denmark
    educational progression 127

exam grades   131
integration   110–12
UK
    educational attainment   141
    unemployment rates   140
work
    illegal, of forced migrants   67
    introduction programmes as   117
    see also labour
work experience: parents   129–30
work permits: Switzerland   97, 100

workers, migrant: global agreements   17
working poor: Switzerland   101
workplace conventions: teaching of   134
World Migration Organization (WMO)
    22
World Trade Organization
    (WTO)   18–19, 22

xenophobia: Switzerland   93, 94, 95–6,
    99, 103